D1270055

Mahler Studies comprises ten innovative essays by leading experts on topics spanning the range of current Mahler research. Herta Blaukopf's probing inquiry into critical influences on Mahler's student years provides a meaningful background for Edward R. Reilly's reassessment of sources for "Opus 1," *Das klagende Lied*. Stephen McClatchie introduces Mahler's previously inaccessible correspondence with family members, chiefly his sister Justine Rosé, while Stuart Feder presents insightful psychoanalytic perspectives on Mahler's relationships to Justine and other women in his life before Alma. Donald Mitchell and Henry-Louis de La Grange explore from complementary standpoints the complex issue of quotation and allusion in Mahler's oeuvre. The long-restricted Seventh Symphony sketchbook provides our first detailed glimpses of that Mahlerian "world" emerging in its earliest stages, as documented by Stephen E. Hefling. Issues of tonal structure and coherence are addressed in state-of-the-art analytical essays by Kofi Agawu and John Williamson, while Peter Franklin on Adorno's Mahler provides the clearest explication to date of that complex author's dialectic engagement with the composer.

Mahler Studies

Mahler Studies

EDITED BY STEPHEN E. HEFLING

CAMBRIDGE
UNIVERSITY PRESS

CAMBRIDGE UNIVERSITY PRESS
Cambridge, New York, Melbourne, Madrid, Cape Town, Singapore, São Paulo

Cambridge University Press
The Edinburgh Building, Cambridge CB2 2RU, UK

Published in the United States of America by Cambridge University Press, New York

www.cambridge.org
Information on this title: www.cambridge.org/9780521471657

© Cambridge University Press 1997
"Das klagende Lied reconsidered" © Edward R. Reilly 1997
"Mahler and Smetana: significant influences or accidental parallels?"
© Donald Mitchell 1997

First published 1997
This digitally printed first paperback version 2006

A catalogue record for this publication is available from the British Library

Library of Congress Cataloguing in Publication data

Mahler Studies / edited by Stephen E. Hefling.
    p. cm.
   Includes bibliographical references.
   ISBN 0 521 47165 6 (hardback)
    1. Mahler, Gustav, 1860–1911. I. Hefling, Stephen E.
  ML410.M23M244   1996
  780'.92–dc20 96–10284 CIP

ISBN-13 978-0-521-47165-7 hardback
ISBN-10 0-521-47165-6 hardback

ISBN-13 978-0-521-03317-6 paperback
ISBN-10 0-521-03317-9 paperback

Contents

R0421572600

Plates

Preface

Mahler Studies comprises ten essays by prominent specialists representing the major trends in Mahler research – documentary biography, source-critical studies, psychoanalytic interpretation, musical antecedents and influences, close analysis of musical structure and syntax, and refraction of Mahler's artistic rays through the prism of Adornian critical theory. The opening chapters by Herta Blaukopf and Edward R. Reilly focus on Mahler's emerging first maturity as a creative artist. By means of the "situational logic" advocated by the Austrian philosopher Karl R. Popper, Blaukopf sheds new light upon the biographical lacuna of Mahler's student years (1875–80). Although his extraordinary gifts were recognized by the time he entered the Vienna Conservatory, Mahler was, in today's parlance, a "late bloomer" whose progress was notably less distinguished than that of many fellow students (including the composer-pianist Hans Rott and Mahler's future brother-in-law, the violinist Arnold Rosé). Unsure of his direction, Mahler changed his major field of study from piano to composition, and then, even before obtaining his conservatory diploma, matriculated to the University of Vienna in 1877 to explore his passion for literature and philosophy; evidently he seriously considered giving up musical composition to become a poet. Only in 1880, in conjunction with his first disappointment in love, his first appointment as a conductor, and the completion of *Das klagende Lied*, his first major work, did Mahler's dreamy extended childhood draw to a close. Reilly examines the sources of *Das klagende Lied* in detail, from the earliest autographs of the poem through the last revisions of the published score – a process of evolution that spanned more than a quarter of a century. Drawing upon documents hitherto restricted, Reilly addresses once again the puzzling question of why Mahler deleted "Waldmärchen," the original opening movement of the cantata, and argues persuasively in support of the composer's decision.

It has long been known that a large cache of Mahler family letters, principally from Gustav to his sister Justine, were in possession of Justine's son Alfred Rosé. Inaccessible until recently, this important correspondence is now being processed at the University of Western Ontario by Stephen McClatchie, who provides us the most detailed account to date of Mahler's fascinating commentaries to "Liebste Justi" on a variety of topics – his troublesome brothers, his blossoming career, encounters with notable contemporaries, and his courtship of Alma Schindler – which, even in excerpts, round out our picture of Mahler in relation to his parents and siblings. The psychoanalyst Stuart Feder presents a finely nuanced review of Mahler's relations to the women in his life before his engagement to Alma – his familial ties to mother and sister, his erotic attachments to the operatic sopranos Johanna Richter and Anna von Mildenburg, and his apparently asexual creative collaboration with Natalie Bauer-Lechner, trusty chronicler of the "*Wunderhorn* years."

Allusions, reminiscences, and seemingly overt borrowings have been noted in Mahler's works since their première performances; "gigantic potspourris" was the critics' cry. Donald Mitchell and Henry-Louis de La Grange address this problematic and multifaceted issue from complementary perspectives. Mitchell focuses on a specific instance not previously identified: the affective and structural influence of the second lullaby from Smetana's *Hubička* (which Mahler must have heard in Prague during 1885–86) upon Mahler's *Wunderhorn* song "Der Schildwache Nachtlied" (composed in 1892); he concludes that Mahler's indebtedness to Czech predecessors remains to be fully assessed. De La Grange presents a broad review of the problem as a whole (including an appendix of more than fifty cases of apparent allusion or borrowing), and surveys it from the differing perspectives of the romantic demand for "pure" originality versus the heterogeneity of emerging neoclassicism on one hand, and Mahler's own "provocative alliance" with trivial music on the other. Surprisingly, yet persuasively, de La Grange concludes by paraphrasing Valéry: the lion consists of all the lambs it has devoured, and the whole of Mahler's musical synthesis surpasses the sum of its frequently heterogeneous sources.

During the past twenty years studies of Mahler's compositional process have advanced considerably, owing in no small part to Edward R. Reilly's pioneering efforts to locate and catalogue the musical manuscripts. The earliest stage in that process, however, has necessarily remained largely unexplored, owing to the scarcity and inaccessibility of Mahler's pocket sketchbooks, only two of which are currently known to survive. Thanks to recent easing of library restrictions, Stephen E. Hefling is able to present a detailed overview of the Seventh Symphony notebook (mistakenly dubbed "Mahler's last sketchbook"), which provides fascinating glimpses of a Mahlerian "symphonic world" growing from its first fragmentary kernels via the unpredictable course Mahler likened to the making of a trumpet: "You take a hole and wrap brass around it; that's about what happens in composing."

How best to grasp the cogency and complexity of Mahler's musical structure and syntax has taxed analysts throughout the twentieth century; the essays of Kofi Agawu and John Williamson both pursue Schenkerian methodology undogmatically, illuminating Mahler's indebtedness to traditional tonal models as well as his departure therefrom. Agawu introduces the topic through examples from Mahler's earlier works (which should prove readily accessible to non-analysts) and then proceeds to insightful explications of passages from later music, in particular "Der Abschied" from *Das Lied von der Erde*. Williamson's focus is the middle-period symphonies, with special attention to baffling segments of the Sixth; he concludes with brief but provocative reflections about the potential compatability of analysis such as he presents with critical approaches to Mahler's oeuvre derived from theories of literary narrative.

The name of the Frankfurt philosopher and sociologist Theodor W. Adorno has long been associated with Mahler criticism; yet owing both to the complexity of Adorno's argument and to his use of language (known as "Adornodeutsch" even among Germans), his dialectical engagement with the composer has been largely neglected in the English-speaking world. Meanwhile, serviceable translations of both *Mahler: Eine musikalische Physiognomik* and Adorno's summary of it in his "Wiener Rede" commemorating the centenary of the composer's birth have appeared during the 1990s; accordingly, Peter Franklin's fine discussion of Adorno's Mahler is especially timely. One cannot sum up Franklin briefly any more than he could Adorno; suffice it to say that this "fanfare and curtain" to the present volume, as well as the essays preceding it, should lead us into deeper understanding of the composer whose time, as he predicted, has indeed come.

Stephen E. Hefling

Acknowledgments

The authors and editor of *Mahler Studies* are grateful to many people who assisted in the preparation of the volume, especially: The Mahler–Rosé Collection, University of Western Ontario, London, William G. Guthrie, head, and also Marina Mahler, for permission to reproduce unpublished family letters and photographs; the James Marshall and Marie-Louise Osborn Collection, Beinecke Library, Yale University, Stephen Parks, curator, for permission to reproduce portions of Mahler's 1879 text of *Das klagende Lied*, and also for the dustjacket photograph, which shows the opening of the "Blumine" movement from the 1893 autograph of Mahler's First Symphony; the Österreichisches Theatermuseum, Vienna, Hofrat Dr. Oskar Pausch, director, and Frau Jarmila Weissenböck, curator of the Mildenburg Nachlaß, for permission to reproduce portions of the Seventh Symphony sketchbook and excerpts from correspondence in their collection; European American Music Distributors Corporation (sole US and Canadian agent for Universal Edition, A.G., Wien), for permission to reproduce excerpts from Mahler's voice-and-piano version of *Das Lied von der Erde* (Kritische Gesamtausgabe, Supplement Band II); the Theodore W. Adorno Archiv, Frankfurt am Main, Dr. Rolf Tiedemann, director, for permission to reproduce Adorno's dedication of *Mahler: Eine musikalische Physiognomik* to his wife; Maria McLeeson, Cleveland, Ohio, for superb work in deciphering Mahler's handwriting and checking translations of German; Kent Quade, Center for Music and Technology, Case Western Reserve University, for expert assistance in computer technology; Deborah M. Hefling, Assistant to the Deputy Director, Cleveland Public Library, for numerous reference questions; and Alice N. Loranth, Head of Special Collections, Cleveland Public Library, for advice on bibliographic description. Special thanks are also due to Penny Souster, music editor, Lucy Carolan, Kathryn Bailey, Caroline Murray, and the staff of Cambridge University Press for their patience and efficiency during the lengthy gestation of the volume.

Bibliographic abbreviations

TAM   Adorno, Theodor W. *Mahler: Eine musikalische Physiognomik*. Frankfurt am
         Main, 1960.

TAME   Adorno, Theodor W. *Mahler: A Musical Physiognomy*. Translated by
         Edmund Jephcott. Chicago, 1992.

NBL2   Bauer-Lechner, Natalie. *Gustav Mahler in den Erinnerungen von Natalie
         Bauer-Lechner*. Edited by Herbert Killian, with annotations by Knud
         Martner. Hamburg, 1984.

NBLE   Bauer-Lechner, Natalie. *Recollections of Gustav Mahler*. Translated by Dika
         Newlin. Edited by Peter Franklin. Cambridge, 1980.

KBD   Blaukopf, Kurt, ed. and comp. *Mahler: A Documentary Study*. With
         contributions by Zoltan Roman. Translated by Paul Baker et al. London,
         1976.

HLGF   De La Grange, Henry-Louis. *Gustav Mahler: Chronique d'une vie*. 3 vols.
         Paris, 1979–84.

HLG 1   De La Grange, Henry-Louis. *Mahler*. Vol. I. Garden City, 1973.

HLG 2   De La Grange, Henry-Louis. *Mahler*. Vol. II: *Vienna: The Years of Challenge,
         1897–1904*. Oxford, 1995.

KG   *Gustav Mahler: Sämtliche Werke, Kritische Gesamtausgabe*. Edited under
         auspices of the Internationale Gustav Mahler Gesellschaft, Vienna, by Erwin
         Ratz, Karl Heinz Füssl, et al. Vienna, etc., 1960–.

AMML4   Mahler, Alma. *Gustav Mahler: Memories and Letters*. 4th edition, revised and
         enlarged by Donald Mitchell and Knud Martner. Translated by Basil
         Creighton. London, 1990.

GMB2   Mahler, Gustav. *Gustav Mahler Briefe*. Revised and enlarged edition by
         Herta Blaukopf. Vienna, 1982.

GMBE   Mahler, Gustav. *Selected Letters of Gustav Mahler*. Edited by Knud Martner.
         Translated by Eithne Wilkins, Ernst Kaiser, and Bill Hopkins. New York,
         1979.

BIBLIOGRAPHIC ABBREVIATIONS

MWY   Mitchell, Donald. *Gustav Mahler: The Wunderhorn Years.* Boulder, Colo., 1976; reprinted, Berkeley and Los Angeles, 1980.

MSSLD   Mitchell, Donald. *Gustav Mahler.* Vol. III: *Songs and Symphonies of Life and Death.* Berkeley and Los Angeles, 1985.

1 The young Mahler, 1875–1880: essay in situational analysis after Karl R. Popper

HERTA BLAUKOPF

translated by Stephen E. Hefling

In the biography of Gustav Mahler, which has been several times chronicled in richly knowledgeable detail, there remains a striking lacuna: the years 1875 through 1880, which Mahler spent in Vienna to study at the Conservatory and the University. In contrast to all other periods of his life, only a few documents and absolutely no personal revelations in conjunction with his development are preserved. As regards Mahler's childhood in the Moravian town of Iglau, we are indirectly enlightened by the composer himself. He readily told those close to him about his earliest musical activities: his own memories, and probably as well the little tales that were recounted to him by family and friends years later. There were two women in Mahler's life – Natalie Bauer-Lechner and Alma Mahler – who wrote down his childhood recollections.[1] Even if this seems somewhat like an instance of stories about stories about stories, there can be scarcely any doubt about their essential kernel of truth. We are told that as a preschooler he already played the harmonica, that he discovered the piano in his grandparents' house, and that he soon completed little compositions, for each of which his mother presented him the honorarium of two *Kreuzer*.[2] We learn what shock the death of younger siblings aroused in him, especially that of

---

[1] *Gustav Mahler in den Erinnerungen von Natalie Bauer-Lechner*, ed. Herbert Killian (Hamburg, 1984) (hereafter cited as NBL2); Alma Mahler, *Gustav Mahler: Memories and Letters*, 4th edn. by Donald Mitchell and Knud Martner (London, 1990) (hereafter cited as AMML4).

[2] NBL2, pp. 69 ff. From the text of this edition it would appear that the reward was in *Kronen* (rather than *Kreuzer*), but that seems to be a misreading of the abbreviation "kr." The *Kronen* currency was introduced in Austria only in the 1890s.

1

his brother Ernst. And we sense too something of his tender relationship with his mother, as well as his problematic connection to his father.[3]

But neither the confidante (Natalie) nor the wife (Alma) gave any particulars about Mahler's student years. As a result we know little more than the bare chronological framework: in 1875 at age fifteen entry into the Vienna Conservatory, where he completed his studies in 1878; enrollment in the University of Vienna in 1877, where he took no degree; in 1880 his first, very modest, position as a Kapellmeister. Concerning the intellectual content of these five years as well as the self-discovery of an extraordinary talent, very little has come down to us: a couple of Mahler's letters, written in stilted style and practically devoid of factual content, and a couple of his poems in the late romantic manner typical of the time.[4] Nothing extraordinary. Nevertheless it was during this student period in Vienna that slowly, as a "late bloomer," he grew toward his future stature.

The Austrian philosopher Karl R. Popper, who was concerned both with the problems of writing history and with the problems of music, urges us in his writings to define the human individual and his actions through so-called situational logic. Among other things, this means explicitly:

> We need studies, based on methodological individualism, of social institutions through which ideas may spread and captivate individuals, of the way in which new traditions may be created, and of the way in which traditions work and break down.[5]

Such an investigation of the existing institutions by which Gustav Mahler was influenced during his early Viennese years will be attempted in the following pages. Through this situational analysis we will be in a position to understand better many a later act and decision. Among the institutions that might be investigated I shall of course limit myself to specific economic and cultural ones, and among the latter to the Conservatory, the Philharmonic Concerts, and the University. Since the known reports and

---

[3] AMML4, pp. 6–11.

[4] Cf. Mahler's letter of 17–19 June 1879 to Joseph Steiner, *Gustav Mahler Briefe*, rev. and enl. edn. by Herta Blaukopf (Vienna, 1982) (hereafter cited as GMB2), no. 5, as well as the poems in Mahler's letters to Anton Krisper, in Hans Holländer, "Unbekannte Jugendbriefe Gustav Mahlers," *Die Musik* 20/11 (1928), 80 ff.

[5] Karl R. Popper, *The Poverty of Historicism* (London, 1979), p. 149.

archives of these institutions have not previously been completely evaluated and have been inaccurately represented in several biographies, the present study can offer conclusions that are in part altogether new. Moreover, in recent years certain previously unknown documents have been discovered that shed additional light upon the darkness of these years.

First, a credibly telling utterance of Mahler's that has been preserved concerning his developmental years:

> It was a time of intellectual absorption that continued quite a long time for me, from childhood into youth. My spirit needed much, and a good deal of time for its building up, and the period of actual being and creating began relatively late for me.[6]

– Thus, one who ripened but slowly. Yet Mahler would not have developed into the great creative artist he was had he not succeeded in holding open forever a door into his childhood. Many who came to know him as a forty-year-old were astounded by the coexistence of intellectual acuteness and childlike naïveté within him. The Austrian historian Friedrich Engel-Janosi, whose memoires were published in 1974, still clearly recalled how Mahler and the elder of his little daughters "with the beautiful corkscrew locks" came into the house and Mahler "despite a tick in his leg" danced with the children. "We liked him very much, although we did not have much sense of his importance, or any great interest in that."[7]

The Vienna of 1875, into which the fifteen-year-old Mahler emigrated from the small town of Iglau, was the capital of a realm that no longer exists: the double monarchy of Austria-Hungary. After Russia and Sweden (at that time united with Norway), it was the largest state in Europe, and also ranked third in population. These nearly forty million inhabitants were made up of twelve different nations (not counting the smaller tribes): Hungarians, Poles, Ruthenians, Czechs, Moravians, Slovaks, Slovenians, Croatians, and Italians (to name only the most prominent), plus the predominating German Austrians, whose speech and culture was also

---

[6] Natalie Bauer-Lechner, "Mahleriana," typescript, private collection, Graz (not consistently paginated, and not textually identical with NBL2). Cf. also Henry-Louis de La Grange, *Mahler*, vol. I (New York, 1973) (hereafter cited as HLG 1), p. 17.

[7] Friedrich Engel-Janosi, . . . *aber ein stolzer Bettler* (Graz, 1974), p. 26 f.

3

professed by the Jews, albeit indifferently, in whatever part of the monarchy they lived. For Jewish Austrians this was a propitious decade. Through statute of the state they enjoyed full civil rights, and political antisemitism had not yet taken root (although there were at all times individual enemies of Jewry).

A dense rail network united the individual kingdoms and duchies that comprised the Habsburg state, such that a letter mailed in Cracow, or, more importantly for us, in Iglau, was delivered in Vienna the following day. When Mahler came to Vienna the city had almost 700,000 inhabitants – in reality almost a million, if one counts the nearby suburbs that would soon thereafter belong to Vienna. The celebrated Ringstraße and many of its representational buildings were still in progress. Already completed in the full splendor of stylistic historicism were the two edifices that must have been most important for a budding musician – the Vienna Court Opera and the Conservatory of the Gesellschaft der Musikfreunde (Society of the Friends of Music).

Three years at the Vienna Conservatory

Unlike other academies, the Conservatory was not one of the state educational establishments. Musically enthusiastic private citizens had founded it at the beginning of the nineteenth century, and continued to manage it well beyond the turn of the twentieth. The necessary means were gathered through membership dues, through donations, including contributions from the imperial court, and not least through rental of the concert halls that belonged to the Gesellschaft der Musikfreunde. During the revolutionary year of 1848 and on several occasions thereafter, the Gesellschaft sought to place the Conservatory in the hands of the state. The state, however, "declined with a nod" and merely granted the institution a relatively modest subvention. Thus, contrary to the original intentions of those who founded the Conservatory, there now remained no choice but to collect a corresponding tuition fee from the students, especially after the stock exchange crash of 1873, when previous revenues sank.[8] Mahler's was

---

[8] See Richard von Perger and Robert Hirschfeld, *Geschichte der k. k. Gesellschaft der Musikfreunde in Wien* (Vienna, 1912).

assessed at the not inconsiderable sum of 120 Gulden per year. In response to his own petition, and based upon recommendation of his professors, his tuition fees were reduced by half for the second and third years of his program;[9] accordingly, he had to pay 60 Gulden – still difficult enough for him. For during Gustav's years of study at the Conservatory the Mahler couple in Iglau had to care for a half-dozen other children; and while they believed in the unusual talent of their eldest, they never sent him as much as he would have needed. It would appear that from the outset, and certainly from his second year on, Gustav was required to teach piano, to pass on what he learned in the Conservatory in order to make ends meet. Conservatory students usually got 1 Gulden for a lesson – not bad, considering that the lowliest bureaucrat made 60 Gulden a month (without additional perquisites), and a worker had to manage with 20.

There are varying reports concerning Mahler's admission to the Conservatory. Immediately after his death, Mahler's professor of piano, Julius Epstein (1832–1926), recalled his first encounter with the pupil who would later become so famous:

> I very well remember the day . . . when Gustav Mahler's father came to see me at the Conservatoire . . . and asked me to examine his son; he wanted to know whether the boy had enough talent to make music his career . . . I asked Mahler to sit down at the piano and play me something. He had already composed several things, so he said, without any previous training, and I asked him to play me one of his own compositions. I let him play for only a few minutes; the composition was immature, and later on he destroyed it himself. But I realized immediately that I was in the presence of a born musician . . .[10]

Seemingly better documented is the account of the rural estate administrator Gustav Schwarz, which was already published during Mahler's lifetime. Evidently it fell to Schwarz early in September of 1875 to persuade the father, Bernhard Mahler, distiller and dealer of spirits in Iglau, that the talent of his son merited a musical education at the Vienna Conservatory.[11]

---

[9] Kurt Blaukopf, ed. and comp., *Mahler: A Documentary Study*, trans. Paul Baker et al. (London, 1976) (hereafter cited as KBD), p. 153.

[10] *Neues Wiener Journal*, 19 May 1911, cited in KBD, p. 151.

[11] Cf. Mahler's letter of 28 August 1875 to Gustav Schwarz, GMB2, no. 1+.

A few days later Schwarz travelled with Gustav to Vienna, to present his protégé to the pianist Julius Epstein:

> when I came to Professor Epstein, I found him anything but delighted, for Mahler's piano playing did not impress him at all. It was only when Mahler played him some of his own compositions that Epstein showed any enthusiasm and said over and over again that they were in direct descent from Wagner . . .[12]

Both versions of the story, although conflicting about who accompanied Gustav, are concordant with respect to essentials. Julius Epstein recognized the eminent musicality of the young man – not, to be sure, in his piano playing, but rather in his compositions. Nevertheless, he immediately placed Mahler in his advanced piano class, not in one of the preparatory classes. In autumn of 1875 there were 648 pupils in the Conservatory (excluding the drama division), and more than half of them – 353 to be precise – were piano students (not including 173 who took piano as a secondary area of study). Most were in rudimentary or preparatory classes; nevertheless, 93, including Mahler, were in the advanced class. Among them were many girls and young women, for the Conservatory, in contrast to the secondary schools and universities, accepted female students, not only in singing and piano classes, but in theoretical studies as well. Mahler's acceptance into the advanced class seems to have been completely justified by the end of his first year, because, together with four of his schoolmates, he received a First Prize, which the jury awarded him unanimously.

"To encourage competition in diligence and progress, prizes are established for which the students of particular departments are permitted to compete if they meet the stipulated requirements pertaining thereto," ceremoniously states paragraph 53 of the "Executive Regulations" concerning competition for prizes. The jury consisted of the director and two professors of the Conservatory, and two connoisseurs not affiliated with the institution; the awards were medals.[13]

---

[12] *Neues Wiener Journal*, 6 August 1905, cited in KBD, p. 151.

[13] All information about activities at the Conservatory is according to *Berichte über das Conservatorium und die Schauspielschule der Gesellschaft der Musikfreunde in Wien*, school year 1875–76 (Vienna, 1876), school year 1876–77 (Vienna, 1877), and school year 1877–78 (Vienna, 1878).

Concerts of the Wiener Philharmoniker

Piano, then, was Mahler's major concentration; as secondary subjects he chose harmony and composition. And during his very first days as a composition student in the class of Professor Franz Krenn, he was drawn into an undertaking that was probably of greatest significance for him. Fifteen young men and women, Mahler amongst them, sent a petition on 19 September 1875 to "The Honorable Society of the Vienna Philharmonic" in which they asked to be admitted to the dress rehearsals for the Philharmonic concerts. The reason advanced was that "only with great difficulty can the efforts of composition students arise to the level of self-reliant accomplishment if the opportunity to be present at the performance of musical masterworks is denied them."[14] Yet this request was formally denied. Just that fall the members of the Philharmonic had chosen a new director, namely Hans Richter, who the following summer would conduct the premiere of Wagner's *Ring* in Bayreuth. Richter, Viennese to be sure, yet new to Vienna as an orchestral conductor, apparently did not want his dress rehearsals to be observed by students. The Philharmonic did, however, promise Professor Krenn a number of tickets for the concerts themselves, to be made available to the composition students. Thus we can assume that during his three years of studies Mahler was able to hear at least a large portion of the Philharmonic concerts, which at that time numbered eight per season.

How delightful and informative it would be at this point if we had one of Mahler's letters, one single letter to his parents or to the rural estate administrator Schwarz, in which he described his impressions from one of these concerts. To be sure, he had already heard orchestral music in Iglau – in the Municipal Theater, in church, in concerts of the military establishment – but certainly nothing approaching the sound of the Philharmonic in the large hall of the Gesellschaft der Musikfreunde. Unfortunately no such letter has survived, and none was probably ever written; according to his own testimony, the young Mahler tended to absorb great artistic events as though they were a matter of course, and to point a finger only at those that were defective.[15]

---

[14] MS, Archive of the Vienna Philharmonic.   [15] HLG 1, p. 42.

Thus, while we have no document of this sort, it may nevertheless be said that the impressions must have been powerful, and in a certain sense, definitive. In particular, if one compares the repertoire Hans Richter offered during the three concert seasons between the fall of 1875 and spring of 1878 with the repertoire Mahler directed twenty years later during his three seasons with the Philharmonic (i.e., 1898 through the beginning of 1901), we are struck by astonishing correspondences.[16] That both Richter and Mahler performed the complete symphonies and most important overtures of Beethoven is hardly telling, for at that time and long thereafter Beethoven's work dominated the programs of all concert organizers in the world. If both had special interest in the C major and "Unfinished" Symphonies of Schubert, that can perhaps be attributed to a binding Viennese tradition. But that Mahler, during the three short seasons he devoted to the Philharmonic, placed the *Symphonie fantastique* and *Roman Carnival Overture* by Berlioz as well as the *Faust Overture* and *Siegfried Idyll* of Wagner on the programs has to be interpreted as the after-effect of his youthful impressions. So, too, with the Brahms *Variations on a Theme by Haydn*. And why would he want to conduct precisely Mendelssohn's Third Symphony and the overture *Meeresstille und glückliche Fahrt*, which the Philharmonic audience had heard just shortly before? The situation was probably obscure even to Mahler himself. He had come to know and marvel over this music during his years of greatest impressionability, and felt compelled to present his own interpretations, which differed from Richter's, as soon as he had the opportunity. If an additional instance were required of how extensively Mahler's choice of repertoire in Vienna was influenced by his youthful impressions – the situation is different as regards his concerts in America – one could cite a concert outside the Philharmonic series at which Franz Liszt played the E♭ ("Emperor") Concerto by Beethoven. During his three years of Philharmonic concerts Mahler offered only a single Beethoven concerto: the E♭, with Ferruccio Busoni as soloist.

At the time he made up his mind to study music, Gustav Mahler probably did not have the intention of becoming a conductor. After all, there was no course of instruction for the budding Kapellmeister at the Vienna

---

[16] Cf. *Wiener Philharmoniker 1842–1942: Statistik*, ed. Hedwig Kraus and Karl Schreinzer (Vienna, 1942).

Conservatory. But what were his professional prospects? Concert pianist? Composer? It would appear that for a long time he himself was unclear about the matter. In Professor Krenn's composition class he distinguished himself in his first year of study, just as he had in the piano class, and in the competition took a first prize for a movement of a piano quintet. During the summer recess of 1876 Gustav Mahler organized a concert in Iglau together with some colleagues from the conservatory. Here as well he presented himself in his double role: as pianist in Schubert's *Wanderer* Fantasy and a Chopin ballade, and as composer with two pieces of chamber music.[17]

During his second conservatory year, however, something must have occurred about which we can merely speculate, and which altered his situation with respect to the institution. It would appear as though Mahler withdrew from the Conservatory in anger, for there is a document in his hand at the Gesellschaft der Musikfreunde in which he characterizes this decision as "over-hasty" and quite meekly asks the director to regard it as though it had not occurred.[18] Given that Mahler's friend and contemporary Hugo Wolf was dismissed from the Conservatory for a breach of discipline during this same school year, it is not unlikely that Mahler's departure and reentry were related to that incident. His school report for the year 1876–77 reflects these upheavals. Mahler arrived too late for a supplementary examination in counterpoint, did not complete the second exercise, and furthermore did not submit an end-of-year assignment. Accordingly, as the register confirms, he was not admitted to the composition competition.[19] In the annual report of the Conservatory, of course, the outcome is represented more considerately: there it states that Mahler "waived" participation in the composition competition.[20]

More a composer than a pianist

Surprisingly, we find that Mahler, whose major concentration had been piano, had changed his major to composition in his third

---

[17] Concert program of 12 September 1876, reproduced in KBD, plate no. 30.
[18] Cited in KBD, p. 154.
[19] "Conservatorium für Musik und darstellende Kunst / der Gesellschaft der Musikfreunde in Wien / Matrikel. / . . . Mahler Gustav . . .," cited in KBD, p. 154.
[20] *Bericht über das Conservatorium* . . ., 1876/1877 (Vienna, 1877).

conservatory year. The idea of pursuing the career of a concert pianist was thus abandoned, if indeed it had ever been entertained. What was the reason for the change? Only shortly before Mahler had finally taken another first prize in the piano competition (although this time, to be sure, the award was not unanimous). Or had the pianistic perfection of Liszt and Rubinstein aroused self-doubt?[21]

We may assume that Mahler decided upon changing concentration from piano to composition with the consent of his teacher, Julius Epstein. If we take at their word the previously cited reports of Epstein and Schwarz, it clearly emerges that from the outset Epstein did not see in Mahler a piano virtuoso. Since music and musicality meant more to Epstein himself than an extremely brilliant piano technique, no rupture emerged in his special liking for Mahler, which he demonstrated throughout the younger man's student years and also long thereafter. Epstein, too, was admired first and foremost as a musician, and only secondarily as a pianist. He did great service as an editor of Schubert's piano music, which also filtered into the repertoire of his students. Mahler acknowledged in later years that playing these pieces he was "filled with enchantment," and that it had been his greatest longing to express in similar vein everything that filled and stirred him.[22] Doubtless this early experience of Schubert left traces in Mahler's songs and symphonies, and this, moreover, was more easily recognized at a distance than in Vienna. In an article on the Paris performance of Mahler's Second Symphony, for example, the composer Alfredo Casella remarked how much he felt reminded of Schubert by Mahler's melodic invention.[23]

Schubert was no more a writer of virtuosic piano music than his editor Epstein was a virtuoso pianist. Here is an excerpt from a review of 1867, when Epstein was at the Conservatory: "As so often before, we must compliment the recitalist on the arrangement of the program. He played only compositions that are very seldom heard, and yet are very much worth hearing. What a blessing . . . to get away from the monotony of the usual piano repertoire!" And about the rendering of Schubert's "Fantasy" Sonata (Op. 78, D. 894) in this concert the critique states: "Mr. Epstein played the

---

[21] HLG 1, p. 42.   [22] Bauer-Lechner, "Mahleriana."

[23] Alfred[o] Casella, "Gustav Mahler et sa deuxième symphonie," *SIM: Revue musicale mensuelle* 6/4 (April 1910), 240 f.

Fantasy with refined feeling, and many passages . . . incomparably beauti-fully. We might of course have wished for more broad and powerful con-trasts in this performance, whereby the sweet contours would only have seemed the more beautiful."[24] The author of this review was Eduard Hanslick, who is known to many music lovers only as an opponent of Richard Wagner's. Unjustly so: he was an enthusiastic and competent critic, and what is more, a musical scholar whose significance as a historian and theorist is being rediscovered only in recent years.

A variety of opportunities detracted from Mahler's development as a piano virtuoso, if that indeed had ever been his goal. During his Iglau years his parents gave him, doubtless at his urging, a library subscription that included the privilege of borrowing music. Every week Mahler received a fresh package of music and played indiscriminately through whatever he had found – opera arrangements, piano albums, salon music, etc.[25] The time invested in this took away from systematic practising. But Mahler was so enthusiastic about the utility of sightreading that as late as 1883 he advised one of his piano students to take out a subscription and "root around diligently in all available music," to play whatever came before her.[26] Naturally neither Mahler nor Fräulein Weiss became technically perfect pianists via this method. Nevertheless, Mahler seems to have acquired through this training the ideal prerequisites to be a vocal coach and conduc-tor. Nor do we know whether Mahler practised extensively during the two years that he was a piano major in Vienna; we do not even know whether he always had a piano at his disposal. For this he would have had to earn money, give lessons, and pay for a rental piano. And in addition, he still had to master the subject matter of the Iglau Gymnasium, where each year the qualifying examinations for private pupils (*Externistenprüfung*) awaited him.

Getting through Gymnasium

Mahler had been a poor student in the lower level of the Gymnasium, while still living in Iglau, and he did even less well in the upper level, which

---

[24] Eduard Hanslick, *Aus dem Concertsaal* (Vienna, 1870), p. 431.
[25] Bauer-Lechner, "Mahleriana"; cf. also HLG 1, p. 17.
[26] Mahler, autograph letter to Hermine Weiss, photocopy, Internationale Gustav Mahler Gesellschaft, Vienna.

he completed in absentia.[27] Nevertheless, he succeeded in passing the matriculation examination, the *Matura* as it is called in Austria, in 1877. A school essay written shortly before this, which is preserved in the Iglau files, shows us an example of young Mahler's absentmindedness – for in those days he was clearly from time to time "lost to the world." The assigned theme for the essay read: "What motives led Wallenstein's various followers to desert him. After Schiller." But Mahler, lost in dreaminess, read the question imprecisely and gave to his work the inscription: "The motives that led Wallenstein to desertion." And then the examinee described the frame of mind of a man bearing no resemblance to either Schiller's Wallenstein or the historical Wallenstein, but who was in a definite sense related to the Gymnasium pupil Mahler:

> When a man is alone and only has his own fantasy for company, he often makes plans without ever thinking of how to put them into practice; they are little more than phantoms born of his poetic fantaisy [!]; he dreams of future greatness and of glory and power, and gradually comes to think that he is actually living in his high-flown ideas and bold plans, which would only appear laughable to him if he considered them in the cold light of reason.[28]

Mahler's essay was deemed "unsatisfactory." That he still ultimately passed the *Matura* was probably attributable only to his intelligence and to the leniency of the teachers toward the musically gifted absentee student. Mahler, however, took his *Matura* certificate and immediately enrolled in the University of Vienna, even though he still had a year at the Conservatory before him.

And in no sense during this final year did Mahler distinguish himself, if one compares him to his closest student companions. Although composition was now his major field, he played the first movement of Xaver Scharwenka's Piano Concerto at one of the sixteen student evening recitals. This was the first and only time that he participated in the numerous student concerts of the Conservatory. When one observes how frequently Mahler's

---

[27] Catalogues of the Iglau State Gymnasium, Bezirksarchiv of Iglau (Jihlava), Latin and German Gymnasium.

[28] Essay clipped into the "Gustav Mahler" folder in the catalogue of the eighth class.

friend Hans Rott or his future brother-in-law Arnold Rosé stepped before the public during this period, Mahler's reticence seems more than unusual. As far as can be ascertained from the annual reports, he made no significant efforts even in composition, his new concentration. His colleagues made fun of him and prophesied that he would never complete a composition, because he never managed to get beyond the first or second movement.[29] In fact the only piece preserved from his conservatory days is the first movement of a piano quartet that apparently was not carried any further. The movement was published in 1973, and has been frequently performed since then.

Mahler's fellow student Rudolf Pichler wrote an orchestra piece during the 1877–78 academic year, and it was performed at one of the Conservatory's public concerts; his female colleague Mathilde von Kralik also had the practical experience of writing a work for orchestra, and both of these students were given the opportunity to conduct their works in public. Yet none other than Mahler, for whom in later years no orchestra was large enough and who above all thought only of orchestral works, once again submitted a movement of chamber music for the competition in 1878. One might be inclined to attribute such non-showings to Mahler's negligence and immaturity, but that would be unjust. His colleagues Pichler and Kralik both came from Vienna and lived there in the bosom of their families, while Mahler had to rely upon favor and disfavor of his land-lords. One of his good friends by the name of Rudolf Krzyzanowski com-posed two lieder in 1878 and won a special prize with them, which carried an honorarium of 20 ducats – nearly 100 Gulden. Mahler evidently com-peted in vain. He was as little understood by the judges of this competition as he would later be by the jurors for the Conservatory's Beethoven Prize (1881); whether in this case the decision was just or unjust cannot be assessed, since both of his competition lieder must be considered lost.[30]

At the competition of the composition class he was once again awarded, although not unanimously, a First Prize in the form of a medal, and at the same time he also received, following a three-year training period, the graduation diploma of the Conservatory.

[29] HLG 1, p.35.
[30] Cf. Ludwig Karpath, *Begegnung mit dem Genius* (Vienna, 1934), p. 62, as well as Robert Fischhof, *Begegnungen auf meinem Lebensweg* (Vienna, 1916), p. 26.

Departure from the Conservatory

What had the three years of study gained him? In later years Mahler himself scarcely said anything about it. His friend and biographer, the musicologist Guido Adler who had himself studied at the Conservatory, wrote the following remarks:

> although he had good teachers in piano playing and harmony, his introduction to the higher theoretical subjects (counterpoint and composition) was anything but profound and purposeful . . . He drew the greatest profit from the stimulating activity of the Director of the institution, for the latter created an especially effective model through the performance of chamber music. The "Hellmesberger Quartet" was a greater influence on us than all instruction. The performance of quartets from Beethoven's last period created deeper impressions than anything then offered in Vienna, and also stylistically affected all students of composition.[31]

Even though many Mahler biographers are inclined to doubt this influence, we cannot rule it out entirely. Thirteen years after Mahler there was a violin student at the Conservatory, a little boy who later became an important virtuoso and composer: the Romanian Georges Enesco. From the rehearsals of the Hellmesberger Quartet he gained valuable and precise hints of how Beethoven and Schubert wanted their music played.[32] For he recognized the significance of stylistic tradition: the father of the Conservatory Director, Hellmesberger, had actually been a musician of the Beethoven era, and Beethoven himself had traversed the narrow alleys of Vienna, just as during Enesco's student days Johannes Brahms strode through the Vienna streets with white beard and wild mien, which instilled the young student with anguish.[33]

Young Mahler must also have encountered Brahms in person on the streets and in the concert hall. He probably regarded him with a certain aversion, since in the passionate quarrel between the Wagnerians and the

---

[31] Guido Adler, *Gustav Mahler* (Vienna, 1916), trans. Edward R. Reilly in his *Gustav Mahler and Guido Adler: Records of a Friendship* (Cambridge, 1982), p. 19.

[32] Bernard Gavoty, *Les Souvenirs de Georges Enesco* (Paris, 1955), p. 58.

[33] Ibid., p. 55.

Brahmsians, Mahler, like many of the students, aligned himself on the side of Richard Wagner. Hugo Wolf declared his Wagnerian enthusiasm in a letter written in the fall of 1875,[34] and we can only suppose that Mahler was equally seized by Wagnerian intoxication. In the year 1877 he joined the Vienna Academic Wagner Society co-founded by Guido Adler, although two years later he left it for unknown reasons.[35] But the cause certainly lay in some sort of dispute within the Society rather than in diminishing veneration of Wagner. Throughout his entire life Mahler admired the Bayreuth master as both artist and man, although he must certainly have been aware of Wagner's antisemitism. Yet in later years Mahler also succeeded in doing justice to Brahms, both as man and artist.

Remarkably, Mahler's encounter with Anton Bruckner took place outside the Conservatory, even though Bruckner taught harmony and counterpoint at that institution. Equally unclear is Mahler's relationship to Bruckner at the University. In December of 1877, during Mahler's last year at the Conservatory and first year at the University, Bruckner conducted the premiere of his own Third Symphony in the large hall of the Gesellschaft der Musikfreunde, which quickly became empty. Among the few who did not flee or hiss were Mahler and his colleague Rudolf Krzyzanowski. Shortly thereafter Mahler undertook, possibly together with Krzyzanowski, the task of preparing a four-hand piano arrangement of this symphony. At that point began the friendship proper between Mahler and Bruckner who, although he enjoyed renown as an organist, was not yet recognized as a composer. There have been several specialized studies concerning the artistic and personal relations between the two; accordingly, that subject may be passed over here.

At the University

In the fall of 1877, although still a pupil at the Conservatory, Mahler matriculated to the University of Vienna. The registration forms, called

[34] Letter of 23 November 1875 from Wolf to his father, cited in Frank Walker, *Hugo Wolf* (New York, 1952), p. 27.
[35] Cf. *Fünfter Jahres-Bericht des Wiener akademischen Wagner-Vereines, für das Jahr 1877* (Vienna, 1878), as well as *Siebenter Jahres-Bericht . . . für das Jahr 1879* (Vienna, 1880).

15

Nationale in Austria, for a total of three semesters are preserved in the archive of the University. But not a single document, no letter, no post-facto account indicates why the developing musician took on a second program of study before completing the Conservatory. Was it the wish of the parents, in whose eyes a university degree had greater weight than the diploma of the Conservatory? Was it Gustav's own decision because he had recognized the inadequacy of his Gymnasium education? In the biography by Richard Specht that appeared in 1905 one reads that "this born musician, during that indeterminate fermentation process of the typical young artist . . . gave up for a long time the thought of musical creativity and instead thought of becoming a poet."[36] Mahler read the text of this small study before it went to press and did not object to this assertion, although both he and Bruno Walter (acting on Mahler's instructions) contested certain other details.[37] Was attendance at the University perchance supposed to aid his development as a poet? Today it is difficult to believe in the sincerity of Mahler's vacillation between music and literature, since his surviving poetic works from this period are lacking both in originality and in fluency of expression. Probably the three university semesters served above all for the still very impressionable young man to become clearer about his own personality.

In later years Mahler gladly made reference to his university studies: at the end of 1884, for example, in that passionate letter to Hans von Bülow, in which he offered himself as student or assistant;[38] then in March 1896, as he answered the letter of an enthusiastic concert-goer: "Moved when 15 to Vienna— *conservatoire* and *university*!";[39] and in December of the same year in a letter to a journalist: "Entered the University of Vienna in my seventeenth year, and instead of lectures (philos[ophical] fac[ulty]), diligently visited the Vienna woods."[40]

---

[36] Richard Specht, *Gustav Mahler* (Berlin [1905]), p. 17 (cf. also KBD, p. 157).
[37] See Mahler's letter to Richard Specht [Fall 1904] in GMB2, no. 336, as well as the accompanying annotation.
[38] Autograph letter in Mahler's personnel file at the Kassel State Theatre, cited in KBD, p. 170.
[39] Letter of 2 March 1896 to Annie Mincieux, *Mahler's Unknown Letters*, ed. Herta Blaukopf et al., trans. Richard Stokes (London, 1986), p. 119.
[40] Letter of 4 December 1896 to Max Marschalk, GMB2, no. 198.

This account sounds more teasing than straightforward, and also contradicts the enthusiastic exclamation point in the letter cited just before. Certainly Mahler, just like other students, may occasionally have cut one or another scheduled lecture to go out walking. Nevertheless it is unlikely that he sacrificed around 15 Gulden per semester from his scanty means chiefly to pass the time in the Vienna woods, where admission was free. His multiple mentions of the University, even including the particular faculty, in the 1880s and '90s lead to the conclusion that Mahler was proud of his university study, even though he did not earn any academic degree and probably also did not aspire to.

Since the individual sources leave us in the lurch, we must rely once again upon the institutions. At first glance the *Nationale* filled out by Mahler for three semesters would suggest that he was not studying for a profession.[41] We find here German literary history, philosophy, art history, and music history. Twice – in the winter term 1877–78 and in the summer semester 1878 – Mahler entered Bruckner's lecture course on harmony in his *Nationale,* and both times it was crossed out, either by his own hand or someone else's. Why? In the first semester its meeting time conflicted with a lecture on general history for which he had also registered. But that, too, was crossed out, and indeed in ink, whereas Bruckner fell victim to a blue pencil. The two cancellations could thus have been undertaken by different persons or at different times. In the second semester, however, there was no such conflict – yet Bruckner's class was entered by Mahler and again crossed out by him or someone else. But that of course does not prove that Mahler did not attend this course every so often, or perhaps even regularly. If he did, however, it would have been unofficial, without attestation and without charge. By dropping the history lecture elected in the winter term of 1877–78 – Bruckner's course was without fee that semester – Mahler's tuition fees were reduced from the previously calculated amount of 20 Gulden 95 Kreuzer to 15 Gulden 70 Kreuzer. The statement of these figures

---

[41] Three *Nationale* filled out by Mahler and stamped by the bursar are preserved in the archive of the University of Vienna, for winter term 1877–78, summer term 1878, and winter term 1879–80 (cf. KBD, plate no. 38). Mahler did not register for the two semesters between the summer term of 1878 and the winter term of 1879–80. This is confirmed not only by the absence of his *Nationale* in the corresponding volumes, but also by an annotation that the winter term of 1879–80 was Mahler's third semester.

is not to suggest, however, that financial reasons alone were decisive for the cancellations.

To be sure, whether or not he attended it, Bruckner's course of instruction can scarcely have been of great importance for the youthful Mahler. It was not listed among the University's academic art offerings, but rather at the end of the catalogue, between choral singing and gymnastics among the so-called "skills" courses (*Fertigkeiten*) provided for the students. The content that Bruckner announced – resolution of chords, exercises in figured bass, simple counterpoint, double counterpoint at the octave, the principal components of fugue, etc. – must long have been familiar to Mahler the composition student.

For two semesters Mahler registered for the lecture "Medieval German Literary History," which was dedicated above all to German medieval love poetry (*Minnesang*), and at the same time for "Studies in Middle High German," which focused on Parsifal. These selections are certainly understandable. Wagner had brought German antiquity to the stage; he had interpreted in new fashion the medival epics "Tannhäuser," "Nibelungen," "Tristan," and most recently "Parsifal,"[42] and now young Mahler, just like his prototype, wanted to get to the sources. He was probably disappointed, because the lecturer, Professor Richard Heinzel, approached the poems and epics without the nationalistic pathos of other Germanists, and did not link them with contemporary philosophies of ruin or salvation. On the contrary, he placed considerable value upon understanding of phonetic laws and the grammar of Middle High German. Moreover, the antiromantic Heinzel, like many Germanists of the period, was anything but a Wagnerian.[43]

The choice of the remaining courses is surprising, since several topics of visual art are among them – yet until his encounter with the Viennese Secession, Mahler showed scarcely any interest in such matters. We have to assume that friends or colleagues recommended these courses to him. Perhaps it was his cousin Gustav Frank, who at that time was studying at the Akademie der bildenden Künste (Academy of Visual Arts), where the

[42] The poem, completed in April 1877, was published in December of that year, although the musical realization was not finished until 1882.
[43] Information concerning university courses is based on the lecture catalogues of the University of Vienna.

University lecture course "Studies of Antique Sculptures on the Basis of Plaster Casts" by Otto Benndorf took place, for which Mahler registered. But perhaps Mahler realized that the overdeveloped musical ear had resulted in detriment to the sense of sight, and wished to compensate for this. In the course of his studies Mahler took "Exercises in Analysis and Interpretation of Artworks" as well as "Greek Art History" and "History of German-Netherlandish Painting."

In his second semester Mahler placed at the top of his *Nationale* the lecture course "Philosophy of History of Philosophy," which Franz Brentano presented to the students, and which was also intended to be the introduction to "Self-Study of Philosophical Writers." It must have had a provocative effect on Mahler, and not only on Mahler. For Brentano, an opponent of metaphysics and one of the fathers of twentieth-century philosophy and psychology, distinguished in each of the great epochs – antiquity, Middle Ages, and modernity – four philosophical phases, as follows: (1) ascent, (2) weakening of scientific interest, (3) skepticism concerning the possibilities of knowledge, and (4) decline into mysticism and mere speculation. And according to Brentano all the philosophers of German Romanticism belonged to the phase of decline, from Fichte to Hegel and, assuredly to Mahler's horror, Schopenhauer as well, the thinker who had played such an important role in Wagner's thought. Not only as a philosopher but also as a devout Catholic, Brentano condemned Schopenhauer's pessimism.[44] In 1879, when Mahler re-enrolled in the University after two semesters' break, he selected a lecture course on Schopenhauer given by the subsequently very well-known Alexius Meinong. Notwithstanding, Franz Brentano, a fascinating figure, a dazzling stylist, a man of passionate disposition, cannot have remained without influence on Mahler. Ultimately Mahler was engaged in philosophical questions through self-study throughout his whole life; like Brentano, he was concerned about modern natural science, and, with a view to both the message of Christ and scientific knowledge, he conferred renunciation upon cultural pessimism. Nor was it insignificant that Franz Brentano was the nephew of the German poet

[44] Franz Brentano, *Die vier Phasen der Philosophie und ihr augenblicklicher Stand* (Stuttgart, 1895); the volume is "sincerely dedicated to the academic youth of Austria-Hungary as an expression of my thankfulness for so many indications of warmest interest."

Clemens Brentano, co-editor of *Des Knaben Wunderhorn*, whose work Mahler read and cherished throughout his life.

Attending Hanslick's lectures

As noted above, following two semesters in which he did not enroll, Mahler returned to the University in the fall of 1879. Above all it should be noted that this time Mahler registered for the lectures of Eduard Hanslick, who held forth that semester on the history of music from the death of Beethoven to the present – an explosive topic, when one recalls the partisan struggles that were fully inflamed during this decade. Wagner, Liszt, and Bruckner stood on one side of the front, with Brahms, Hanslick, and all those belittled by Wagner on the other, including (posthumously) Mendelssohn and Schumann. We can assume that in his lectures, just as in his reviews, Hanslick distinguished between the Wagner of *Tannhäuser* and *Meistersinger*, two works which he treasured, and the Wagner of the *Ring*. Yet that did not redeem him either in Wagner's own eyes or in the view of Wagner's partisans, who were much more intolerant than Hanslick. How Mahler took all of this we do not know. We can only confirm from his later concert repertoire that the conflicting tendencies found symbiosis in Mahler. Moreover, Hanslick expressly exercised his influence on behalf of his former student when Mahler's appointment to the Vienna Opera was pending in the year 1897.

But what was Mahler doing during the two semesters that he did not pass his days at the University, yet had already left the Conservatory? Perhaps it was at this juncture that the Vienna woods replaced the lecture hall. We know only that, as earlier, he was active as a piano teacher, and that in this capacity he spent a couple of months in the Hungarian steppe region (*Puszta*). Presumably he occupied himself there with literary projects. Probably as early as 1877, steeped in his Middle High German studies, he had written a "Ballad of the Blond and Dark-haired Horseman" ("Ballade vom blonden und braunen Reitersmann"), which he incorporated under the title "Waldmärchen" ("Forest Legend") into the first draft of the text for *Das klagende Lied*. The title comes from the German compiler of *Märchen* Ludwig Bechstein, but the content was reworked by Mahler himself. During his first year at the Conservatory a version of *Das klagende Lied* by the

German poet Martin Greif was presented as part of a student evening recital, with roles assigned to five of the first-year acting pupils. Perhaps the designation "Märchenspiel" that Mahler originally gave his work stemmed from remembrance of that performance. In contrast to the polished verses of Greif the young Mahler produced a linguistically raw version of the tale, which would not be lacking in unintentional comedy had Mahler not subsequently overlaid it with music far more promising than the material of the text. Whether he already thought to set it to music when the text was fully assembled in March of 1878 is questionable. In February of 1879 – and note well the period in question – the plan for a setting seems to have advanced further. For at that point Mahler carefully copied out the text of *Das klagende Lied,* gave it the title "Ballade," and marked at least for Part One at which points the chorus was to repeat the last words of a stanza as an echo. It is, of course, not certain that he intended a singing rather than a speaking chorus.[45]

It seems likely that 1879 was also the year in which he was occupied with the libretto of an opera that, unlike *Das klagende Lied,* never achieved musical manifestation: *Rübezahl.* The idea came from Mahler's conservatory colleague Hugo Wolf, and led to a serious dispute between the two friends.[46] In contrast to the tragically gruesome *Das klagende Lied,* Mahler's *Rübezahl,* the text of which has survived, was intended to be a cheerful work. The story is quite childish; the characters are like clichés; the language, both prose and poetry, seems in part very clumsy, yet not altogether lacking in wit. In the cantilena of the lover, Ratibor, there are two lines that we encounter once again, only slightly altered, in the *Lieder eines fahrenden Gesellen,* for which Mahler himself also wrote the text. The lines in question read thus in *Rübezahl*: "Im Busch seh' ich ihr Haar nur weh'n / am Himmel ihr blauen Augen steh'n" ("I see her hair wafting in the bush / her blue eyes are yonder in the heavens"). In the third of the *Gesellen-Lieder* we hear: "Wenn ich in den Himmel seh / seh ich zwei blaue Augen stehn. / Wenn ich

---

45 Further on the genesis of *Das klagende Lied* see Edward R. Reilly, pp. 25–52 below.

46 NBL2, p. 70 f. The autograph libretto is located in the Osborn Collection of Beinecke Library at Yale University; see also Stephen E. Hefling, "The Road Not Taken: Mahler's Rübezahl," *Yale University Library Gazette* 57/3–4 (1983), 145–70.

im gelben Felde geh / seh ich das blonde Haar im Winde wehn." ("When I look into the heavens / I see yonder two blue eyes. / When I traverse the golden fields / I see her blond hair wafting in the wind.") In this unpretentious passage one can readily detect how Mahler's sense of language has developed during the intervening years.

A piano for *Das klagende Lied*

Where Mahler lived during his first two conservatory years is unknown. When he registered for the first time at the University in the fall of 1877, he gave an address in the fourth district: Margarethenstraße 7, second stairway – a convenient location, five to six minutes' walk from the Conservatory and at most twenty from the University. At the beginning of the second semester, in the spring of 1878, he lived in the eighth district, again near the inner city, yet farther from both the Conservatory and the University. As he began his third university semester in the fall of 1879, he was living at Rennweg No. 3, which is noteworthy in that two decades later as Director of the Vienna Opera he took rooms at Rennweg No. 5. These are only three of the dozens of addresses Mahler went through in the course of a few years, either alone or together with a friend. Which is to say that Mahler felt himself obliged to move every couple of weeks, at least from the fall of 1877 on. "I have now been in Vienna three months already," he wrote in 1880 to one of his former colleagues at the Conservatory, "and, not counting various hotels, am now in my fifth lodging."[47]

Perhaps this is the place to say a few words about the Viennese subtenant room, an institution under the jurisdiction of civil law; such a room will spread no ideas in Karl Popper's sense, but may hinder the formation of any ideas. The Viennese subtenant room had nothing to do with the Parisian garret widely known from *La Bohème*, or with the English boarding house, and least of all with the student hostels of famous small university towns. It was a room in an average Viennese residence that the so-called head renter, who rented directly from the owner of the house, would sublet to unmarried men. The design of such dwellings was almost never intended for this purpose, for there was almost never direct access from the staircase, and

---

[47] Holländer, "Unbekannte Jugendbriefe," p. 813.

seldom enough was there an entry from the hallway situated within the flat. Isolation, therefore, was hardly possible. The ideal "gentleman lodger" (*Zimmerherr*), as he was called in Vienna, left his room at seven o'clock in the morning, did not return before nine at night, and then, without creating any sort of stir, went directly to bed. In no wise did Gustav Mahler and his colleagues match such a model. They of course spent many hours at home, raged at the piano, sometimes even singing with it, yet complained if, God forbid, a few notes from the keyboard came through from a neighboring apartment. Thus the conflicts between landlord (often a widowed land-lady) and gentlemen lodgers were pre-programmed. And once the conflict had broken out, there was nothing for it but to change rooms – moving again.

Under such circumstances was it conceivably possible to practise the piano for the number of hours that would have been necessary for a future concert pianist? Was it possible to work on a complicated score? And what happened to the piano at moving time? Certainly there were landlords who placed their own pianos at the disposal of music students who lived with them. It seems that occasionally the renowned Viennese piano manufac-turer Bösendorfer would make a piano available to a Conservatory pupil without charge; we know of this from a letter probably dating from 1882 in which Mahler once again turned to Bösendorfer for such a loan.[48] But for the most part Mahler had to rent an instrument, and it is altogether imagin-able that during periods when he changed lodgings especially frequently, no piano was available at all.

In the second half of February 1880, however, he had a piano. By chance the invoice from the "Fortepiano-Fabrik Jacob Czapka & Sohn" has survived, dated 18 February, on which Mahler signed for the receipt of a baby grand from that firm. The piano was valued at 420 Gulden; Mahler's rental fee was 7 Gulden per month. At that time he lived in the sixth district, Windmühlgasse 39, first floor, door 18, in the apartment of Frau Kaglmeier.[49] Mahler badly needed the piano, for he was in love and had decided to dedicate five songs with piano accompaniment to his beloved

---

[48] Autograph letter, undated, Gesellschaft der Musikfreunde, Vienna, cited in KBD, p. 165.

[49] Invoice in private collection, Vienna; photocopy at the Internationale Gustav Mahler Gesellschaft, Vienna.

Josephine in Iglau. The first of these was produced on 19 February – precisely the day after the piano's delivery – the second on 27 February, and a third on 5 March. The projected fourth and fifth songs were never composed, perhaps because Mahler realized the hopelessness of his love affair, or perhaps because, as his colleagues maintained, he never brought a work to conclusion. But perhaps because another, greater project detracted from it: in fact, he was working on the setting of *Das klagende Lied*. Already on 21 March the short score of the second part, "Der Spielmann," was finished; for the first part, "Waldmärchen," no dates have come down to us.

Around this same time other changes indicative of the future began to take place. Mahler, it appears, had slowly outgrown boyhood. Aside from piano instruction, he sought some other musical occupation. We know that his friend Guido Adler was looking around on his behalf and recommended him for a choirmaster's position that he did not obtain.[50] On 12 May, on the other hand, Mahler signed a contract with the theatrical agent Gustav Lewy and departed several days later for Hall in Upper Austria, where he was engaged as Kapellmeister at the spa theater. That engagement was not a happy one and did not last long. Following his return to Vienna he pressed ahead with *Das klagende Lied* and was able to report the completion of the work in November 1880.[51]

Therewith ended Mahler's prolonged childhood, the time of dreamlike wandering and searching for identity. He himself changed, and so, too, his letter-writing style was tellingly transformed from world-worn self-expression to objective communication. Inadvertently he had found the two callings he would pursue until the end of his days: composer and conductor. Still ahead lay a painful apprenticeship, and he still had to give piano lessons when he was without an engagement. But in themselves his goals remained unwavering.

---

[50] Reilly, *Gustav Mahler and Guido Adler*, p. 82 f.
[51] Letter of 1 November 1880 to Emil Freund, GMB2, no. 11.

2   *Das klagende Lied* reconsidered

EDWARD R. REILLY

Das klagende Lied (1880) is the first large-scale work by Mahler that survives. In 1896, more than fifteen years after the work was first drafted, he explained the reasons for this to his friend and confidante Natalie Bauer-Lechner:

> The compositions of my student days, where I still relied on inspiration from other sources, are lost or have never been performed. And what I did later, beginning with *Das klagende Lied*, is already so "Mahlerish," so distinctively and completely marked with my personal style, different as it is from all others, that there is no longer any connection between them and the earlier works.[1]

Later that same year he wrote in similar vein to the critic and composer Max Marschalk:

> The first work in which I really came into my own as "Mahler" was a *fairy-tale* [*Märchen*] for choir, soloists and orchestra: "Das klagende Lied." I number that work Opus 1.[2]

These now-familiar assessments by the composer of his first distinctive work prompt this reexamination of its background, creation, and substantial revision, which entailed completely omitting "Waldmärchen," the original first part. In the course of this essay I suggest a somewhat different view of why that was done, and offer new details about a number of other issues.

---

[1] NBLE, pp. 54 and 233–34 (NBL2, p. 50), 2–6 April 1896.
[2] GMBE, no. 189 (GMB2, no. 198) [4 December 1896].

EDWARD R. REILLY

Sources for *Das klagende Lied*: an overview

Das klagende Lied is also the first of Mahler's compositions for which we have manuscripts that reflect several of the important stages through which it progressed. The identifiable literary and musical sources, some of which have been lost, are summarized in tabular form below as a prelude to reviewing the history of the work's gestation. The three earliest musical manuscripts – short-score drafts of "Der Spielmann" and "Hochzeitsstück" plus the first orchestral fair copy of "Der Spielmann" – provide notable evidence that already at age twenty Mahler had established some of the working habits which would remain relatively constant throughout his development as a composer. These same compositional stages are still apparent in the sources for the incomplete Tenth Symphony (1910).

Source materials for Das klagende Lied

Text (*sources are assigned Arabic numerals*)

1. Autograph fair copy, complete text of the three-part version, with alterations; dated 18 March 1878. (New Haven, Conn., Yale University, Beinecke Library, James Marshall and Marie-Louise Osborn Collection; bound in with Music Ms. 507 – see below under "Music," source F.)

2. Complete autograph text of the three-part version, entitled "Ballade," signed by Mahler and dated 27 February 1879. (Yale University, Beinecke Library, James Marshall and Marie-Louise Osborn Collection, 90.5.3; see Plate 2.1.) Formerly owned by Dr. Felix Steiner, son of Mahler's youthful friend Josef Steiner.[3]

3. Text of the first part, autograph, with the title "Ballade vom blonden und braunen Reitersmann." Present location unknown. Apparently sent by Mahler to his friend Anton Krisper in a letter dated 3 March 1880.[4]

---

[3] The manuscript is listed for sale and illustrated in Sotheby's auction catalogue *Fine Books and Manuscripts, New York, Tuesday, June 27, 1989*, lot 106; part of the last page, including signature and date, is reproduced in AMML4, p. 222.

[4] Quoted in full in Hans Holländer, "Unbekannte Jugendbriefe Gustav Mahlers," *Die Musik* 20/11 (August 1928), 807–13.

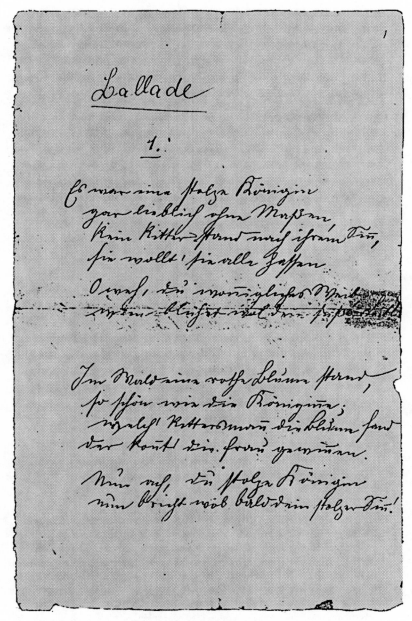

Plate 2.1   Mahler, *Das klagende Lied*, text of part I ("Waldmärchen"), autograph dated 27 February 1879

4. Unsigned autograph text of the revised two-part version. (Jerusalem, Jewish National and University Library.)[5] Although dated 18 March 1878, the text itself and the notation next to the date – "war also 17½ Jahre alt!" ("thus I was 17½ years old!") – make it clear that this copy was made at a much later date. It is possibly the one that Mahler mentions that he is sending to Natalie Bauer-Lechner in a letter of 9 December 1893 (see below, p. 44).

5. Printed text. As pointed out by Rudolf Stephan, the full score of the first edition of *Das klagende Lied* (and the later study score of 1914) presents the text of the poem before the musical score, and this text does not agree precisely with that set to music, or, I would add, with the other texts listed above. In the introduction to his critical edition, Stephan includes this printed version of the text in parallel columns with that found in the score.[6]

Music (*sources are assigned upper-case letters*)

A. Preliminary sketches. None have been traced thus far.

B. Preliminary draft.
  1. Autograph draft of "Der Spielmann," the original second part of *Das klagende Lied*, in *Particell* format. (Vienna, Stadt- und Landesbibliothek, MH 4076/c.) Inscribed "Ende des Spielmanns! Sonntag 21. März 1880."[7] At the end of the manuscript is a sketch for a passage not yet worked out in the main body of the autograph; this material is elaborated somewhat differently in the fair copy of the orchestra score (see item D below) and also in the copyist's manuscript (see F below). The passage was finally substantially cut and modified in the revision of 1893–94 (see G 1 and 2 in this table, and also pp. 48–50 below).

  2. Autograph preliminary draft of the beginning of "Hochzeitsstück," also in *Particell* format. (New York, collection of Mr. Jerry Bruck.) "Ende October u Anfang November 1880" appears on the upper part of this page

---

[5] I am indebted to Stephen Hefling for drawing my attention to this manuscript.

[6] See KG, vol. XII (Vienna, 1978), unnumbered pages of the foreword.

[7] See Ernst Hilmar, "Mahleriana in der Wiener Stadt- und Landesbibliothek," *News About Mahler Research*, no. 5 (June 1979), 3. The dated page is reproduced in Kurt Blaukopf, ed. and comp. (with contributions by Zoltan Roman), *Mahler: Sein Leben, sein Werk und seine Welt in zeitgenössischen Bildern und Texten* (Vienna, 1976), and KBD, plate 41. Martin Zenck ("Mahlers Streichung des 'Waldmärchens' aus dem 'Klagenden Lied': Zum Verhältnis von philologischer Erkenntnis und Interpretation," *Archiv für Musikwissenschaft* 38 [1981], 182) mistakenly gives the year as 1881.

in Mahler's hand. The manuscript is titled "3. [clearly written over 4.] Stück. / 'Hochzeitsstück.'"[8] According to Henry-Louis de La Grange, the continuation of this draft was at one time still in the collection of Alma Mahler,[9] but it had already disappeared at the time this leaf was given to Mr. Bruck.

C. Preliminary orchestral draft. None has survived.

D. Fair copy of the first orchestral version of "Der Spielmann." (Vienna, Stadt- und Landesbibliothek, MH 4077/c.) "2. Stück / 'Spielmann'" appears on a separate title page. "Monat März 1880" is found in the upper right side of the title page, but is not in Mahler's hand, and probably derives from the date in source B l above; that date may be incorrect for this stage in the composition. Both B l and this manuscript at one time belonged to Natalie Bauer-Lechner. The opening pages of music are missing, and the pagination shows that it was originally part of a larger manuscript, perhaps of the entire work. The surviving music begins with bar 32 of the published score.[10]

E. Fair copies, presumably autograph, complete orchestral score of the three-part version of *Das klagende Lied.*
   l. A manuscript formerly in the possession of Baroness Marion von Weber, probably given to her in 1888 during her affair with Mahler. Examined by Willem Mengelberg and mentioned in a letter of 10 July 1907 written to his wife from Dresden.[11] Possibly destroyed during World War II when Dresden was bombed.

   2. Another manuscript of the three-part version, sent to Dr. Ludwig Strecker, the proprietor of B. Schott's Söhne in Mainz between October 1891 and February 1892, to be considered for publication. The title page, which lists the three parts by name, survives in Schott's archives,[12] but the remainder has disappeared. This title page confirms that at that point the

---

[8] The title and the single page of music are reproduced in Jack Diether, "Notes on Some Mahler Juvenilia," *Chord and Discord* 3/1 (1969), plate I following p. 48. Although several indications of instrumentation are found in the manuscript, it is a preliminary *Particell* draft, rather than an orchestral sketch as suggested in HLG 1, p. 730 (HLGF 1, p. 943).   [9] HLG 1, p. 730 (HLGF 1, p. 943).

[10] See also Hilmar, "Mahleriana." Stephen Hefling reports that the ink in this manuscript appears to be the same as that in the preliminary draft in the same library. The date, however, is added in purple ink.

[11] See Eduard Reeser, *Gustav Mahler und Holland: Briefe,* Bibliothek der Internationalen Gustav Mahler Gesellschaft (Vienna, 1980), p. 90.

[12] Quoted in Rudolf Stephan, ed., *Gustav Mahler: Werk und Interpretation* (Cologne, 1979), p. 26; see also Knud Martner and Robert Becqué, "Zwölf

first part had not yet been eliminated. (Or perhaps Mahler may have sent
Strecker the copyist's manuscript listed in F below with an additional title
page.)

F. Copyist's manuscript, complete orchestral score of the three-part version.
(New Haven, Conn., James Marshall and Marie-Louise Osborn Collection,
Beinecke Library, Yale University, Music Ms. 507.)[13] "'Das klagende Lied.' /
Ein Märchen / in drei Abtheilungen / von / Gustav Mahler" appears on the
title page, which precedes the manuscript of the text cited in l above. Each
part also has its own title page. This is the only surviving manuscript
currently known to preserve "Waldmärchen."

G. The revision of *Das klagende Lied*: the first two-part version.

l. Sketches for a passage in "Der Spielmann." (New York, collection of Mr.
Jerry Bruck.) The sketches are preserved in a signature marked
"Dummheiten!" that was probably at one time used as a cover for other
materials. Both sketches pertain to a revision of the passage beginning
at bar 219 (fig. 15) in the published score.[14]

2. Autograph of the complete two-part version of *Das klagende Lied*.
(New York, the Dannie and Hettie Heineman Collection in the Pierpont
Morgan Library.)[15] Formerly in the collection of Alma Mahler, who
probably added the title (otherwise lacking) on the verso of the leaf
preceding the first page of music. This revision almost certainly dates
from late 1893 and early 1894 in Hamburg (see below, pp. 45–46), and
eliminates the offstage orchestra in "Hochzeitsstück."

H. Copy of the preceding revision. In a postcard postmarked 4 January 1893
to his sister Justine, Mahler mentions that his completed revision is "already
at the copyist's" (see below). This copy has disappeared. It may have been

---

unbekannte Briefe Gustav Mahlers an Ludwig Strecker," *Archiv für
Musikwissenschaft* 34 (1977), 287–97.

[13] See Diane Boito, "Manuscript Music in the James Marshall and Marie-Louise
Osborn Collection," *Notes* 27 (1970), 243–44.

[14] The sketches are to be reproduced, with transcriptions, in my article "Two
Sketches for *Das klagende Lied*," *Neue Mahleriana: Festschrift für Henry-Louis de
La Grange*, ed. Günther Weiss (Regensburg, forthcoming).

[15] See J. Rigbie Turner, *Nineteenth-Century Music Manuscripts in The Pierpont
Morgan library: A Check List* (New York, 1982), p. 33 (this is a slightly revised
version of the listing published in *19th Century Music* 4 (1980), 49–69 and
157–83; see esp. p. 163). This manuscript is not in the Osborn Collection at
Yale, as mistakenly indicated in KG XII.

used to make the revisions planned in the fall of 1898 and chronicled by Bauer-Lechner (see below).

I. Autograph or partial autograph, revised form of the two-part version of *Das klagende Lied*. Since the revisions center primarily upon the restoration of the offstage orchestra, Mahler may have rewritten only the appropriate passages and inserted them into the copyist's manuscript mentioned in H above. The autograph of these revisions has not been found.

J. Copyist's manuscript of the whole two-part version, or of those portions associated in the 1898 or 1899 revisions, used as a *Stichvorlage* for the published edition. Such a copy would almost certainly include some autograph alterations or additions. Untraced.

K. The published Weinberger full score (Plate No. 26), issued together with a piano reduction by Josef Venantius von Wöss (Plate No. 25), in 1899 or 1902.[16]

L. Printed copy of the full score with alterations by Mahler. (Vienna, Stadt- und Landesbibliothek [Universal Archive].)[17] The changes indicated by Mahler are detailed by Rudolf Stephan in the foreword to KG XII. The majority of these revisions were included in the study score issued by Universal in 1914.

In addition to these items, one other autograph should be mentioned that, although not actually part of *Das klagende Lied*, is related to it through an important aspect of Mahler's oeuvre: self-borrowing. "Im Lenz [In Spring]," one of Mahler's early songs dedicated to Josephine Poisl (which have only recently been published) contains material in bars 21–27 and 42–53 parallel to what is heard at figure **21** in "Der Spielmann," and subsequently at figure **59** in "Hochzeitsstück." This is evidently the earliest of the overt borrowings in various forms that would crop up in Mahler's first four symphonies and, somewhat more subtly, in his later works as well. The date on the autograph of "Im Lenz" is 18 February 1880, which indicates

---

[16] Rudolf Stephan gives the date 1899 in his foreword to KG XII, but 1902 is indicated by Donald Mitchell (*The New Grove Turn of the Century Masters* [New York, 1985], p. 165) and Henry-Louis de La Grange (HLG 2, p. 722 [HLGF 1, p. 917]). The anonymous publication *100 Years Remembered: A History of the Theatre and Music Publishers Josef Weinberger, Vienna, Frankfurt am Main, London, 1885–1985* (London: Josef Weinberger Ltd, 1985), p. 9, also gives the year as 1902.   [17] See Hilmar, "Mahleriana," p. 6.

that it was written at the same time Mahler was working on "Der Spielmann" (see item B 1 above).[18]

The poetic text

Mahler's dramatic *Märchen* or *Ballade* (as he called it on different occasions) may have drawn upon various literary sources – Ludwig Bechstein, the brothers Grimm, and Martin Greif – which have been reviewed on several occasions (notably by Donald Mitchell and Henry-Louis de La Grange).[19] But his principal source seems to have been Bechstein's version of the tale, also entitled "Das klagende Lied," which appeared in his *Neues deutsches Märchenbuch* of 1856.[20] Bechstein's influence seems particularly apparent if we compare the bone flute's recurring accusations of murder in his version with Mahler's treatment of them in the manuscript of the poem dated 27 February 1879 (item 2 above). Particularly telling are the repeated form of address in the first line (which Mahler later modified) and the image of "playing upon my dead bone [*Todtenbein*]":

---

[18] See KG XIII/5, *Verschiedene Lieder für eine Singstimme mit Klavier* (Mainz, 1990), pp. 2 and 4; KG XII, *Das klagende Lied*, pp. 27–28 and 79–81; and Donald Mitchell, *Gustav Mahler: The Early Years*, rev. and ed. Paul Banks and David Matthews (Berkeley, 1980), pp. 180 and 312–13. In their appendix to this volume, Paul Banks and David Matthews suggest "It seems likely that the song quotes from the cantata rather than the other way round, as the tempo direction *Noch einmal so langsam* found in both is more appropriate to the cantata than to the song; in the latter it cannot really be understood without reference to the equivalent passage in the cantata." But see also below, n. 30.

[19] Mitchell, *Mahler*, pp. 141–43; HLG 1, pp. 731–33 (HLGF 1, 945–46). See also Wolf Rosenberg, "Die Moritat vom singenden Knochen: Das klagende Lied," in *Mahler: Eine Herausforderung*, ed. Peter Ruzicka (Wiesbaden, 1977), pp. 135–49, which places the story in a broader mythological context.

[20] Modern edn. in Bechstein, *Sämtliche Märchen*, 3rd edn. (Munich, 1985), pp. 487–93. The text of Mahler's *Märchen* opera *Rübezahl*, which he worked on at the same time as *Das klagende Lied*, also relies chiefly upon one well-known source of its folk tale; see Stephen E. Hefling, "The Road Not Taken: Mahler's Rübezahl," *Yale University Library Gazette* 57/3–4 (1983), 145–70.

Bechstein

Mahler (Osborn MS 90.5.3, 27 February 1879)[21]

"O Hirte [Ritter, Mutter] mein, o
Hirte mein,
Du flötest auf meinem Totenbein!
Mein Bruder erschlug mich im
  Haine.
Nahm aus meiner Hand
Die Blum, die ich fand
Und sprach, sie wäre die seine.
Er schlug mich im Schlaf, er schlug
  mich so hart –
Hat ein Grab gewühlt, hat mich
  hier verscharrt –
Mein Bruder – in jungen Tagen . . ."

"Ach Spielmann mein, ach Spielmann
  mein,
das muß ich dir nun klagen:
um ein schönfarbig Blümelein,
hat mich mein Bruder erschlagen:
Im Walde bleicht mein junger Leib –
– Mein Bruder freit ein wonnig' Weib!
O Leide, weh, o Leide!["]

"Ach Bruder mein, ach Bruder mein,
Du hast mich ja verschlagen,
nun bläst du auf meinen Todtenbein,
Deß' muß ich ewig klagen!
Was hast du mein junges Leben
dem Tode schon gegeben
O Jammer, weh, o Jammer."

"O shepherd [knight, mother]
  mine, o shepherd mine,
You play flute upon my dead bone!
My brother struck me dead in the
  grove.
He took from my hand
The flower, which I'd found
And declared that it was his.
He struck me in sleep, he struck me
  so hard –
Raked out a grave, and quickly
  buried me here –
My brother – in youthful days."

"Ah, minstrel mine, ah minstrel mine,
this I must now lament to you:
For the sake of a beautifully colored
  little flower,
My brother struck me down:
In the forest my young body is
  bleaching –
My brother woos a delightful woman!
O sorrow, woe, o sorrow!["]

"Ah, brother mine, ah brother mine,
You indeed knocked me off course,
now you blow upon my dead bone,
Of this must I ever lament!
Why indeed did you
give my young body to Death
O misery, woe, o misery."

---

21 Reproduced through kind permission of the James Marshall and Marie-Louise Osborn Collection, Beinecke Library, Yale University, Stephen Parks, curator.

Mahler's major departures from his model were to eliminate Bechstein's character of the old queen, and to focus guilt and sorrow upon the fratricidal king and his arrogant wife. Mahler also changed the nature of the contest and the contestants: in his version, two brothers (rather than a brother and sister) are in competition, vying for the hand of the haughty young queen, whose proud disposition is to be broken by marriage. The well-known Grimm brothers' tale "Der singende Knochen [The Singing Bone]"[22] is a version of the legend involving two brothers – the elder crafty and prideful, the younger innocent and simple – who compete for the hand of a princess: very likely this was the antecedent of Mahler's changes in characters and contest. Several of his alterations, however, are distinctly his own, and it should be remembered that during Mahler's childhood "Nanni," the nurse of his friend Theodor Fischer, told the children stories, including one called "*Das klagende Lied*, which may have given rise to one of Mahler's subsequent compositions."[23] Thus, as is also the case for some of the *Wunderhorn* songs, Mahler may have been acquainted with the story through an oral tradition that differed in various ways from the published texts.

To what extent the *dramatic* work of Martin Greif (pseudonym for Friedrich Hermann Frey [1839–1911]) performed by the drama students at the Vienna Conservatory on 3 May 1876[24] may have influenced Mahler remains uncertain. Its text has not been located, and there is in fact no positive proof that Mahler saw it. Greif's *poem* on the subject, however, hardly suggests that the dramatized version would have departed very far from Bechstein: the published Greif text is a poetic rendering of Bechstein's tale.[25] It explicitly quotes Bechstein's narrative of the bone flute, "O Hirte mein, O Hirte mein, Du flötest auf meinem Totenbein! [O shepherd mine, O shepherd mine, you play flute upon my dead bone!]" plus the ensuing eleven

[22] Jacob and Wilhelm Grimm, "Der singende Knochen," *Kinder- und Hausmärchen* (Göttingen, 1857), no. 28 (variously reprinted and translated).
[23] Fischer, "Aus Gustav Mahlers Jugendzeit," *Deutsche Heimat* 7 (1931), 264–68, trans. in Norman Lebrecht, *Mahler Remembered* (New York, 1987), pp. 17–18.
[24] HLG 1, p. 731 (HLGF 1, pp. 945–46); cf. also Herta Blaukopf, "The Young Mahler," pp. 20–21 above.
[25] See Martin Greif, *Gedichte*, 5th edn. (Stuttgart, 1889), pp. 198–206, and Bechstein, *Sämtliche Märchen*.

lines, as well as the recurring variants of this refrain. Thus, any distinctive influence from Greif appears unlikely.

Mahler himself is responsible for the remark, which misled most early commentators, to the effect that *Das klagende Lied* "was initially thought of as a fairy tale for the stage [*Märchenspiel für die Bühne*]."[26] He had already used the ambiguous term *Märchenspiel*, which might imply a stage work, as early as 1880 (see below). Donald Mitchell offers the most probable interpretation of what Mahler actually meant: "Taking that 'thought of' in its strictest sense, the statement is probably correct. Mahler, when first turning the project over in his mind, may have considered a stage setting as a possibility. But this intention was never represented at any creative level."[27] Indeed, all of the surviving textual and musical documents listed above indicate that, when work was actually begun on *Das klagende Lied*, the poetry and the music were created as a dramatic cantata. The libretto for a true *Märchenspiel* by Mahler, *Rübezahl*, does survive, and clearly demonstrates how differently he conceived such a work for the stage at the very time he was composing *Das klagende Lied*.[28]

Possibly the earliest preserved document connected with the work is the autograph of the entire text, dated 18 March 1878 (see Text item 1 above). As noted, it is bound with the complete copyist's manuscript of the composition. This fair copy of the poem appears to have been very carefully prepared, but exactly when it was made cannot be firmly established. Mahler may have written it out after the music was complete, retaining the original date of the poem (as he did in item 4 above). The other sources for the poem, together with the musical manuscripts, preserve numerous variants. Some of these are purely literary in origin, and may precede the fair copy already cited, but other alterations were made during composition or reworking of the music. Thus, in the Hamburg revision (ca. 1893–94), line 10 of "Der Spielmann" was altered from "Er

---

26 Mahler in a conversation recounted by Ernst Decsey, "Stunden mit Mahler," *Die Musik* 10/18 (June 1911), 352–56, and 10/21 (August 1911), 143–53, trans. Lebrecht, *Mahler Remembered*, p. 256. The statement was also repeated by Guido Adler in his 1916 monograph, *Gustav Mahler* (see Edward R. Reilly, *Gustav Mahler and Guido Adler: Records of a Friendship* [Cambridge, 1982], p. 60).

27 Mitchell, *Mahler: The Early Years*, p. 145.

28 See Hefling, "The Road Not Taken."

hob es auf. – es war nicht schwer [He lifted it up – it was not heavy]" to "Er hob es auf, als wär's ein Rohr [He picked it up as though it were a reed]," while "O ließest du das Flöten sein! [O leave flute-playing alone!]" (line 13) was changed first to "das wird ein seltsam Melodei'n [that will be strange melodizing],"[29] and finally to "das wird ein seltsam Spielen sein! [that will be strange playing!]." At a stage before actual composition, the lines that read "Es klingt wie Lachen und Weinen, doch sagen könnt' ich es Keinem! [It sounds like laughing and crying, but I could tell this to no one!]" in the "1878" copy of the poem were changed to "Es tönt so traurig und doch so schön, wer's hört, der möchte weinen geh'n: [It sounds so sad and yet so beautiful, whoever hears it wants to go and weep:]."[30] Much later the end of the line was altered to "vor Leid vergeh'n! [expire from sorrow!]" as it is in the published score, although this change is not yet apparent either in the revised Hamburg score (Music item G 2, 1893–94) or in the two-part version of the poem probably associated with that revision (Text item 4).

Cantata in three parts: the earlier musical sources

We can only estimate when Mahler began setting text to music. From the known musical manuscripts listed earlier, it is certain that the preliminary draft of the second part, "Der Spielmann," was completed on 21 March 1880 "beim Einzug des Frühlings! [with the arrival of Spring!],"[31] almost two years after the earliest date found among the texts.

---

[29] At some point Mahler entered the two alterations just mentioned into the fair copy of the poem dated 18 March 1878 (Text item 1).

[30] Most interestingly, the song "Im Lenz" (which, as noted on p. 31 above, shares the same musical material found in this passage of the cantata) includes two lines of text very similar to those just cited from Text item 1, dated "1878": "Könnt' lachen und könnte weinen, / doch sagen könnt ich es keinem." In the earliest musical manuscripts of the cantata, however, the lines of text in question are closer to what appears in the 1879 version of the poem (Text item 2), except that the word "tönt" has been changed to "klingt" in the earliest fair copy of the music (Music item D, autograph). This may indicate that the song was in fact written before the cantata, in contrast to the views of Banks and Matthews cited in n. 18 above.

[31] See n. 7 above.

The inscription "Monat März 1880" on the first surviving orchestral score of "Der Spielmann" is certainly a later addition. Mahler announces the completion of *Das klagende Lied* in a letter of 1 November 1880 to his good friend Emil Freund, and says that it cost him "more than a whole year's labor."[32] This statement would place the beginning of composition sometime in the late summer or fall of 1879, a time that would be congruent with 21 March 1880 as the date for the completion of "Der Spielmann." Preliminary sketching almost certainly preceded formal composition,[33] which for Mahler usually meant working out his preliminary drafts in *Particell* format. His announcement that *Das klagende Lied* was finished also indicates completion of a preliminary draft, since the opening of "Hochzeitsstück" in the earliest surviving manuscript (also a preliminary draft) is dated by Mahler (after the fact?) "end of October and beginning of November 1880" (Music item B 2 above). In later years, too, "completion" often referred to this essential stage. Working out, developing, solving specific compositional problems and then orchestrating the whole (often in two stages) were frequently viewed as more purely technical matters.

The intensity with which Mahler worked is reflected in some of the stories he himself reported. Concerning the creation of *Das klagende Lied*, he told Bauer-Lechner the following (many years after the fact):

> He confessed to me that, while writing this piece [the Third Symphony], he was struck with the most uncanny sense of awe . . .

> In his youth, he had a similar experience with a seemingly insignificant passage in *Das klagende Lied*. He could never get through it without being profoundly shaken and overcome by intense excitement. Whenever he reached it, he always had a vision of himself emerging out of the wall in a dark corner of the room. He felt such intense physical pain, when this "double" [Doppelgänger] tried to force its way through the wall, that he

---

[32] GMB2, no. 11 (GMBE, no. 11).

[33] Bauer-Lechner provides a glimpse of Mahler at work during the earlier stages of *Das klagende Lied*; in recounting his preliminary work on the Fourth Symphony (1899) she notes that "He even composes when out walking (alone, or often with us, when he will lag a little) – a thing he has never done since *Das klagende Lied*" (NBLE, p. 132 [NBL2, pp. 138–39]).

could not go on with his work and had to rush from the room – until one morning, while working on this same passage, he collapsed in a nervous fever. (Admittedly, he had been working for weeks under the utmost pressure, and at the same time had undermined his strong constitution by a strictly vegetarian diet.)[34]

In 1881 Mahler entered the completed cantata in the competition for the Beethoven Prize sponsored by the Gesellschaft der Musikfreunde.[35] Since the meeting to decide the winner took place in December, Mahler would have had some time to complete and orchestrate the draft, and then have the whole work copied. The judges included Brahms and Goldmark, the conductors Wilhelm Gericke (1845–1925), Johann Nepomuk Fuchs (1842–99), Josef Hellmesberger (1829–93) and Hans Richter (1843–1916), as well as Franz Krenn (1816–97), one of Mahler's former teachers at the conservatory. He did not, however, obtain the prize, which was awarded to to Robert Fuchs (1847–1927). It is possible that the copyist's manuscript of *Das klagende Lied* in its full three-part form (now at Yale, Music item F above) was the score submitted for the competition; but this source may also have been prepared on a later occasion to be discussed presently. Preceding this copy was a relatively fair autograph full score, the "Spielmann" portion of which survives in the Vienna Stadtbibliothek (Music item D). That score, however, is not in a form suitable either for a contest or for performance: as in many of Mahler's later manuscripts, numerous details are abbreviated – e.g., key signatures are indicated only at major points of change, full-bar rests are rarely filled in, etc.

Meanwhile, Mahler had begun his conducting career in the summer of 1880, and took up his second post (his first important one) at the town of Laibach (present-day Ljubljana) in September 1881, before the Beethoven Prize contest was decided. In later years he looked back upon his failure to win as a major turning point in his life, complaining that had he been successful, he might have been spared "this hellish life in the theatre."[36] Despite confusion about certain details and possibly clouded hindsight, the essential emotional truth of what Mahler remembered may be to the point:

[34] NBLE, p. 53 (NBL2, pp. 49–50).
[35] This is the contest Mahler discussed with Bauer-Lechner in April 1898, but by then he no longer remembered the chronology of events accurately; see NBLE, p. 116 (NBL2, p. 117).   [36] NBLE, p. 116 (NBL2, p. 117).

in 1881 he was still just beginning work as a conductor; a major success with
Das klagende Lied might have given him greater confidence in his compositional powers, and could perhaps have opened practical alternatives to conducting opera. Brahms was the obvious example of an independently
successful composer; yet Mahler's contemporary Richard Strauss, whose
early compositions met with enormous acclaim, nevertheless pursued a
very active career as a conductor.

In any case, Mahler did not immediately give up trying to gain
recognition for his "Schmerzenskind [child of sorrow]." In 1883 he submitted it for possible performance at the festival of the Allgemeiner
Deutscher Musikverein. Again it was turned down by an eminent contemporary – in this case one by no means musically conservative: Franz Liszt. In
brief and rather abruptly dismissive manner, Liszt wrote to Mahler (see also
Plates 2.2 and 2.3):

> Sehr geehrter Herr!
> Ihre mir freundlichst / zugesandte Composition / "Waldmärchen" enthält /
> manches Werthvolle. / Das Gedicht scheint jedoch / nicht derart, derselben /
> einen Erfolg zu verbürgen. /
> Mit ausgezeichneter / Achtung.
>
> F. Liszt
>
> Weimar
> 13 Septb.
> 1883[37]
>
> Dear Sir,
>
> "Waldmärchen," the composition which you so kindly sent to me, contains
> much of value. The poem, however, does not seem to be of a kind to
> guarantee it a success.
>
> With highest regards.
>
> F. Liszt

---

[37] This letter is in the Mahler–Rosé Collection, University of Western Ontario,
London. I am most indebted to William G. Guthrie, Head of the Music Library,
and to Marina Mahler, for permission to reproduce and quote the letter here.
It is mentioned (but not quoted) in HLG 1, p. 850, n. 20 (HLGF 1, p. 168).

Plate 2.2 Franz Liszt, envelope of autograph letter to Mahler

It is not clear whether Mahler sent Liszt only the first part of *Das klagende Lied*, or whether Liszt proceeded no further than reading through the opening. To have been rejected not only by Brahms but also by Liszt, however, must have deeply wounded Mahler and weakened his self-confidence as a composer. Adding insult to injury, Liszt singled out Mahler's own poetry as the weak point. It would be ten years before the composer returned to the piece. And although we will never know with certainty, Liszt's specific rejection of "Waldmärchen" may have influenced Mahler's subsequent decision to excise it.

Revision: cantata in two parts (1893–94)

Precisely when Mahler took renewed interest in his cantata and began to revise it was clouded in confusion by his longtime friend Guido Adler, who, in a single sentence of his influential memorial Mahler monograph (1916), conveyed a considerable amount of misinformation. Who or what

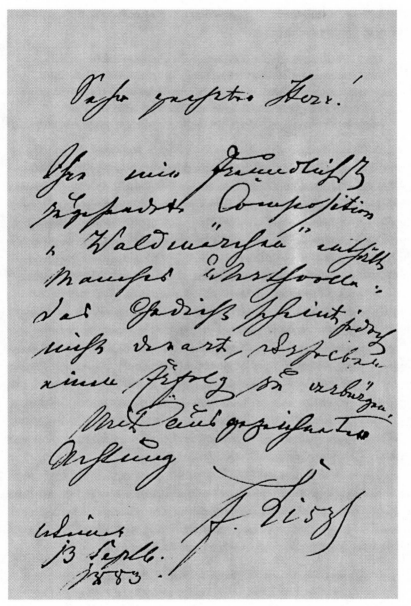

Plate 2.3 Franz Liszt, autograph letter to Mahler, dated "13 Septb. 1883"

Adler's sources may have been remains uncertain, but he described the history of the work as follows:

> *Das klagende Lied*, composed at the age of eighteen to twenty years, in 1888 underwent a thorough remodeling through omission of the third part, contraction of the first two parts and shortening of the instrumental interludes and, after a considerable time, a further revision of the instrumentation. Its relationship to the first version cannot be established.[38]

Virtually every feature of the first sentence is incorrect. The surviving autograph title page of the manuscript that Mahler sent to the publisher Schott in 1891 (item E 2) clearly indicates that the work was still in three-part form at that time. When revisions were made, it was the first part (rather than the third) that was deleted. And as we shall see below, one interlude in "Der Spielmann" was shortened, but not more than one; there is no other evidence that the remaining two parts were contracted. Adler's reference to a "further revision," however, accurately recounts one aspect of what actually transpired.

Schott's publication of Mahler's early songs in 1892 may have been one of the factors motivating the reworking of *Das klagende Lied*. Although the publisher had rejected the cantata together with several other works submitted, Mahler came to the conclusion that revising these pieces would improve their chances for performance, as letters both to his sister Justine and to Natalie Bauer-Lechner confirm (see below). But whatever the reasons, there was an unmistakable upsurge in his creative activity during the years 1892 and 1893: he composed the first of the orchestral *Wunderhorn* songs, resumed work on the Second Symphony, and revised both the First Symphony and *Das klagende Lied*.

The date of the cantata's first reworking was established by Henry-Louis de La Grange from references in unpublished letters and documents. Evidently the earliest indication of Mahler's renewed interest in it is found in Natalie Bauer-Lechner's diary entry for 28 August 1893, which suggests that Mahler had been looking over his youthful work again:

> Gustav said to me about his "Klagendes Lied": This earliest composition is already completely original, but still rather inflated and overloaded. Too much decoration. Indeed, later, when I took it up again, I corrected a lot. But

[38] See Reilly, *Gustav Mahler and Guido Adler*, p. 60 and n. 76 on pp. 135–36.

I could not remove too much of the finery and decoration because that would have obliterated the lines themselves.[39]

These comments are somewhat ambiguous in that it is not at all clear when he "took it up again." Had Mahler already begun work on the revision earlier that year, or had the corrections referred to been made much earlier, perhaps when a copy (or copies) had been made for the Beethoven competition or the Allgemeiner Deutscher Musikverein? The next reports of the work's revision are the composer's own, in a series of letters written between 5 December 1893 and 4 January 1894. Five are to his sister Justine (then in Italy), and one is addressed to Natalie Bauer-Lechner; they contain the following references to the cantata:[40]

[5 December 1893: to Justine Mahler]
Ich bereite jetzt das klagende Lied vor, wie seinerzeit den Titan um es eventuell zu[r] Aufführung parat zu haben. – Du kannst Dir denken, was das für Nachmittage und Abend[e] kostet. – Dazu studi[e]re ich jetz[t] 2 Novitäten ein – also überlege Du, wie viel Muße zum Briefschreiben ich habe. –

I am now preparing *Das klagende Lied*, as also in due time *Titan*, in order eventually to have it ready for performance. – You can imagine what that costs in afternoons and evenings. – In addition, I am rehearsing two new works – so consider how much spare time I have for letter writing. –

[9 December 1893: to Justine Mahler]
Ich arbeite eben fleissig [an] dem "klagenden Lied" – und so was consumirt [konsumiert] immer alle meine Zeit und Kräfte, wie Du weißt.

I am working diligently just now on the "Klagendes Lied" – and something like that consumes all of my time and energy, as you know.

[9 December 1893: to Natalie Bauer-Lechner. After mentioning that he was "preparing the score for possible performance," Mahler continues:]

---

[39] NBL2, p. 34 (my translation; not in NBLE).
[40] Once again I am indebted to the Mahler–Rosé Collection at the University of Western Ontario, to William G. Guthrie, Head of the Music Library, and to Marina Mahler for permission to quote from these letters. I am also most grateful to Dr. Stephen McClatchie for extracting the relevant passages from the originals. Brief citations from these letters have already appeared in HLG 1, pp. 284–85 (HLGF 1, pp. 436–37).

I see that the only progress I have made since then [i.e., his early years] is technical. But for the essentials, all the "Mahler" whom you know was revealed at one stroke. What surprises me most is that even in the instrumentation, nothing has to be altered, it is so characteristic and new; only some small details that I could not see at the time must be modified.

In addition, I send you the poem so that you may know it too. Tell me what changes Trik [an unidentified friend] wanted to introduce! I find nothing that could be changed, and I am certain that if Trik had found this text in an old collection of ballads like the *Knaben Wunderhorn*, such an idea would never have occurred to him. You will see that at a time when I did not even suspect the existence of the *Wunderhorn*, I already lived completely in its spirit. Oh, dear God, if only I could have a little peace within my family![41]

[17 December 1893: to Justine Mahler]

Liebste Justi!

Hoffentlich hast du auch die kleinen Photographien erhalten!

Ich bin jetzt fest über dem <u>Klagenden Lied</u>! d. h. – eigentlich ist [*sic*] besteht meine ganze Arbeit in verständnißvollem Copiren und und [*sic*] dem Appretiren des ganzen mit Hilfe meiner Erfahrungen als Dirigenten. – Denn <u>ändern</u> kann ich gar nichts (im ganzen) an der Sache.

Ich kann Dir sagen ich bin <u>paff</u> über dieses Werk, seitdem ich es wieder unter den Händen habe. Wenn ich bedenke, daß das ein 20–21 jähriger Mensch geschrieben, kann ich es nicht begreifen, – so <u>eigenartig</u> und <u>gewaltig</u> ist es! Die Nüsse, die ich da aufzuknacken gegeben habe sind vielleicht die härteste, die mein Baum je hervorgebracht. – Ob ich <u>das</u> je zur Aufführung bringen kann weiß Gott.

Dearest Justi,

Let us hope you have also received the little photographs!

I am now certain about the <u>Klagendes Lied</u>! That is to say, all my work actually consists in intelligent copying and the dressing of the whole with the help of my experiences as a conductor. For (on the whole) I can <u>alter</u> nothing at all in the piece.

I can tell you that I am <u>delighted</u> about this work since I have taken it up again. When I consider that a 20/21-year-old wrote it, I can not imagine it, – it is so <u>original</u> and <u>powerful</u>! The nuts that I have given to be cracked open in it are perhaps the hardest that my tree has yet produced. – Whether I can ever bring <u>this</u> to performance, God knows.

---

[41] Cited in HLG 1, p. 285 (HLGF 1, p. 436), apparently from a copy in the possession of de La Grange.

[24 December 1893: to Justine Mahler]

Die Arbeit am "Kl. Lied" schreitet sehr langsam, aber stetig fort. Ich hoffe noch vor Beginn des neuen Jahres damit fertig zu sein. Denn schnell copirt und Stimmen ausgezogen.

The work on the "Klagendes Lied" moves ahead very slowly, but steadily. I hope to be finished with it before the beginning of the New Year. Then [have it] copied quickly and parts extracted.

[Postmarked 4 January 1894: postcard to Justine Mahler. Postscript:]

Klagende Lied ganz fertig gestellt und schon beim Copisten!
Klagende Lied entirely finished and already at the copyist's!

As matters developed, Mahler would have to wait seven more years to hear his work performed, and eight to see it published. His chronicle of revising the score contains a certain amount of characteristic exaggeration, but there is no doubt that the composition was indeed remarkable and distinctive, reflecting many of the stylistic traits that would reappear in later pieces. What is curious is that he does not specifically mention the changes that, in all likelihood, he made in the score during December of 1893. For although other explanations may be possible, the evidence of the manuscripts strongly suggests that at this time (or just before) Mahler eliminated "Waldmärchen" and prepared the two-part version that was a major step toward his final conception of the work. As noted above, when he submitted *Das klagende Lied* to Schott, it still comprised three parts; thus, "Waldmärchen" was dropped at some point between 1891 and late 1893. Mahler's silence about this, both to his sister and to Bauer-Lechner, may indicate that he had already decided to excise the first part before setting to work on the revision of the remainder.

Mahler's letters to Justine do reveal, however, that he was influenced by the practical realities of getting new works performed: such considerations may also have reinforced an earlier decision about "Waldmärchen." Mahler also sacrificed the offstage band in "Hochzeitsstück" (now part II of the composition) "in order to make the performance possible" as he later told Bauer-Lechner, because "I knew no one would ever do *that*!"[42] He also revised the orchestration in a variety of other ways. These alterations are clearly represented in the autograph now located in the Heineman

---

[42] NBLE, p. 118 (NBL2, p. 124), fall of 1898.

Collection at the Pierpont Morgan Library (item G 2), and it is apparent that Mahler used the much earlier copyist's manuscript (item F, Osborn Collection, Yale) in making at least some of these changes. The music papers in the autograph at the Morgan also strongly suggest a date contemporary with the letters and diary from 1893–94 quoted above: other manuscripts from this time also contain varying combinations of papers bearing the colophon of "Joh. Aug. Böhme, Hamburg" as well as sheets lacking any manufacturer's identification.[43] Only two songs, "Der Schildwache Nachtlied" and "Das irdische Leben," plus a cover folder for a group of *Wunderhorn* songs, are written on paper marked with the distinctive "B. C." colophon that also appears in portions of the Morgan's *Klagendes Lied* manuscript, and these songs unquestionably date from the years 1892 and 1893.[44] While the possibility that the composer used music paper only long after it was purchased cannot be entirely excluded, it would certainly appear that the two-part autograph version of *Das klagende Lied* dates from the period 1892–94.

Additional revisions (1898)

No currently known document indicates any further changes to *Das klagende Lied* prior to 1898, at which point Mahler decided to restore the offstage orchestra in "Hochzeitsstück." In an important passage of Bauer-Lechner's reminiscences written shortly after 26 September 1898 (briefly quoted above), Mahler makes several explicit statements about the revisions he had made in Hamburg – yet again, however, there is no mention of deleting "Waldmärchen":

> Mahler complained to me that, with the masses of work he had to get through at the Opera, he could not get *Das klagende Lied* ready for printing. "I shall have to alter a whole passage, that is restore it to its original form from which I once changed it in Hamburg. Unfortunately, in the meantime I've lost the original version! It is the part where I use two orchestras, one

[43] E.g., the 1893 autograph revision of the First Symphony, Osborn Collection, Music Ms. 506, Beinecke Library, Yale University.
[44] "Der Schildwache Nachtlied" and the cover folder just mentioned are in the Staatsbibliothek Preußischer Kulturbesitz in Berlin; "Das irdische Leben" is in the Pierpont Morgan Library, New York.

46

of them in the distance outside the hall. I knew no one would ever do *that*! In order to make performance possible, I cut out the second orchestra and gave its part to the first. When I saw the passage again, however, I immediately realized that this change had been detrimental to the work, which I must now restore to its original form – whether they play it or not![45]

These comments suggest that nothing had been altered since the two-part version emerged in 1893–94; so, too, does Ernst Decsey's report of his conversations with Mahler: "In Hamburg he looked at it [*Das klagende Lied*] with a conductor's eye, and shortened and simplified it into its present form."[46] Decsey's unspecific "shortened" may refer to the excision of "Waldmärchen."

How long Mahler worked on the 1898 revision remains uncertain. No autograph of this final version has been traced, and the copyist's manuscript that Mahler normally had prepared for the engraver (the *Stichvorlage*) also appears to be lost. Thus we must depend upon the printed score issued by Weinberger in 1902 (item K) for what we know of the changes made between 1898 and the time of publication. The offstage orchestra is restored in this score, but Mahler did not revert completely to his first version of the passage (as he had told Bauer-Lechner he would). Rather, he re-orchestrated it afresh, as becomes apparent by comparing the early copyist's manuscript at Yale (F) with the published score. By that point he may have lost track of the Yale manuscript (as Bauer-Lechner's chronicle would suggest) and simply worked from his own two-part version (G 2).

Thoughts about the deletion of "Waldmärchen"

The second re-discovery of "Waldmärchen"[47] has provoked a variety of responses, from the hope that it be permanently restored, to vigorous

---

[45] See n. 42 above. See also NBL2, pp. 182–83 for an account of the first performance on 17 February 1901 (not in NBLE).

[46] Quoted in Lebrecht, *Mahler Remembered*, pp. 256–57.

[47] "Waldmärchen" was performed for radio broadcasts in Brno (28 November and 2 December 1934) and Vienna (8 April 1935) under the direction of Alfred Rosé, the composer's nephew, and it was discussed in an article by Hans Holländer, "Ein unbekannter Teil von Mahlers 'Klagendem Lied,'" *Auftakt* 14 (1934), 200–02. Renewed interest in the piece began when Thomas and Marshall Osborn acquired the copyist's manuscript in 1969.

approval (for several diverse reasons) of Mahler's major surgery.[48] As Martin Zenck has demonstrated in his thoughtful study of the issue, a whole network of musical and dramatic allusions is lost when "Waldmärchen" is not heard. In my opinion, however, the composer's decision reflects a distinct logic of its own, and ought accordingly to be respected. (Such a position does not, of course, rule out study and occasional performance of the original three-part score.) As I have already suggested, rejection of the work by both Brahms and Liszt may have influenced Mahler. Yet in the end he surely trusted his own musical judgment, and was not swayed solely by practical considerations: so much is clear from his final restoration of the offstage orchestra (which still challenges performers today, when the conductor can be watched via closed-circuit television). The greater concision and stronger dramatic momentum of the final version, which result from striking the redundant recounting of the fratricide, are obvious.[49] And although certain connections to "Waldmärchen" are lost, the remaining two parts have for nearly a century stood as a quite satisfying musical and dramatic whole without the original first part.

Zenck has drawn attention to the integral connection between a fairly substantial passage in "Der Spielmann," eventually cut by Mahler, and material presented earlier in "Waldmärchen." But I am not convinced that he fully explores either the background of the passage or Mahler's possible reasons for recasting it. The episode in question, found in the copyist's manuscript at Yale (F), consists of twenty-one bars preceding figure 15 in the printed score.[50] This segment was problematic from the earliest stages of the movement's genesis: the preliminary draft at the Stadtbibliothek in Vienna (B 1) shows an altogether different attempt to set the words "O Spielmann mein," which has been canceled.[51] But there is

---

[48]   See Jack Diether, "Mahler's *Klagende Lied* – Genesis and Evolution," *Music Review* 29 (1968), 268–87, as well as his foreword to the full and vocal scores of the movement (New York, 1973); Donald Mitchell, "Mahler's Waldmärchen: The Unpublished First Part of 'Das klagende Lied,'" *Musical Times* 111 (1970), 375–79, as well as MWY, pp. 56–68; and Martin Zenck, "Mahlers Streichung" (see n. 7 above).

[49]   See Mitchell, "Mahler's Waldmärchen," and MWY, pp. 58–60.

[50]   The relevant pages from the Yale manuscript are reproduced in Zenck.

[51]   Reproduced in Zenck, "Mahlers Streichung," and also in Rudolph Stephan, ed., *Werk und Interpretation*, p. 27.

no replacement for it. The draft simply continues with an earlier version of the material found at 15, now with the text "O ließest du das Flöten sein." At the very end of the manuscript, however – after the dated inscription "Ende des Spielmanns" – one finds what looks very much like an early sketch for the interlude that materializes in the Stadtbibliothek's orchestral score of "Der Spielmann" (item D). Here the episode is developed into a setting of the lines "O Spielmann, lieber Spielmann mein, O ließest du das Flöten [sein]" (the second line partly canceled), and an eight-bar orchestral interlude. Then in four bars he eventually cut, before the entrance of the chorus, Mahler has inserted "O Spielmann, lieber Spielmann mein" into the solo soprano part; the chorus follows with "O ließest du..."[52]

In the Yale manuscript (F) we find a further development of the episode: in essence, this is an elaboration of the Stadtbibliothek score, with the introduction of new fanfare figures and further working out of material that is to suggest distant bell sounds. But quite curiously, in this version Mahler begins with only the single line "O Spielmann" and follows it with fifteen bars of instrumental interlude before introducing the chorus singing "O ließest du . . ." This interlude certainly provides a network of connections with "Waldmärchen," and with other parts of "Der Spielmann" as well; but it also obviously disrupts the narrative and breaks up the setting of the stanza. Mahler further complicates the situation by removing the repetition of the opening line in the Yale copy. Later he seems to have realized that the interlude appeared in the wrong place and was simply unnecessary. Condensation of the passage to what is found in the published score yields a sense of hushed anticipation, built up by the repeated notes over the sustained F pedal, which makes the first line (replacing the original "O ließest du . . .") a chanted collective summons, almost in the manner of Greek tragedy, from the chorus to the minstrel: "O Spielmann, lieber Spielmann mein [O minstrel, my beloved minstrel]." The music also underscores the "strangeness" of the new second line "Das wird ein seltsam Spielen sein [that will be strange playing]" through a new harmonic shift. Thus Mahler had very good reasons – intelligibility,

---

[52] This concluding page of the episode is also reproduced in Zenck, "Mahlers Streichung."

economy, and mood – for altering a passage that had caused him difficulties for quite some time. Other changes appear to be equally well grounded.

A great deal of attention has been focused upon the fratricidal struggle in the cantata (chiefly owing to Jack Diether's instigation);[53] as a result, commentators often fail to grasp that the dramatic center of the work is not the crime itself, but rather the retribution that follows the crime. Indeed, this is inherent in the title: although *Das klagende Lied* is sometimes translated as *The Song of Lamentation*, "klagen" means, besides "to lament," to accuse, charge, complain, or indict, as Wolf Rosenberg and others have pointed out.[54] (In legal cases, *der Klagende* is the plaintiff.) And the work is indeed the story of the murderer's indictment and the demise of the queen who instigated the conflict in the first place. Surely it is no accident that the central figure is neither the murderer nor the queen, but the lowly minstrel (*Spielmann*) whose skill as creator and performer – in fashioning the bone flute and then playing on it – enables the dead brother to utter his accusation against the survivor. Through his art the minstrel exposes the crime and thus overthrows a corrupt regime.[55]

Such a story, in which a folk figure brings aristocratic criminals to justice, might well appeal to a young man strongly influenced by Wagnerian and Nietzschean notions about the dramatic potential of myths and the significance of music and musicians in the redemption of society. Wagner was and remained a most central influence in Mahler's musical and

---

[53] See n. 48 above. Diether's position has not gone unchallenged; cf., e.g., Dika Newlin, "The 'Mahler's Brother Syndrome': Necropsychiatry and the Artist," *Musical Quarterly* 66 (1980), 296–304.

[54] Rosenberg, "Die Moritat," pp. 135–49. I am indebted to Philip Winters for stimulating discussions of this point before I encountered Rosenberg's article.

[55] Donald Mitchell (*Mahler*, pp. 143–44) draws attention to the different role of the queen in Bechstein's story: "the figure of the mother . . . destroys the son who has offended against nature (in the Shakespearean sense)." In Mahler's version, brother kills brother rather than sister (see above, p. 34), which may be related to notions of crimes against brotherhood rather than to fratricide in the familial sense. And Mahler allows the dead brother to speak only through the playing of the *Spielmann*, whereas in Bechstein (and Greif) the bone flute passes from the shepherd who discovered it to a knight, and finally to the queen herself.

intellectual development, and it is certain that he absorbed Wagner's writings as well as his music. (Indeed, following Wagner's precepts, he temporarily became a vegetarian in 1880, just at the time he was composing *Das klagende Lied*.)[56] Wagner had not only written about revolution, he had been a revolutionary. And *Das klagende Lied* can be read as a political allegory in which a ruler stirs up fratricidal strife among her subjects, whereupon a bold musician, implicitly from the lower classes, brings about the collapse of an evil competitive society through his special gifts.

By eliminating "Waldmärchen," Mahler reasserts in one bold stroke the main theme of his ballad. For "Waldmärchen," evocative and appealing though it may be, is not only redundant, but actually draws attention away from the theme of retribution. The movement overplays both the initial forest setting of the story and the first account of the murder. As a result, when the minstrel finally appears, he seems much less central to the tale than he truly is. Thus Mahler may have reached his decision to cut "Waldmärchen" for dramatic and philosophical as well musical reasons.

Late retouchings

The final stage in the history of *Das klagende Lied* during Mahler's lifetime is documented by autograph revisions in a copy of the printed Weinberger score now located in the Stadt- und Landesbibliothek in Vienna.[57] These reportedly date from 1906, and may stem in part from the performance in Amsterdam by the Concertgebouw Orchestra and the Toonkunst choir that Mahler conducted on 10 March 1906.[58] The majority of these alterations were included in the posthumously published edition of the work issued by Universal in 1914. For some unknown reason,

---

[56] See Bauer-Lechner's commentary on pp. 37–38 above. Wagner advocated vegetarianism in his essay "Religion and Art," which appeared in the *Bayreuther Blätter* in October 1880; for further discussion of Wagner's influence on Mahler and his circle at this time, see William J. McGrath, *Dionysian Art and Populist Politics in Austria* (New Haven, 1974), chaps. 1–4.

[57] See Hilmar, "Mahleriana," p. 6.

[58] See Knud Martner, *Gustav Mahler im Konzertsaal: Eine Dokumentation seiner Konzerttätigkeit 1870–1911* (Copenhagen, 1985), p. 93.

however, Mahler's important added indication at figure **63** – "if possible, to be sung by a boy's voice" – was omitted. Both here and in the closely related passage at **26**, Mahler reverted to the vocal sonority as he had initially composed it more than twenty years earlier: the boy alto is called for in the first autograph full score of "Der Spielmann" (ca. 1880) preserved at the Stadtbibliothek in Vienna (item D above).

3 "Liebste Justi!": the family letters of Gustav Mahler

STEPHEN McCLATCHIE

To Mrs. Maria Rosé, in gratitude

"Since I am now very engaged with posterity, the here-and-now (*Mitwelt*) must have a little patience."[1] So wrote Mahler to his sister Justine on Christmas Eve, 1893, when he was deeply engrossed with revisions of his youthful cantata, *Das klagende Lied*. But such was not his usual attitude toward his family, as the hundreds of surviving letters to his siblings and parents clearly reveal. These letters form the bulk of the Gustav Mahler–Alfred Rosé Collection in the Music Library at the University of Western Ontario. In addition, the Mahler–Rosé Collection includes musical manuscripts, letters, cards, photographs, and other memorabilia relating to Gustav Mahler, his sister Justine Mahler-Rosé, and her husband Arnold Rosé, long-time concertmaster of the Vienna Philharmonic and leader of the renowned Rosé Quartet. The scope and contents of the Collection have not become widely known, owing to restricted access. Fortunately, this situation has now changed: research is underway on various aspects of the Collection, and an edition of the family letters is in progress.[2]

---

[1] Letter from Gustav to Justine, 24 December 1893, E3-MJ-131. "Da ich jetzt bei der Nachwelt sehr engagirt bin, muß sich die Mitwelt ein wenig gedulden."

[2] An abridged version of my inventory of the Mahler–Rosé Collection appears in the December 1995 issue of *Notes*; the complete inventory may be consulted at the Music Library, The University of Western Ontario. The following history of the Collection and introduction to the letters is based upon the inventory.

Among the more interesting items in the Collection is a copyist's manuscript of Mahler's First Symphony that transmits the work as it was first performed in Budapest in 1889, and contains numerous autograph revisions and reorchestrations. A detailed report will be forthcoming in another publication.

Plate 3.1 Photograph of Mahler inscribed "To my dear friend and / 'Kindred Spirit' Arnold Rosé / Vienna June 98 Gust. Mahler" (an allusion to Goethe's *Wahlverwandschaften* [*Elective Affinities*])

Plate 3.2   Photograph of Justine Mahler-Rosé

A brief history of the Collection

That the Mahler–Rosé Collection ended up in London, Ontario is due to a chain of events set in motion by the social upheaval of World War II. Hitler invaded Austria in March of 1938; the following September Alfred Rosé, the son of Justine and Arnold, fled to the United States with his wife Maria, just one month after Justine had died at the age of seventy (cf. also Fig. 3.1, "The Rosé Family Tree," below). A few months later Arnold and his daughter Alma found refuge in England, taking the Collection with them in steamer trunks. Alma subsequently went to Holland to play and conduct, and became trapped by the Nazi occupation; in 1944 she perished in Auschwitz-Birkenau, where she had bravely served as conductor of a women's orchestra in the camp. After learning of his daughter's fate in 1946, the eighty-three-year-old Arnold, who was preparing to join his son Alfred in the United States, passed away in England. The Mahler–Rosé Collection was then shipped to Cincinnati, where Alfred and Maria had settled in 1938. There it might have remained, had a former pupil of Arnold Rosé not recommended Alfred to inaugurate an opera workshop at the Conservatory in London, Ontario. After running this workshop during the summers of 1946 and 1947, Alfred was offered a permanent teaching position at the Music Teacher's College, newly affiliated with the University. (The College would undergo several metamorphoses, and eventually became the Faculty of Music in 1968.) The Rosés moved to London in 1948, bringing the Collection with them. For over three decades it remained in a London bank vault until it was deposited in the Mahler–Rosé Room at the Music Library of the University of Western Ontario by Maria Rosé in 1983, eight years after her husband's death.

By all accounts, Alfred Rosé was adamant that the Collection never be returned to Vienna after his death. Rather, he insisted that, like himself, it would remain forever exiled from the land that rejected him in 1938. Alfred was equally firm in refusing to allow publication of the family letters during his lifetime, owing to the private nature of their contents. He was especially uneasy about Mahler's frequent reproaches to his sister, Justine (Alfred's mother). As a result, with only few exceptions, the letters remain

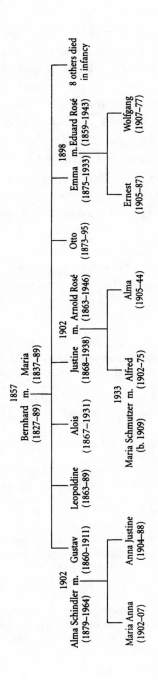

Fig. 3.1   The Mahler–Rosé family tree

unpublished to this day.[3] Many of them, however, are familiar in essence to Mahler scholars from the summaries and translated excerpts in Henry-Louis de La Grange's monumental Mahler biography.[4] In the late 1950s Alfred allowed de La Grange to examine and photograph many of the letters, and also granted permission for their use in the biography.

Sometime after de La Grange examined the collection, Alfred Rosé sold or gave away a number of letters.[5] Thirty-five were purchased by the University of Western Ontario and now form the first supplement of the Mahler–Rosé Collection.[6] One was willed by Alfred to de La Grange, and the precise history of a further ten is unclear. Fortunately, copies of all these letters have survived, so that they may be included in an edition.[7]

Nature and distribution of the letters

As the list on p. 59 indicates, almost 85 percent of the letters in the Collection are from Mahler to his younger sister Justine. This is because

---

[3] Nevertheless, four letters from Mahler to his parents were published (under circumstances unknown to me) by Hans Holländer, "Gustav Mahler vollendet eine Oper von Carl Maria von Weber: Vier unbekannte Briefe Mahlers," *Neue Zeitschrift für Musik* 116 (1955), 130*–132*, and four letters from Mahler to Justine are published in *Gustav Mahler: Unbekannte Briefe*, ed. Herta Blaukopf (Vienna, 1983), pp. 109–16.

[4] HLG and HLGF. De La Grange does not always indicate when he is citing a letter from the Mahler–Rosé Collection.

[5] One seems to have been given away by Justine long before this, as only a copy survives in the Collection, with "Originalbrief an Mrs. Lanier in New York geschenkt" written on the back in Justine's hand.

[6] There are five supplements to the main Collection (which comprises the material deposited in 1983): (1) the letters sold to the University of Western Ontario by Alfred Rosé in 1971 (38 in total, including 3 non-family letters); (2) material purchased by the Music Library at Sotheby's sale of the Ernest Rosé collection (No. 5256, 12 December 1984); (3, 4, & 5) material given to the University by Mrs. Rosé in 1989 and 1995 (scores, photographs, memorabilia).

[7] Of these ten, one is now in the Pierpont Morgan Library in New York, four are (or were) in the collection of one of Arnold Rosé's former students, Felix Eyle (and have been published in *Gustav Mahler: Unbekannte Briefe*), and one or two were owned by David Stivender in New York. The present whereabouts of the other three or four is unknown.

both Mahler's parents (as well as a sister, Leopoldine) died in 1889; thereupon Gustav and Justine assumed joint responsibility for their brothers Alois and Otto, and their sister Emma. For the next several years Justine served as acting head-of-household in Vienna while the younger siblings (supposedly) pursued their studies; meanwhile Mahler continued his career as a conductor in Budapest and later Hamburg, thereby providing financial support. Most of the remaining letters from Mahler to family members are to his parents, but a few are addressed to his brothers and his other sister, Emma.

The Mahler family letters

Letters from Gustav Mahler

56	letters to parents (53 original letters + 3 copies)
437	letters to Justine (428 original letters + 9 copies)
1	letter to Alois
1	letter to Otto
2	letters to Emma
1	postcard from Gustav, Alma, and Justine to Emma
1	letter to Leopoldine
1	letter to Uncle and Aunt
10	letters to Arnold Rosé
10	letters from Alma and Gustav to Justine and Arnold Rosé
1	postcard from Alma and Gustav to Alfred Rosé
521	(509 original letters + 12 copies)

Letters from other family members

1	letter from Maria Mahler to unknown correspondent
1	letter from Otto Mahler to unknown correspondent
5	letters from Justine to Gustav
3	letters from Alma to Justine
6	letters from Justine to Emma
1	letter from Alma Mahler-Werfel to Alfred Rosé
17	

In addition to Mahler's letters home, there are another sixteen written from and to various family members. Especially notable are the five from Justine to Gustav – the sole remnant of what must have been hundreds

Fig. 3.2 Concentration of the Mahler family letters

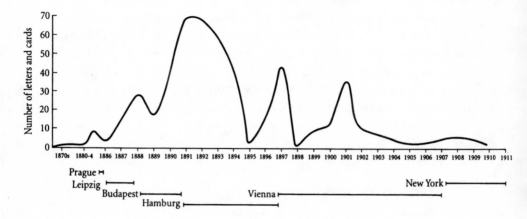

of letters she wrote to her older brother. The rest, like most of the correspondence Mahler received during his lifetime, were destroyed during the Second World War when a bomb struck the second story of Alma Mahler's house in Vienna.

The vast majority of the family letters were written between 1888 and 1894; accordingly, they are among the most important material surviving from the period when Mahler was establishing himself as a seasoned young professional (see Fig. 3.2). The letters prior to 1889 are mainly to his parents, written from Kassel, Prague, and Leipzig, cities where Mahler successively held conducting posts. Those to Justine come mainly from the Budapest and early Hamburg years, and are preoccupied with household accounts, finances, worries about schooling, family crises, and other day-to-day news, as well as the odd tidbit about Mahler's own works. They also document Mahler's summer trips – his pilgrimages to Bayreuth, his vacation in Scandinavia in 1891, and his conducting engagement in London in the summer of 1892.

In the mid 1890s the character of Mahler's letters to Justine changes; they are much less focused upon quotidian matters, and there is a marked decrease in their number. The reason is that the family situation had evolved: following a period of considerable resentment on the part of

60

both Mahler and his brothers, Otto and Alois had finally begun to earn a living.[8] Since an apartment in Vienna was no longer necessary, in the autumn of 1894 Justine and her younger sister Emma moved to Hamburg to keep house for Mahler, thus removing the need to communicate regularly by letter. Consequently, Mahler's letters to Justine after September or October 1894 were generally written when he was away from Hamburg. They document such matters as the 1895 première of his Second Symphony in Berlin, the many concerts he conducted in the winter of 1897 (Dresden, Berlin, Moscow, Munich, and Budapest), and also his frequent trips to Vienna during his campaign to become Director of the Vienna Court Opera. Around 1900 the number of his letters to Justine increases as the widening fame of Mahler the composer takes him to Prague, Liège, Paris, Munich, Dresden, and Berlin. After Mahler's marriage to Alma Schindler on 9 March 1902 (Justine and Arnold Rosé were wed the next day), there is a second marked decrease in letters.

These family letters provide an intimate counterpoint to the more public image of Mahler that emerges from many other surviving documents. In addition to chronicling family history, such as the illness and death of his parents and sister in 1889, Alois's illness in 1892, and Justine's trips to Italy in the winters of 1892–93 and 1893–94, the letters also reveal Mahler's private reactions to events and people around him. Of particular interest are his comments on his own conducting and composing, as well as his views of musical contemporaries.

Conductor and composer: a career blossoms

The earliest of Mahler's letters to his parents reveal the excitement of a young man embarked upon his course and enjoying his first successes. For example, in October or November 1885 Mahler wrote the following home to Iglau:

> Today I can give you the welcome news that Director Neumann has begun negotiations regarding the extension of my contract. Since we are both sharp fellows, this matter should take some time. – In the meantime, I will rehearse and conduct "Meistersinger," "Rheingold," "Walküre," and "Tristan" here, and

[8] See HLGF 1, 435–36, 446–47, and 499–501.

my career has taken a great upturn. As you see, everything has turned out better than we might have hoped.[9]

Likewise, the stunning success of his completion of Carl Maria von Weber's *Die drei Pintos* precipitated a considerable correspondence with his parents; the morning after the première on 20 January 1888 he was able to report that

> Everything went magnificently. The cheering was frenzied. Today the house is again sold out. Don't be surprised if my contribution is somewhat minimized by the newspapers. For "business considerations," it must be kept secret up front what is by me and what is by Weber. This much I can already tell you, that two of the most successful numbers, which the newspapers everywhere mention especially (No. 1: Student chorus, and the Ballad of Kater Mansor), are by me, as well as many other things. – All this must be kept secret, however, until the opera is performed everywhere. For now it means the less the prestige, the more the money! That is how it will be until all is revealed. In any case, from this day on I am a man of world renown.[10]

At times Mahler's earliest letters foreshadow the mature man, the self-assured future autocrat of the Vienna Opera, as do the following lines

[9] Letter from Gustav to his parents, October or November 1885, E17-MF-627. "Heute kann ich Euch die erfreuliche Mittheilung machen[,] daß Dir. Neumann mit mir betreffs Contraktverlängerung in Unterhandlung getreten ist. Da wir beide geriebene Kerls sind, so dürfte sich die Angelegenheit in die Länge ziehen. – Unterdessen werde ich 'Meistersinger,' 'Rheingold,' 'Walküre,' und 'Tristan' hier einstudiren und dirigiren – und meine Carriere hat einen großen Aufschwung genommen. – Wie ihr seht, ist alles besser ausgefallen, als wir es alle gehofft hätten."

[10] Letter from Gustav to his parents, 21 January 1888, E13-MF-540. "Alles gieng großartig. Der Jubel war frenetisch. Heute ist das Haus wieder ausverkauft. Wundert Euch nicht, wenn mein Verdienst in den Zeitungen etwas geschmälert wird. Aus 'Geschäftsrücksichten' muß es vorderhand verheimlicht werden, was von mir und was von Weber ist. So viel kann ich Euch schon sagen, daß 2 Lieblingsnummern, welche gerade in den Zeitungen überall erwähnt werden (Nro. I Student[en]chor und die Ballade von Kater Mansor) von mir sind, wie noch vieles andere. – Das muß Alles aber geheim gehalten werden, bis die Oper überall aufgeführt worden ist. – Jetzt heißt es, je weniger Ehre, desto mehr Geld! Das kommt dann noch, bis die Enthüllungen folgen. Jedenfalls bin ich vom heutigen Tage an ein weltberühmter Mann."

addressed to his parents on the day he first conducted Mozart's *Don Giovanni* in Prague:

> Tonight I conduct <u>Don Juan</u>, and it is a sign of Neumann's particular
> confidence that he hands over to me just this opera, because it is of great
> significance for Prague since Mozart composed it specifically for Prague, and
> he himself rehearsed and conducted it here. The citizens of Prague especially
> make the greatest demands. The newspapers – mainly the <u>Tagblatt</u> – will
> probably tear me to pieces, for I predict now that they will all cry "Oh! Oh!
> 'Tradition' has gone to the devil!" With this word, one means in fact the
> long-standing habit – or rather, rut – of performing a work on a stage. I have
> been concerned with none of this, and tonight I will calmly follow <u>my own</u>
> path.[11]

Several years later, Mahler's conducting of *Don Giovanni* in Budapest
attracted the attention of none other than Johannes Brahms, who seems to
have been quite taken with the younger musician's interpretation of the
work. On 17 December 1890 Mahler wrote to Justine that Brahms and
d'Albert had been at the previous evening's performance, and that Brahms
"was <u>really delighted</u> with my conducting ... He said that many things had
been revealed to him for the first time, and that he had <u>never</u> heard Mozart
performed so stylishly. From Brahms, this really means something, because
he belongs completely to the old school."[12] Almost a year later, Brahms was
still talking about that performance:

---

[11] Letter from Gustav to his parents, 6 September 1885, E13-MF-538. "Heute
Abend dirigire ich <u>Don Juan</u>, und ist dies ein Zeichen des besonderen
Vertrauens Neumann[s], daß er mir gerade diese Oper übergibt, weil dieselbe
für Prag von großer Bedeutung ist, denn sie ist von Mozart für Prag selbst
componirt, und von ihm selbst hier einstudirt und dirigirt worden. Die Prager
machen gerade da die größten Ansprüche. Die Zeitungen[,] hauptsächlich das
<u>Tagblatt</u>[,] werden voraussichtlich über mich herfallen, denn das sage ich schon
voraus, daß sie Alle schreien werden: Wehe! Wehe! die 'Tradition' ist beim
Teufel! Mit diesem Wort bezeichnet man nämlich die langjährige Gepflogenheit
(resp. Schlendrian) an einer Bühne[,] ein Werk aufzuführen. Ich habe mich um
Nichts gekümmert und werde heute Abend ruhig <u>meine</u> Bahnen gehen."

[12] Letter from Gustav to Justine, 17 December 1890, E12-MJ-483. "von meiner
Direktion <u>ganz entzückt</u> war ... Manches, sagte er, habe er zum erstenmale
kennengelernt, und noch <u>nie</u> Mozart so stylvoll vortragen hören. – Von
Brahms will das was heißen, der ganz den alten Richtung angehört."

Yesterday Brahms was at the Bülow Concert [Hamburg Abonnement concert series], where, to the amusement of the audience, Bülow, who also usually makes all kinds of jokes with me, called down from his first-floor box that I should come up right away: Brahms was asking for me. – There both Brahms and Bülow treated me in the most reverential way. Brahms especially had been raving all day long to all who would listen about my Don Juan performance in Budapest . . . – Afterwards, I was together with Brahms at the inn; it is really rare that Brahms, the notorious ironist, takes someone else so seriously and treats him so warmly and sincerely – especially a musician![13]

In subsequent years, it was Mahler's habit to visit the older musician at Bad Ischl during the summer; these visits are often referred to in letters and postcards to Justine.

Several of Mahler's letters to Justine from the second half of January 1894 discuss his relationship with his most famous contemporary, Richard Strauss.[14] Strauss was in Hamburg to conduct the Abonnement concert scheduled for the twenty-second of the month because the director of this subscription series, Strauss's mentor Hans von Bülow, had been forced to abandon the season owing to declining health. Mahler took advantage of

---

[13] Letter from Mahler to Justine, 1 December 1891, E10-MJ-418. "Gestern war Brahms im Bülow-Concert, da mir zu Belustigung des Publikums Bülow, der auch sonst allerlei Scherze mit mir zum Besten giebt, aus der Logen im 1. Stock herunter rief, ich solle gleich heraufkommen: Brahms verlangt nach mir. – Daselbst wurde mir nun sowie von Seiten Brahms als auch Bülow die huldvollste Behandlung zu Theil. Brahms besonders hatte sehr den ganzen Tag zu allen, die es hören wollten, von meiner Don Juan Aufführung in Pest geschwärmt . . . – Nachher war ich mit Brahms im Wirtshaus zusammen; es ist wirklich höchst selten, das[s] der berüchtigte Ironiker Brahms einen anderen, namentlich Musiker! so ernst nimmt und so aufrichtig herzlich behandelt."

[14] For additional information on the relationship between Strauss and Mahler, see Herta Blaukopf, "Rivalry and Friendship: An Essay on the Mahler–Strauss Relationship," in *Gustav Mahler–Richard Strauss: Correspondence 1888–1911*, ed. Herta Blaukopf (London, 1984), 103–63, and Stephen E. Hefling, "Miners Digging from Opposite Sides: Mahler, Strauss, and the Problem of Program Music," in *Richard Strauss: New Perspectives on the Composer and his Work*, ed. Bryan Gilliam (Durham, 1992), 41–53.

In the fall of 1889 Mahler sent Strauss's autograph to Justine with the following comment: "Enclosed, an autograph from <u>Richard Strauss</u>, one of the most famous young composers, who probably has a great future" (E13-MJ-519). ("Beiliegend ein Autograph von <u>Richard Strauss</u>, einem der namhaftesten jungen Componisten, der wahrscheinlich eine große Zukunft hat.")

the occasion to play Strauss some of his compositions: "Strauss is here now; yesterday I played my Humoresken for him. He was very delighted, and, hopefully, will do something for them."[15] After his colleague's departure, however, Mahler reflected upon how he differed from Strauss, and indeed from most of his contemporaries:

> I was often together with Strauss. I would be lying, however, if I were to say that many points of contact arose between us. – More and more I see that I stand entirely alone among present-day musicians. Our goals diverge. From my point of view, I can only see everywhere either old-classical or New-German pedants. Hardly has Wagner been recognized and understood when yet again the priests of the only accepted true faith come forth and surround the whole terrain with fortresses against real life, which thus always consists of the fact that one always reshapes the Old (even if it is greater and more significant than the New) and creates it anew out of the necessity of the moment. Strauss in particular is just such a Pope! But, at any rate, a likeable chap, insofar as I could find out. Whether it all is real remains to be seen. All this is said strictly between us, because he is "my only friend among all the gods" – and I do not want to ruin everything with him.[16]

[15] Letter from Gustav to Justine, ca. 22 January 1894, E3-MJ-134. "Strauss ist jetzt hier; gestern spielte ich ihm meine Humoresken vor. Er war sehr entzückt, und wird dafür hoffentlich etwas thun."

On 14 January, Mahler had written to Justine that "Strauss conducts here next, and has announced himself to me in a friendly manner – 'among all the gods my only friend'" (E3-MJ-132). Mahler alludes to Wotan's lines addressed to Loge at the beginning of the second scene of *Das Rheingold*: "Von allen Göttern / dein einz'ger Freund." ("Nächstens dirigirt Strauss hier, und hat sich mir freundschaftlich angekündigt[,] 'unter allen Göttern mein einziger Freund.'")

[16] Letter from Gustav to Justine, late January 1894, S1-MJ-748. Mahler's Wagner allusion is identified in n. 15 above. This letter was among those sold to the University of Western Ontario by Alfred Rosé in 1975, and has been published in Blaukopf, "Rivalry and Friendship," pp. 116–17. "Mit Strauss war ich sehr viel beisammen. Ich müßte jedoch lügen, wenn ich sagen sollte, daß zwischen uns sich viel[e] Berührungspunkte ergeben haben. – Ich sehe immer mehr und mehr, daß ich unter den heutigen Musikern ganz allein dastehe. Unsere Ziele gehen auseinander. Ich von meinem Standpunkt kann überall nur entweder altclassischen oder neudeutschen Zopf erkennen. Kaum ist Wagner anerkannt und verstanden, so kommen schon wieder die allein seligmachenden Pfaffen und führen auf dem ganzen Terrain die Schutzwälle gegen das wahre Leben auf, das doch immer darin besteht, daß man das Alte, selbst wenn [es] auch größer und bedeutender ist, als das Neue, immer wieder umgestaltet und aus den Bedürfnißen des Moments neu erschafft. Strauss vornehmlich ist ganz Pope,

Just over two years earlier, Mahler had also taken the opportunity to play one of his compositions for Hans von Bülow – with disastrous results. Covering his ears in distress, Bülow declared that next to Mahler's "Todtenfeier," *Tristan* had the effect of a Haydn symphony; from then on, the mutual admiration between the two men was mingled with resentment on both sides.[17] Bülow died on 12 February 1894, and it was decided that the next of the Hamburg Abonnement concerts on the twenty-second should be dedicated to his memory, and conducted by his protégé Richard Strauss. In the event, Strauss bowed out for political reasons, claiming ill health, and Mahler, who had long been anxious to supplement his opera conducting with more concert performances, was called in to substitute.[18] His wry comment to Justine on this affair sums up his mixed feelings: "it is curious that someone always has to become ill or die before I can conduct a symphony."[19]

Apart from these letters of 1894, Strauss is mentioned only infrequently in the family correspondence, although in March 1897 Mahler again played one of his own compositions for him:

> Strauss, with whom I was together yesterday, and to whom I played the last movement of my Second [Symphony] (he was downright <u>enthusiastic</u>), also thinks that I am already on the right path, and that my triumph is now only a question of a very short time.[20]

Mahler's letters to his parents and Justine also allude to aspects of his own creative life, although generally in a rather incidental fashion. The progress or completion of *Die drei Pintos*, the First Symphony, "Todtenfeier," the *Wunderhorn* songs, and the revision of *Das klagende Lied*

Papst! Aber immerhin ein lieber Kerl, soweit ich ihn erkennen konnte. Ob alles echt ist, muß sich erst erweisen. Dies ist alles <u>unter uns</u> gesagt, denn er ist 'unter allen Göttern mein einziger Freund' – und ich will mir es nicht noch mit dem verderben."   [17] HLGF 1, 369–74.   [18] HLGF 1, 449–50.

[19] Letter from Gustav to Justine, third week of February 1894, E15-MJ-581. "[e]s ist eigenthümlich, daß immer jemand krank werden oder sterben muß, damit ich eine Symphonie dirigiren darf."

[20] Letter from Gustav to Justine, 21 March 1897, E14-MJ-562. "Strauss, mit dem ich gestern beisammen war, und dem ich den letzten Satz aus meiner II. vorgespielt [habe] (er war geradezu <u>begeistert</u>), meint auch, daß ich bereits am besten Wege [bin], und daß mein Sieg nun nur noch eine Frage der kürzesten Zeit ist."

are mentioned, and as research on the letters continues, perhaps these brief references will provide additional details concerning the chronology of Mahler's compositional activities. His comments to Justine during the revision of *Das klagende Lied* can but make one wish that he had been similarly discursive about other of his works:

> I am now resolved about <u>Das klagende Lied</u>! . . . I can tell you that I am <u>absolutely astounded</u> by this work, ever since I have had it in front of me again. When I consider that it was written by a 20/21-year-old man, I cannot understand it; it is so <u>idiosyncratic</u> and <u>powerful</u>! The nuts which I have given to crack here are perhaps the toughest that my imagination has yet brought forth.[21]

The later letters give a strong indication of his somewhat ambivalent relationship with the Vienna Philharmonic (Wiener Philharmoniker), for on several occasions Mahler punningly refers to them as the "Viehharmoniker."[22] In one such letter, written in the autumn of 1907 during the brief Russian tour Mahler made just after his final performances at the Vienna Court Opera,[23] he offers an interesting comparison between the orchestras of St. Petersburg and Vienna:

> By the way, the orchestra here is really tremendous and reminds me of the Viennese one – in its scampishness too! However, I have it firmly by the reins, and they would like to engage me for some concerts. I seem to have more esteem with them than with our own dear *Viehharmoniker*.[24]

---

[21] Letter from Gustav to Justine, 17 December 1893, E15-MJ-579. "Ich bin jetzt fest über dem <u>klagenden Lied</u>! . . . Ich kann Dir sagen[,] ich bin <u>paff</u> über dieses Werk, seitdem ich es wieder unter den Händen habe. Wenn ich bedenke, daß das ein 20/21-jähriger Mensch geschrieben [hat], kann ich es nicht begreifen – so <u>eigenartig</u> und <u>gewaltig</u> ist es! Die Nüsse, die ich da aufzuknacken gegeben habe, sind vielleicht die härtesten, die mein Boden je hervorgebracht."

[22] This pun on philharmonic is untranslatable into English – *Vieh* means cattle, livestock, or "animal" in general.

[23] HLGF 3, 129 ff.

[24] Letter from Gustav to Justine, 7 November 1907, E6-MJ-294. "Das Orchester hier ist übrigens wirklich großartig, und erinnert mich an die Wiener – auch in der Lausbüberei. Aber ich habe sie doch straff am Bandel, und sie möchten mich für eigene Concerte gerne engagiren. Ich scheine bei denen mehr Anwerth zu besitzen als bei unseren lieben Viehharmonikern."

Mahler and his brothers

Perhaps the most constant refrain in the family letters of the early 1890s is Mahler's difficulties with his brothers Alois and Otto. The following lines from Mahler to Justine, written in the spring of 1893, sum up the tone of these letters:

> I am beginning to get absolutely fed up with being dragged behind, continually, through thick and thin, tied to the stirrup of my lord brothers' winged horse. – I have no desire to follow this bold flight any farther. I, too, am still young, and not in the mood to be a grumpy moralist. I, too, would enjoy my life, and am not ready to wheeze around with the cares of a nearly dead old man. – I still have my flight, damn it all. – I now believe that it was a big mistake that I was so forbearing and trusting with those two fellows.[25]

It appears that both Alois and Otto were weak, stubborn, irresponsible, and constantly in debt, and Mahler's letters to Justine teem with exasperated and often angry references to them both. But Mahler was also continually concerned with their well-being; in particular, the earlier letters reveal his active involvement in their education. When Alois and Otto were older, Mahler frequently attempted to secure positions for them, but was often rebuffed for his efforts.

Of the two, it was the older, Alois, who caused Mahler the most trouble. He seems to have been entirely without discipline, negligent and proud – not to mention dishonest, as a letter from the second half of April 1892 suggests:

> First, the letter from Alois. According to this letter, the young man was not arrested, and that scare was only a later addition. That is the worst of it, that I cannot put any faith in his words. – A frivolous prank I would gladly

---

[25] Letter from Gustav to Justine, Spring 1893, E3-MJ-144. "Ich fange an, es überhaupt satt zu bekommen, mich von meinen Herrn Brüdern so unaufhörlich durch dick und dünn[,] so zu schlingen am Bügel ihres geflügelten Roßes dahinschleifen zu laßen. – Diesem kühnen Fluge weiter zu folgen, habe ich keine Lust. Ich bin auch noch jung, und zum griesgrämigen Moralisten nicht gelaunt. Ich will mein Leben auch noch geniessen, und nicht bereits mit den Sorgen eines abgelebten Greises herumkeuchen. – Ich habe auch meinen Flug, zum Donnerwetter noch einmal. – Ich glaube es nun, daß es ein großer Fehler war, daß ich immer so nachsichtig und vertrauensvoll gegen die Burschen war."

excuse – but not to be able to <u>believe</u> a person, that makes every relationship impossible . . . If he only had some <u>Mahler</u>ish blood in his veins, I could do so much for him here in <u>Hamburg</u>.[26]

The Mahler–Rosé Collection includes one letter from Alois to Gustav that, after two pages of complaints, closes thus: "I have a heart so full of bitterness that I would have to write you twenty more pages, but I shall prefer to remain silent." This letter has survived because Mahler immediately sent it to Justine, with the following message on the verso: "As you see, we are thus all agreed to let Alois go his own way now."[27] While he had expressed this sentiment several times previously, in this case it was followed through. A letter of 23 August 1893 to Alois (perhaps a copy sent to Justine) makes Mahler's position perfectly clear:

> When your savings are exhausted, do not, under any circumstances, count on getting even a kreuzer more from me. I assure you categorically that I am neither in a position to support you financially, nor have I the slightest intention of doing so, and you would make a severe – and for you, disastrous – error if you secretly held to that idea . . . It only remains for me to express to you my best wishes for your well-being, and my hope above all to see you yet as a useful member of human society.[28]

[26] Letter from Gustav to Justine, second half of April 1892, E6-MJ-290. "<u>Erstens</u> den Brief von Alois. Nach <u>diesem</u> Brief also war der junge Mann <u>nicht</u> Arrestant[,] und <u>der</u> Schreck war nur Draufgabe. Das ist das Schrecklichste, daß ich keinen Glauben in seine Worte setzen kann. – Einen leichtsinnigen Streich würde ich ihm gerne verzeihen – aber einem Menschen nicht <u>glauben</u> zu können, das macht jedes Verhältniß [sic] unmöglich . . . Wenn er nur etwas vom <u>Mahler</u>schen Blut in den Adern hätte – wie viel könnte ich hier in <u>Hamburg</u> für ihn wirken."

[27] Letter from Alois to Gustav, May 1893, E10-[F]MJ-437. "Ich habe ein solch von Bitterkeit erfülltes Herz, daß ich Dir 20 Seiten schreiben müßte, doch will ich vorziehen zu schweigen." Gustav's comment to Justine on verso: "Wie Du siehst, sind wir also Alle darin einig, den Alois jetzt laufen zu laßen."

[28] Letter from Gustav to Alois, 23 August 1893, E15-MF-597. "Rechne unter keiner Bedingung darauf[,] wenn dein Geld zur Neige gegangen ist, auch nur einen Kreuzer von mir zu erhalten. Ich versichere Dich auf das entschiedenste, daß ich weder in der Lage bin, noch im Geringsten die Absicht habe, Dich mit Geld zu unterstützen; und Du würdest einen argen, und für Dich verhängnißvollen Fehltritt begehen, wenn Du Dich aber im Stillen darauf verlaßen würdest . . . Es erübrigt also mir, Dir meine besten Wünsche für Dein Wolergehen und die Hoffnung auszusprechen, Dich doch noch meist als brauchbares Mitglied der menschlichen Gesellschaft wiederzusehen."

After this date, Alois is only infrequently mentioned in any of Mahler's correspondence. He emigrated to the United States in 1907 and died of cancer in Chicago in 1931.

The greatest failing of Mahler's second brother, Otto, was his aversion to any type of work. His continual laziness drove Mahler to distraction, for by all accounts, Otto was possessed of a sharp intelligence and a decided gift for music. When he left the Vienna Conservatory in early 1892 without completing the program, Otto and Justine managed for several months to conceal the news from Mahler, who was, of course, furious when the truth eventually emerged. Nevertheless, he was sufficiently convinced of Otto's musical gifts to obtain positions for him in at least two German theatres; Otto, true to form, was never satisfied. In a letter of February 1893, Mahler discussed Otto's character with Justine:

> About Otto, I am now absolutely at my wit's end! It's an awful shame about the boor! Incompetent, ignorant, and respectful of no one! What is there to do? . . . I think that you should not send him my letters, and make it quite clear to him that I know everything about him. And that I know about his wanton thoughtlessness as well, and also that he strikes such a presumptuous tone in his letters to me, and – despite the fact that he denies it – is so insincere towards me, that I am very angry about it all.[29]

The Collection includes a draft in Justine's hand for a letter of 1 October 1894, ostensibly from her to Otto, but covered with Mahler's own comments and marginal scribblings. This angry but fair communiqué is the last mention of this wayward brother: on 6 February 1895 Otto Mahler shot himself in Vienna (in his pocket was found a lock of his mother's hair, now in the Mahler–Rosé Collection). Although Mahler's letters to Justine are silent about Otto's death, they do reveal that the possibility of such a tragedy had occurred to Mahler more than a year before it came to pass:

---

[29] Letter from Gustav to Justine, February 1893, E5-MJ-251. "Für Otto weiß ich jetzt überhaupt keinen Rath mehr! Es ist ein Jammer mit dem Schliffel. Nichts können, nichts wissen und vor Niemandem Respekt! Was läßt sich da thun? . . . Ich denke, Du schickst ihm meine Briefe nicht, und läßt ihn überhaupt merken, daß ich über ihn alles weiß. Und daß ich über seinen frevelhaften Leichtsinn sowol [Bescheid weiß], wie auch darüber, daß er in seinen Briefen an mich einen so anmaßenden Ton anschlägt, und trotzdem er es läugnet, – so unwahr gegen mich ist, daß ich über alles das sehr erzürnt bin."

I don't really understand what you mean by the "stupid things" that he [Otto] could undertake. Do you perhaps mean suicide? That I do not believe – but <u>even if</u> – <u>how</u> am I supposed to prevent such a thing from happening in the future to an undisciplined person? I shall certainly not be prepared always to tremble and quake about whether or not Mr. Otto is satisfied with me. – My <u>righteous indignation</u> towards him (you know how patient I was) has reached its climax![30]

It is quite probable that Justine destroyed a great deal of her correspondence, either immediately upon receipt or at a later date. The only letter from Otto in the Mahler–Rosé Collection is not to a family member, and the single example from Alois was preserved because Mahler responded to Justine on its reverse; likewise, the draft letter to Otto was kept owing to Mahler's participation in its composition. Since Justine's letters to Mahler have been destroyed, and Alois's and Otto's as well, it is often difficult to reconstruct the details of these family crises, although it is very likely that certain aspects will be clarified as research on the letters continues.

Alma and Justine

A second important area of Mahler studies that the family letters clarify concerns the relationship between Mahler's wife and his closest sister. Alma Mahler's books paint a decidedly negative picture of Justine. In *Gustav Mahler: Memories and Letters*, for example, she describes the arrangements that were made after the deaths of Mahler's parents as follows:

He took a large flat for the family in Vienna, and Justine, the eldest, was put in charge. It was too much for a scatter-brained girl of twenty . . . Letters

[30] Letter from Gustav to Justine, December 1893 or January 1894, E5-MJ-243. "Was ihr für 'Dummheiten' meint, die er [Otto] anstellen könnte, verstehe ich nicht recht. – Meint Ihr vielleicht einen Selbstmord? Das glaube ich nicht – aber <u>wenn auch</u> – <u>wie</u> soll ich in Zukunft solches bei einem disciplinlosen Menschen verhindern können? Ich werde mir es doch nicht einrichten, nur immer zu zittern und zagen, ob Herr Otto mit mir auch zufrieden oder nicht. – Meine <u>gerechte Empörung</u> über ihn (Du weißt, wie langmüthig ich war) hat ihren Höhepunkt erreicht!"

71

flew to and fro, bearing demands for money from the one side and exhortations to economy from the other.[31]

Immediately after this passage, Alma writes that Mahler confided in Justine concerning his relationship with Anna von Mildenburg, but that she "clung to him jealously, and therefore did all she could to inject his feelings with suspicion." Her account of the events surrounding Mahler's marriage is similarly couched: Justine is depicted as a jealous shrew who sought to deny her brother his happiness, yet was all the while engaged in a clandestine affair with Mahler's own concertmaster, Arnold Rosé. According to Alma, for fear of his sister's jealousy Mahler did not tell her of his engagement, but instead

> sent for Justine to join him at Dresden and put her on the rack . . . by firing off questions such as: "Should a middle-aged man marry a young girl?" "Has he the right to do so?" "Can autumn chain spring to its side?"

> Justine, feeling herself narrowly observed, was filled with foreboding . . .[32]

All of these tales are called into question by correspondence in the Mahler–Rosé Collection.

Five letters from Mahler to Justine survive from the crucial days of his courtship during early December 1901; in addition, there are four from Justine to Mahler. It may be that Justine, keenly aware of her brother's place in history, kept copies of these important letters for herself; at any rate, for once we have access to both sides of the correspondence. From this exchange it is quite clear that Gustav had solicited Justine's advice and enlisted her aid regarding Alma; at one point he writes, "if you can, stay calm and consider, or rather, help me consider."[33] Clearly, then, there was no secrecy surrounding the matter; the questions mentioned by Alma were indeed asked, but directly in reference to Alma:

> I must still consider carefully! The dear girl is herself now badly stirred up, and finds herself in such an uncustomary situation, one in which I must

---

[31] AMML4, 11.   [32] Ibid., p. 22.

[33] Letter from Gustav to Justine, 12 December 1901, E3-MJ-139. "Wenn Du kannst so bleibe ruhig und prüfe – resp. helfe mir prüfen."

keep my eyes open for us both. She would still need to mature a great deal – as I have just clearly seen once more – before a step of such great consequence could be seriously faced on my part.[34]

Mahler's next remark in this letter can only refer to Justine's liaison with Arnold Rosé,[35] and the sentence after that removes any suggestion of strained relations between brother and sister:

> You, on the other hand, naturally, are entirely the ruler of your own decisions. And whatever happens, the two of us will remain bound for life; I want to see you happy, and help you with everything that you need for your settling and contentment.

Justine, for her part, reveals nothing in her letters other than a generally favorable impression of Alma coupled with a natural concern for her brother – perhaps mixed with a bit of understandable jealousy. She appears quite practical and rational. In her answer to the letter from Mahler just quoted, Justine writes that

[34] Letter from Gustav to Justine, ?10 December 1901, collection of Henry-Louis de La Grange, Paris (copy: OS-MD-683). "Ich muß noch <u>sehr</u> prüfen! Das liebe Mädel ist jetzt selbst arg aufgewirbelt und befindet sich in einer – für sie doch so sehr ungewohnten – Situation, in der ich für uns Beide die Augen offen halten muß. Sie müßte noch sehr heranreifen, wie ich neuerdings wieder deutlich sehe, bevor meinerseits ein so folgenreicher Schritt ins Auge gefaßt werden könnte. Du andererseits bist natürlich ganz Herrin Deiner Entschlüße. Und wie es auch ausfällt, bleiben wir Beide doch verbunden für's Leben[,] und ich will Dich glücklich sehen, und Dir in Allem helfen, was Du zu Deiner Klärung und Befriedung brauchst."

[35] Alma claims that Natalie Bauer-Lechner, Mahler's longtime friend and confidante who hoped eventually to marry him, made an agreement with Justine to conceal her liaison with Arnold Rosé in exchange for help in Natalie's efforts to be alone with Mahler, "until, as had to happen, they all betrayed each other" (AMML4, 13). Although the letters in the Collection do not confirm this, they do contain many incidental and friendly references to Rosé, which document his close connection with the family. Mahler did, however, have a decisive confrontation with Natalie in September 1901; he wrote to Justine that "With Natalie, it's beginning again. It hurts me terribly, but now I must tell her the unvarnished truth and, of course, shatter her. But hopefully she'll get herself back on her feet again" (E19-MJ-658). ("Mit Natalie geht es wieder los. Sie thut mir schrecklich leid, aber ich müßte ihr jetzt ungeschminkte Wahrheit sagen, die sie freilich niederschmettert. Aber hoffentlich wird sie sich doch wieder auf die Beine helfen.")

I am now very curious about tomorrow when Alma will be alone with me. For me it all comes down to one thing. That I can only repeat again and again: that she is good, and that she loves you, for then you can educate her, as you have already educated me. If she loves you, she will make you happy . . . You know that I must marry; I feel this an absolute necessity for us both. You will also marry, and that will be the solution for everything. Your wife will not be able to help but love you passionately; you already compel everyone to it, man and woman. I maintain that my Arnold loves you more than me.[36]

In another letter, she does admit to Mahler that "I am afraid that for me, any woman whom I imagine as your wife would never, never be satisfactory," but she immediately goes on to say that "the main thing must be that she loves you, and totally subjects herself to you."[37]

Mahler's next letter to Justine does in fact express concern about the age difference between him and his beloved, in exactly the same terms Alma later reported; Mahler wonders

whether a man on the verge of getting old has the right to chain so much youth and freshness of life to his overripeness – uniting spring to autumn, forcing it to skip over summer – that frightens me.[38]

Far from being mute in response to Mahler's questioning, as Alma suggests, Justine replied quite eloquently:

[36] Letter from Justine to Gustav, 13 December 1901, E8-JM-400. "Ich bin schon sehr neugierig auf Morgen, wenn A[lma] allein bei mir sein wird. Es kommt mir auf Einiges an. Das kann ich immer nur wiederholen, daß sie gut ist und Dich liebt, denn dann kannst Du Dir sie erziehen, wie Du mich ja erzogen hast. Wenn sie Dich liebt, wird sie Dich glücklich machen . . . Weißt Du, daß ich heirathen muß, fühle ich als eine absolute Notwendigkeit für uns beide. Du wirst eben auch heirathen[,] und das wird die Lösung für Alles sein. Deine Frau wird nicht anderes können[,] als Dich leidenschaftlich lieben, Du zwingst ja jeden dazu, Frau und Mann. Ich behaupte[,] meiner [sic] Arnold liebt Dich mehr wie mich."

[37] Letter from Justine to Gustav, 15 December 1901, E8-JM-401. "ich fürchte, daß mir jede Frau, die ich mir als Deine Frau denke, eben nie nie genügen wird . . . die Hauptsache muß sein, daß sie Dich liebt und sich Dir total unterordnet."

[38] Letter from Gustav to Justine, 15 December 1901, E19-MJ-653. "[O]b ein Mensch, der im Begriffe steht, alt zu werden, das Recht hat, so viel Jugend und Lebensfrische an seine Überreife – den Frühling an den Herbst zu ketten[,] ihn zu zwingen, den Sommer zu überspringen – das macht mir bang."

Your letter from Sunday just arrived. I can really sympathize that you
are anxious about the great difference in age, but believe me, men like
you are not to be measured like others. It does not worry me at all. You
will remain young in every respect longer than she will. You must
remember that a woman becomes a mother, and these duties even
everything out.[39]

There is no question that Alma's later relations with Justine and Arnold
were occasionally strained – Mahler chides Justine about this in a 1903
letter in the Collection – but the surviving documents simply do not bear
out many of Alma's stories.

Except for one. It does appear that, during her twenties, Justine was a
bit flighty. Mahler's letters to her are indeed – just as Alma says – full of
exhortations to thriftiness in response to her demands for money. One
such letter from Justine has survived, because it so distressed Mahler that
he sent it back to her with the comment, "Sensitivity of the most immature
sort! Complete misunderstanding of my views and intentions!"[40] At the
same time, he wrote to Ernestine Löhr, a close family friend, about Justine's
letter:

You have probably read my last letter to Justi, and of you I can suppose
that you have read it correctly. Justi's answer seems to me to have been
written in the <u>heat of the moment</u>, and I am less annoyed about its
somewhat brusque form (which I naturally attribute only to the
momentary mood) than I am about the content, i.e. the fundamental way of
thinking (<u>not</u> the way of feeling), which I find so <u>immature</u>. Furthermore,
she knows that nothing irritates me more than this type of childish
sensibility – from which I had really hoped <u>she</u> had long ago emancipated
herself.

---

[39] Letter from Justine to Gustav, 16 December 1901, E8-JM-402. "Soeben
kommt Dein Brief von Sonntag. Ich kann Dir so sehr nachfühlen, daß Du vor
dem großen Altersunterschied bangst. Aber glaube mir, Menschen wie Du
sind doch nicht wie andere zu messen. Das macht mir wieder gar nicht
bange. Du wirst länger jung bleiben, in jeder Beziehung, wie sie. Du mußt
Dir doch denken, daß eine Frau Mutter wird und diese Pflichten gleichen alles
aus."

[40] Letter from Justine to Gustav, with Gustav's marginal annotations, ?April 1892,
E7-JM-353. "Empfindlichkeit Unreifer Sorte! Gänzliches Misverstehen [*sic*]
meiner Ansichten und Absichten!"

Today I sent her letter back to her with my marginal notes, and I beg you to go to her and look at my answer for yourselves, and wash her childish head, and read through my letter with her one more time.[41]

In a subsequent letter to Justine, written immediately after the exchange just cited, Mahler explains his angry reaction to her:

Money, after all, is only money, and as regards the <u>future</u>, I am truly not accustomed to deem the <u>present</u> so trifling!. . . Note one thing: if you were to write to me today "I have spent such and such for my <u>pleasure</u> – I have ordered a pretty dress for myself" and so on, I would only be <u>pleased</u> about it. But if you now write: we have nothing to wear – we are stinting on food, you must send us more money again because (for example) the lessons have again become more complicated, then I would simply like to fling it all down out of anger . . . Incidently, I never write you in this manner to reproach you, but <u>only</u> to make you aware in the <u>future</u>! Moreover, I am not at all <u>edgy</u> about it – to the contrary, once I have expressed something like this, I am done with it, and I don't think of it at all . . . Above all, <u>damn it</u>, don't <u>spare</u> me, you dope, you only <u>upset</u> me that way!![42]

---

[41] Letter from Gustav to Ernestine Löhr, between 9 and 13 April 1892, S3-MC-776. Ernestine must have shown Mahler's letter to Justine, who either kept or was given it. "Sie haben jedenfalls meinen letzten Brief an die Justi gelesen, und ich kann mir von Ihnen denken, daß Sie ihn richtig gelesen. Die Antwort Justis scheint mir in der ersten Rage verfaßt zu sein, und ärgert mich nicht so sehr wegen der etwas brüsken Form (welche ich natürlich nur der momentanen Stimmung zuschreibe) als weil ich den Inhalt respectiv die demselben zu Grunde liegende Denk- (<u>nicht</u> Empfindungs-) weise so <u>unreif</u> finde. Sie weiß übrigens, daß mich nicht mehr aufbringt, als diese Art kindischer Empfindlichkeit – da ich doch wirklich gehofft hätte, daß <u>sie</u> sich davon schon lange emancipirt hat. Ich habe ihr heute ihren Brief mit meinen Randbemerkungen zurückgeschickt, und bitte Sie gehen Sie nur zu ihr, und sehen Sie sich meine Antwort an, und waschen Sie ihr den kindischen Kopf, und lesen Sie mit ihr meinen Brief noch einmal durch."

[42] Letter from Gustav to Justine, April or May 1892, E10-MJ-422. "Geld ist ja endlich doch nur Geld, und über die <u>Zukunft</u> bin ich wahrlich nicht gewöhnt, die <u>Gegenwart</u> gering zu achten! . . . Merk Dir nur eins! Wenn Du mir heute schreibst "ich habe zu meinem <u>Vergnügen</u> das und das ausgegeben – ich habe mir ein schönes Kleid machen lassen" – etc. so werde ich mich darüber nur <u>freuen</u>. Wenn Du mir aber nun schreibst: wir haben nichts anzuziehen – wir sparen uns das Essen vom Mund ab, aber Du mußt mir wieder mehr Geld schicken, weil z.B. der Unterricht wieder complicirter geworden ist, so möchte ich einfach vor Ärger Alles hinschmeißen . . . Übrigens schreibe ich sowas nie,

The preceding highlights can but hint at the scope and breadth of the Mahler family letters. Additional research remains to be done, particularly to establish dates for many of them, and to further unravel the tangled skeins of the family debates and disputes. The forthcoming complete edition of these letters will add immeasurably to our knowledge of Mahler the man, and will illuminate as well his relationships with family, contemporaries, and the world around him.

um Dir Vorwürfe zu machen, sondern <u>nur</u> um Dich für die <u>Zukunft</u> darauf aufmerksam zu machen! Übrigens bin ich gar nicht <u>nervös</u>, sondern im Gegentheil, wenn ich so etwas ausgesprochen habe, ist es für mich abgethan, und ich denke gar nicht [mehr] daran! . . . Und vor Allem <u>zum Teufel,</u> <u>verschone</u> mich doch nicht, Du Schaf, dadurch <u>beunruhigst</u> Du mich doch bloß!!"

4 Before Alma ... Gustav Mahler and "Das Ewig-Weibliche"

STUART FEDER, M.D.

"My wife ..."

"You must understand," Mahler told his friend the Czech composer Josef Foerster in 1894, "that I could not bear the sight of an untidy woman with messy hair and neglected appearance. I must also admit that solitude is essential to me when I am composing; as a creative artist I require it without conditions. My wife would have to agree to my living apart from her, possibly several rooms away, and to my having a separate entrance. She would have to consent to sharing my company only at certain times, decided in advance, and then I would expect her to be perfectly groomed and well dressed ... In a word, she would need qualities that even the best and most devoted women do not possess."[1] Such stringent requirements reflect a curious compromise between a romantic artistic ideal ("Bohemian" in the social sense of the word) on one hand, and a contrastingly bourgeois outlook on the other. There is as well no small measure of the haughtily aristocratic in Mahler's statement. Above all, these remarks reveal how little the thirty-four-year-old composer – as yet relatively inexperienced in affairs of the heart – knew about himself.

In addition to the specific preconditions universally dictated by the individual psyche, Mahler consciously shared with those of his generation and culture a variety of views about women, love, and marriage. One such attitude, of typically bourgeois origin, was ingenuously stated by his contemporary Sigmund Freud in a letter to his betrothed: "And everything must be kept in good order, else the *Hausfrau,* who had divided her heart

---

[1] Josef Bohuslav Foerster, *Der Pilger: Erinnerungen eines Musikers,* trans. Pavel Eisner (Prague, 1955), pp. 444–45; Eng. trans. in HLG 1, pp. 313–14.

78

up in little bits, one for each piece of furniture, will object."[2] Another prevalent belief, Hegelian in its codified form, was that marriage transcends individuality. Nevertheless, the union also results in inequality between the partners because a woman's individuality is renounced in favor of her natural destiny in marriage and motherhood; the man's sphere remains the wider world, owing to his superior rationality.[3] Schopenhauer, whose works considerably influenced Mahler, wrote a classic of misogyny entitled "On Women," which particularly emphasizes "The Weakness of Women."[4] A remarkable young contemporary of Mahler's, Otto Weininger (1880–1903), put forth a hypothesis of human bisexuality (which was probably derived from Freud), and then developed it in the direction of virulent antipathy toward women, in the course of which he conflated women and Jews for good measure.[5] Generally speaking, the privileged among this generation were bound by a common education and experience whereby the *lingua franca* of the cultured man was the handy quotation from Schiller or Goethe. When Mahler set the concluding scene of *Faust* in the Finale of his colossal Eighth Symphony, it summed up for that era its greatest idealization of the feminine – an idealization that, although coexisting with those counter-currents noted above, was at least equally influential. The premiere of the Eighth in Munich on 12 September 1910, attended by so many distinguished members of Mahler's generation, was a quasi-religious event, ending with the chorale setting of:

> Alles Vergängliche
> Ist nur ein Gleichnis;
> Das Unzulängliche,
> Hier wird's Ereignis;
> Das Unbeschreibliche,
> Hier ist's getan;

---

[2] Ernest Jones, *The Life and Work of Sigmund Freud*, 2 vols. (New York, 1953–57), vol. I, p. 140.

[3] Rosemary Agonito, *History of Ideas on Woman: A Sourcebook* (New York, 1977), pp. 159–60.

[4] Ibid., esp. "The Weakness of Women," p. 193.

[5] William M. Johnston, *The Austrian Mind: An Intellectual and Social History, 1848–1938* (Berkeley, 1972), p. 159.

STUART FEDER, M.D.

Das Ewig-Weibliche
Zieht uns hinan.[6]

When the younger Mahler declared his bill of particulars for the perfect woman in 1894, his friend Foerster wisely counseled that he would soon forget all that when he fell in love. And as Mahler's biographer Henry-Louis de La Grange has observed, it is noteworthy "how little the two women who were to play an essential role in his life resembled his feminine ideal of modesty and selflessness."[7] They were, respectively, Anna von Mildenburg, whom he would encounter the following year (1895), and Alma Schindler, destined to become his wife six-and-a-half years later. It was to Alma that Mahler would eventually dedicate the Eighth Symphony with its crowning idealization of the womanly. But it was an older, humbler Mahler who did so, under less than happy circumstances, a man of fifty who revealed intensified aspects of his psychological relation to women of which he was unaware when he spoke so arrogantly of his earlier ideal. For by 1910, much had changed for Mahler; at that point the ideal of the womanly symbolized by Goethe's "Das Ewig-Weibliche" could not have lacked an ironic dimension in the mind of the composer.

In the following pages we will consider Mahler's most significant relationships with women from his early life up to 1901, when at the age of forty-one he married Alma Schindler. That final chapter, which occupied the decade preceding his death in 1911, requires a study of its own.[8] The past is, however, truly prelude, and there is little emotional content in Mahler's involvement with Alma that is not foreshadowed in his earlier relationships with women. Indeed, identifying and tracking these elements can only enrich our understanding of Mahler's marriage. Hence the purview of this study: "Before Alma…"

But first a caveat: To infer the nature of Mahler's relationships with women from only a few examples is to do injustice to the richness of the man's interpersonal life overall. For the single most impressive feature of

[6] "All that is transitory / is only a symbol; / what seems unachievable / here is seen done; / what's indescribable / here becomes fact; / Woman, eternally / shows us the way." Johann Wolfgang von Goethe, *Faust I & II*, ed. and trans. Stuart Atkins (Cambridge, Mass., 1985), p. 305.   [7] HLG 1, p. 314.

[8] A work in progress by the present author focuses upon the final year of Mahler's life, including detailed consideration of his marriage.

80

Mahler's interaction with other human beings was its variety and complexity. He was the polar opposite of the stereotypically withdrawn, schizoid, phobic "sensitive artist." On the contrary, Mahler's human involvements were generally vigorous yet finely textured, and his narcissism was of a different nature. While he may have considered himself (and by extension, his art) to be central, there was not merely a place for others in his life, but indeed an intense need for them on every level, personal as well as artistic. His work as artistic director and the exacting standards he brought to it made him aware of such needs at every turn, and rendered him characteristically demanding. However, artistic demands and those that were personal – in particular, those stemming from childhood that were fundamentally infantile – could be conflated. Need turned on neediness in personal relationships, and Mahler did not hesitate to call upon family and friends for attention and aid in his multiple personal endeavors and responsibilities. Indeed, the closer the relationship, the greater his expectations. In addition, the quantity of energy devoted to relationships – family, friendship, business, political, artistic, and love relationships – is impressive, and perhaps secondary only to his investment in his dual career as conductor and composer. The intensity and durability of his relationships is also noteworthy, as is their variety. Boyhood friends became lifelong friends, and their wives, too, were eventually drawn into Mahler's circle. Mahler had not only many male friends during various stages of his life, but also equally respected female friends. He had a need for confidantes, and women such as Adele Marcus filled this role. Although her connection with Mahler will not be considered in any detail here, suffice to say that at various points Mahler cultivated a circle including other such women friends. Several might attend Mahler's concerts (even those outside of Vienna), often in the company of Mahler's sister, Justine.

At times, Mahler's relationship with an individual could undergo a fundamental change in character without dissolving. And such a change could be either toward greater flexibility or rigidity, which increased the multifaceted nature of Mahler's mental life. For example, erotic attachments could eventually mellow into mutually respectful artistic relationships, as was the case with both Anna von Mildenburg and Selma Kurtz.[9]

[9] Concerning Mahler's liaison with Selma Kurz, see HLG 2, pp. 224–31 and 243.

Rarely was someone cut or abandoned, except at the time of Mahler's marriage, when Alma's distaste for several old friends resulted in a degree of detachment from them. Sadly, the estrangement of his singularly devoted friend Natalie Bauer-Lechner – who, as we will see, initiated the break – was Mahler's responsibility as well.

Finally, in considering Mahler and "Das Ewig-Weibliche," it should be noted that his attitude toward the feminine and the masculine was complex. Perhaps this is nowhere more apparent than in his music, where, however, it is expressed in very subtle form. As noted above, the rather stiff-necked and male-chauvinist vision of the feminine Mahler confided to Foerster dates from 1894. But Mahler never lacked the perspective provided by humor; on the contrary, it enriched the ironic side of his nature in both life and art. The following year (1895) he composed the *Wunderhorn* song "Lied des Verfolgten im Turm [Song of the Prisoner in the Tower]," in which a philosophical and super-idealistic prisoner (*Der Gefangene*) projects a somewhat exaggerated masculinity (which was, nevertheless, in keeping with the times); "Die Gedanken sind frei . . . [Thoughts are free . . .]" is his recurring motto. The contrastingly feminine *Mädchen* responds by invoking the joys of everyday life – summer pleasures, intimacy, and human attachment: "Im Sommer ist gut lustig sein . . . von dir mag ich nicht scheiden [In summer it is good to be merry . . . I do not want to part from you]." Mahler, the ironist, satirizes the bombastic, arrogant male in music, rationalizing his isolation and detachment safe from the sexuality, tenderness, and intimacy embodied in the feminine. Indeed, we perceive in both text and musical treatment the very "devotion," unconditional "solitude," and isolation from women (save for prearranged visits) that Mahler specified in his earlier comments to Foerster! Thus we hear the prisoner as something of a dolt who has made his own prison; perhaps we also hear an insightful Mahler laughing at himself.

The family Mahler

The origin and nature of Mahler's relationships with women must be sought in his earliest family relationships. De La Grange's biography offers the fullest presentation of the available data, yet three factors cloud the picture. First, the most detailed account of Mahler's childhood, that written by his wife Alma, is characteristically histrionic and undoubtedly biased.[10] Second, the "psychoanalytic" vignettes of his childhood that have come down to us from Mahler's single "session" with Sigmund Freud are problematic. That meeting was hardly comprehensive, and revealed only certain anecdotal aspects of Mahler's background and emotional life; as Freud himself put it, "It was as if you would dig a single shaft through a mysterious building."[11] Finally and most fundamentally, the ultimate source of all the stories is Mahler himself, who was subject to the inevitable distortions that regularly insinuate memory, motivated by self-justification and aggrandizement as well as the need to create personal myths.

Something remains to be told beyond the tales of his parents' tension-filled, loveless relationship and the multiple instances of childhood trauma, which ranged from sadomasochistic encounters with his father, to abuses suffered while a student boarder, to the numerous sibling deaths. For in spite of all, Mahler came from a close and cohesive family that was bourgeois from the economic perspective and Jewish as regards religion and culture. Among the values by which he was raised were the primary importance of education as well as caring responsibility for others, based upon both love and guilt. In addition, esteem within such families accorded just as much to the actual and anticipated accomplishments of offspring as to the honorable heritage of forbears. The Mahlers were the typical sort of Eastern European family that, described by a number of sociologists and psychologists, has been characterized by Herz and Rosen as "placing primary emphasis on (1) centrality of the family; (2) suffering as a shared value; (3) intellectual achievement and financial success; and (4) verbal expression of feelings."[12] In addition to the nuclear family, many of Mahler's close relationships were marked by these same features, both with respect to what he gave and what he expected. (It may be noted that, generally speaking, family characteristics such as these create a potential for certain kinds of individual psychopathology. Despite the

---

[10] AMML4, pp. 6–11.

[11] Theodore Reik, *The Haunting Melody: Psychoanalytic Experiences in Life and Music* (New York, 1953), p. 343.

[12] Fredda M. Herz and Elliott J. Rosen, "Jewish Families," in *Ethnicity and Family Therapy*, ed. Monica McGoldrick, John K. Pearce, and Joseph Giordano (New York, 1982), p. 365.

often health-promoting discharge afforded by verbal expression and ventilation, certain factors – high family expectations, pressures of constant striving, and the tendency toward inducing and experiencing guilt plus the seemingly paradoxical gratifications of suffering – all tend to create stress and intrapsychic tensions manifested particularly by depression and psychosomatic illness. Mahler suffered from both categories of emotional illness.)

As might be expected, all of Mahler's later relationships were to be colored by his relationship to the first woman – Marie Hermann Mahler. Equally to be expected was the special role Gustav played in his mother's life: he was doubly loved by her because he served as the replacement for her first child, Isadore, born in 1858, who had died in an accident during his first year, the year immediately preceding Gustav's birth in July of 1860. The following October the Mahlers moved from Kalischt to Iglau, away from the only family Marie had previously known. This separation would have drawn her even closer to her child during his crucial first year, when her husband was preoccupied with establishing himself in business. Another son, Ernst, was born in 1861, but remained sickly throughout his short life; the next child was a girl, Leopoldine (born in 1863), followed by two boys who died in infancy (in 1865 and 1866 respectively). Thus, there is little question of Gustav's priority among his siblings, and that priority would soon be reinforced by the emergence of his musical gift and his ensuing accomplishments, which brought prominence to the family within the community. Much in Mahler's mental life overall can be understood from Freud's adage: "A man who has been the indisputable favorite of his mother keeps for life the feeling of a conqueror, that confidence of success that often induces real success."[13]

Echoes of Mahler's mother would resound throughout his life, in details such as his wife's name, Alma Maria, and the naming of his first child, Maria (called "Putzi"), as well as in his special tenderness toward both his daughters. The death of the elder in 1907 was devastating; two years later Mahler decided that he would be buried in the same grave.[14]

---

[13] Sigmund Freud, *The Standard Edition of the Complete Psychological Works of Sigmund Freud*, trans. and ed. James Strachey et al. (London, 1953–74), vol. XII, p. 26.   [14] HLGF 3, pp. 83 and 541.

During serious crises such as this he turned to another mother – Alma's mother Anna Moll (previously Schindler) – even as he would when his own death approached.

Mahler's music is repeatedly informed by this primary and enduring relationship in mental life, from his musical identification with the grieving parent of the *Kindertotenlieder* (e.g., the third song, "Wenn dein Mütterlein... [When your dear mother...]" to the ultimate idealization of the eternal feminine in the Eighth Symphony. Through the transformations of her son's art, modest Marie Hermann was destined to endow representations of the quotidian-tragic mother as well as the most noble symbol of motherhood: Marie become Mary, the Mater Gloriosa of *Faust*.

Justi, 1889–1901

The importance of the family in the emotional life of its members is amply confirmed by the response of Mahler and his sister Justine to the deaths of their parents, and by the special relationship in which they engaged for several critical years thereafter. Justi was the second daughter, eight years younger than Gustav. The year 1889 was a tragically decisive one for the Mahler family. In February the father, Bernhard Mahler, died; his wife Marie survived him only until October. According to Alma's later account, "Justine nursed her until her death and Mahler loved her [Justine] as his beloved mother's dying bequest."[15] In the meantime, Leopoldine (called Poldi), the elder daughter and only married sibling, had died in September of a brain tumor. Upon his father's death, Gustav, now director of the Royal Budapest Opera, had assumed responsibility for his musically talented younger brother Otto, and had arranged for him to live with sister Poldi in Vienna, where Otto could pursue studies at the Conservatory. With Poldi's death Otto was consigned to the family of Gustav's close boyhood friend Fritz Löhr, and twenty-one-year-old Justi was to come to Budapest to keep house for Gustav, who was now the tyro *paterfamilias* at age twenty-nine. By the following year, he had placed his brothers Alois and Otto plus his younger sister Emma under Justi's supervision in Vienna, where

---

[15] AMML4, p. 10.

together they weathered continuing family crises that I have discussed elsewhere.[16]

Justi's devotion to her brother was unstinting, driven by an underlying intensity that was fueled by social as well as psychological factors. Gustav, their family, "their" children, his work, his circle had become the central focus of her life as she entered her twenties. Mahler depended upon her as a matter of course; she, in turn, was dependent upon him psychologically as well as economically. Thus began a new stage in their relationship, whereby Justi assumed the curiously hybrid role of sister, daughter, and wife. Mahler's behavior toward her could be caring, encouraging, demanding, critical and sarcastic in turn; nor did his relationship with Justi lack respect and consideration for her. The first spring after their parents' death he took the exhausted Justi with him on a tour to Italy, during which he was continually solicitous about her health, and just as anxiety-ridden over any sign of illness in her as he was in himself. He urged her to see doctors, followed her progress carefully from wherever he was, and sent her to spas when she needed rest. Reciprocally, he shared his concern about his many ailments frankly with her.

Although numerous letters from Mahler to Justine from the 1890s survive, regrettably few of Justine's answers have surfaced to date.[17] However, it is clear from Mahler's correspondence that their exchanges were hardly limited to everyday family matters. Mahler also shared his musical experiences with her in intelligently detailed letters, which are devoid of the patronizing attitude evident in those where he criticizes her housekeeping and parenting. Justi was also knowledgeable about the intricacies of the musical politics that were a constant part of Mahler's life; she knew who all of the participants were, and held her own opinions. Brother and sister also shared reading, and Mahler frequently recommended books and provided her with periodicals he thought would interest her.

It is not known where Justine received her education. Young women

---

[16] Stuart Feder, "Gustav Mahler: The Music of Fratricide," *International Review of Psycho-Analysis* 8 (1981), 257–84, reprinted in Stuart Feder, Richard Karmel, and George H. Pollock, eds., *Psychoanalytic Explorations in Music: First Series* (Madison, Conn., 1990), pp. 341–90.

[17] The surviving letters are located principally in the Gustav Mahler–Alfred Rosé Collection, Music Library, University of Western Ontario, London; see Stephen McClatchie, "'Liebste Justi!': The Family Letters of Gustav Mahler," pp. 53–77 above.

of the time were not admitted to *Gymnasium,* and beyond the state-supported primary school there was no regular course to follow; further education depended upon the values and resources of the family.[18] But Justi clearly possessed the kind of high intelligence Mahler respected. The surprising degree of her worldliness, which seems apparent from Mahler's letters, very likely developed from the practical education he provided and from her vicarious involvement in the affairs of her brother. (Indeed, in a revealing letter to Mahler from the time he was courting Alma, she writes: "you can educate her, just as you have educated me."[19])

To a certain degree, Justi was also privy to Mahler's romantic life, and was evidently quite opinionated about whatever she knew. Some women, such as Anna von Mildenburg, were her natural rivals; others, such as Natalie Bauer-Lechner, were warmly safe, and as much "family" to her as to Mahler himself. In the Mildenburg affair, which we will come to shortly, Justine was an influential third party whom the couple had to take into account regarding many of their actions and plans.

For Mahler was not unaware that Justine was sacrificing her youth for him. Moreover, in diligently assuming the responsibilities thrust upon her, she was moving in a counter-cultural direction that might threaten to impair chances for marriage later. Stephan Zweig has described what society of the day generally expected of young women: to remain "silly and untaught, well-educated and innocent, curious and shy, uncertain and unpractical, and predisposed to this education without knowledge of the world from the very beginning, to be led and formed by a man in marriage without any will of their own . . . But what a tragedy it was if one of these young women missed her time, if she was not yet married at twenty-five or thirty."[20] In a sense, Justi no longer resembled such a "cultural virgin," having already been "led and formed" by Mahler. Although there is no evidence that she ever attempted to exact guilt, he must inevitably have felt that something was owed her. For her part, their relationship may have been gratifying in different ways, including the promise of a lifetime brother–sister commitment, which was, after all, one of several life paths open to her. In any event,

---

[18] See Hannah Decker, *Freud, Dora, and Vienna 1900* (New York, 1990), pp. 56–58.

[19] See McClatchie, "'Liebste Justi!'," p. 74 above.

[20] Stefan Zweig, *The World of Yesterday* (New York, 1943), p. 78.

through their bargain Mahler had found in Justine a partner for the discharge of familial obligations, and by that same token someone to saddle with the often considerable responsibility of taking care of *him* as well. At the very least, any romantic liaison between Mahler and another woman would severely unsettle the equilibrium he and Justi had achieved, which had been instrumental in the preservation of the family and its values.

In the end, a solution was found which permitted both of them to progress in their lives without the undesirable alternatives that loomed earlier, which would have meant for Justi a compromise that would arrest her own life's course through renunciation of marriage and family in favor of remaining her brother's mate, and for Gustav, either the pursuit of a guilt-ridden relationship with another woman, or perhaps a series of them ultimately leading to embittered, depressed resignation. The denouement in this drama occurred in 1901, and we will consider it presently.

Romance

First we must confront another complexity of Mahler's mental life: For Mahler, love, art, and mood were intimately related. Accordingly, a word about his tendency toward depression is appropriate. Anecdotal evidence from childhood suggests he experienced the kind of episodic moodiness that eventually becomes chronically entrenched in personality and gives rise to enduring traits of character even as periodic episodes of more severe depression might recur from time to time. Stimulated by the deaths of several siblings, the chronic mourning of the family, and intensely experienced personal losses (such as that of his beloved younger brother Ernst), Mahler's disposition toward depression was probably familial and ultimately biological (i.e., genetic) in nature. Its importance here stems from its intimate connection to love objects.

A prime case in point is the nineteen-year-old Mahler's very first adolescent relationship – with Josephine Poisl of Iglau, who had been his piano student. The tempestuousness of Mahler's outpourings, in contrast to the banal and conventional responses from his idealized "darling of the gods,"[21]

---

[21] See Mahler's letter to Anton Krisper of November and 14 December 1879, GMB2, no. 8 (GMBE, no. 6).

suggests that what transpired was largely the one-sided reflection of a young man's as yet unfocused passion and fertile imagination. As de La Grange shrewdly observes, certain of Mahler's phrases in describing his sufferings to a fellow conservatory student, Anton Krisper, "could have come from Hoffmann's Kapellmeister Kreisler."[22] Mahler became infatuated with Josephine in the autumn of 1879, a few months after he wrote the well-known "literary" and philosophical letter to Josef Steiner in which his melancholy is revealed in a pervading *Sehnsucht* and an idealization of sorrow and death.[23] That same mood fueled his sudden attachment to Josephine, and only intensified following the perceived loss of the young woman, who seemed hardly engaged in the affair to begin with. A sensible and comforting letter to Mahler from Josephine's well-meaning mother reproaches him for his unremitting gloom and isolation.[24] From a misery that was endogenous, yet to a degree self-inflicted – even self-consciously cultivated – there emerged three early lieder, dedicated to Josephine.[25] In addition, Mahler worked intensively on *Das klagende Lied* during this period. Overall, the situation represented the prototype of a characteristic triad in Mahler's life: love and its loss, depression, and creativity.

In what is generally believed to be his first reciprocal affair (and perhaps his first sexual relationship) – with the singer Johanna Richter three years later in Kassel – many characteristics of Mahler's youthful passion for Josephine can still be observed, particularly his intensity once the relationship was under way. But his response to Josephine's apparently immature lack of involvement began to yield to something different with Johanna and subsequent lovers: this was Mahler's own penchant for sensing the slightest coolness or indifference, or even the momentary lapse of a lover's being as passionately involved with him as he was with her. Deeply pained by such circumstances, Mahler demanded certainty in love. Flaws in such a relationship, which threatened yet another loss, elicited a profound pessimism about the future, plus the potential for depression.

On the other hand, creativity flourished in Mahler's efforts to master

---

[22] HLG 1, p. 61.
[23] GMB2, no. 5 (GMBE, no. 2), 17–19 June 1879; cf. also HLG 1, pp. 55–60.
[24] HLG 1, p. 62.
[25] Now published in KG, XIII/5 (Vienna, 1990); cf. also HLG 1, pp. 724–29.

and repair the psychic wounds he experienced. During the breakup with Johanna (as also with Josephine), he wrote both poems and music.[26] In addition, he continued to pen letters in "literary" style, now addressed to Fritz Löhr, which appear contrived on some occasions, yet warm or intimate on others. Mahler complains to Löhr that Johanna is "enigmatic as always." And one wonders whether his "dread of the inevitable"[27] – namely separation – was in some measure a wish, one that by now anticipated the creative impetus such events brought to his life.

In one of the "literary" letters to Löhr, dated 1 January 1885, Mahler recounts the conflict-laden drama of the previous night, when he and Johanna had broken off their year-and-a-half-old relationship. His description is rather like a dramatic *mise-en-scène*. "Ah, my dear Fritz," he writes, "it was as if the Great Stage-Manager of the Universe wanted everything arranged by the rules of art."[28] By that point some of Mahler's ardor had begun to cool; there was, moreover, the ever-present Justi to consider. Despite residual inner conflict stemming from his own difficulties with separation, Mahler was already planning his next professional move: out of Kassel, *sans* Johanna. Indeed, to be the more active party in terminating a relationship (in which both partners may have had mixed feelings) was part of Mahler's mastery of loss. – But not without a creative souvenir, one in which love, its loss, and the ensuing melancholy were again reordered according to "the rules of art": this was, of course, the *Lieder eines fahrenden Gesellen*, Mahler's autobiographical song cycle. And the same triadic plot, with minor variants, was re-enacted at the close of his illicit affair with Marion von Weber in Leipzig during 1887–88; in that instance, the artistic memorials were Mahler's First Symphony (including the "Blumine" andante for Marion's birthday) and the "Todtenfeier" movement of his Second.[29]

---

26 Mahler's poems to both Josephine Poisl and Johanna Richter are printed in HLG 1, pp. 824–34.
27 GMB2, no. 31 (GMBE, no. 28) [late August 1884]; cf. also HLG 1, p. 117.
28 GMB2, no. 32 (GMBE, no. 29), 1 January 1885; cf. also HLG 1, p. 120.
29 See Stephen E. Hefling, "Mahler's 'Todtenfeier' and the Problem of Program Music," *19th Century Music* 12 (1988): 27–39.

Anna and the Pygmalion of the opera

Mahler's propensity to impose "the rules of art" upon human relationships was evident at the onset of his relationship with Anna von Mildenburg. In the summer of 1895 Anna had been engaged as a dramatic soprano at the Hamburg opera by its impresario, Bernhard Pollini, even though Principal Conductor Mahler had not heard her audition. Returning from his summer holiday, Mahler dropped in unexpectedly on one of her rehearsals; dismissing the accompanist and taking over the piano himself, he terrorized the young singer, bringing her to tears.[30] Yet during the next two years he was instrumental in preparing her for a brilliant superstar career. Mahler's education of Mildenburg reveals that there was much of the Pygmalion in him; indeed, therein may lie the psychological underpinnings of his achievements as an opera director. For a Pygmalion's success depends in large measure on his ability to identify with the Aphrodite he creates – a projection of the feminine in himself. *Psychological* bisexuality is a constant element in human mental life, and one of particular importance for artists, who can humanly enrich what they create through their access to aspects of both sexes within themselves. Mahler's capacity to do so is apparent in the male–female polarity manifest in his *Wunderhorn* song "Lied des Verfolgten im Turm," as discussed above. Now we observe it enacted within a relationship – one that was at first apparently only professional, but soon became intimate and erotic in nature. Thus, when at an early point in their artistic collaboration Mahler himself taught Anna how to apply her stage makeup, he unconsciously exercised a feminine side of himself. Owing to inexperience Anna had applied everything too thickly, whereupon Mahler rubbed his own face as if the superfluous layer of paint were there, crying "It is abominable...Take all that off!"[31]

Of greater artistic significance was Mahler's attunement to women singers and the roles they created. The performance notes he made for Mildenburg were more than detailed and empathic; to further her Wagnerian studies during her first year as a professional, he went beyond mere characterization, observing, for example, that her singing in

---

[30] Anna Bahr-Mildenburg, *Erinnerungen* (Vienna, 1921), pp. 11–14; cf. also HLG 1, p. 333.   [31] Bahr-Mildenburg, p. 23; cf. also HLG 1, pp. 335–36.

Lohengrin "was not the proper color, for Ortrud is all secrecy, deceit, and false <u>humility</u>." He goes on, "Your appearance in the second act was superb in the first costume, much less so in the second because your deportment was careless. For heaven's sake, in such roles, let your imposing [height] make its effect."[32] In another note discussing her singing while he conducted, he writes: "I breathe each breath with you."[33] And later he would boast to Justi and Natalie, "Do you really think that Mildenburg, for instance, whom you now admire as the greatest truly classic actress, was always so successful?" Obsessed with her body as much as her vocal technique, Mahler cited his many efforts in dealing with her "clumsiness" and making her "strong, rather heavy body supple and easily responsive in every movement":

> Much the same way that I drilled her musically, I made her study every
> expression and gesture of her mime and acting in front of a mirror . . . When
> she had memorized her part, I had a grand piano moved onstage and there
> showed her every step, every pose, and every movement, and rehearsed her
> very precisely in relation to the music. Thus I studied the Wagner scores
> with her from A to Z.[34]

And thus, visualize Gustav Mahler himself in the role of Ortrud or Isolde!

Like Pygmalion, Mahler fell in love with his creation. But this time he was completely smitten – not only with the diva into whom he had breathed life, but with the living, breathing woman. Through examination of Mildenburg's published memoirs plus the 180-odd letters and telegrams from Mahler she preserved, de La Grange has traced the course of this affair, which was "one of the longest and most violent in Mahler's life."[35] During the two years of their liaison the lovers' emotional involvement ranged

---

[32] GMB2, no. 161 (GMBE, no. 152), dated 31 December 1895; the word "height [*Größe*]" is missing from the original, which reads simply "Lassen Sie doch um Gottes willen in solchen Rollen Ihre imposante wirken." Given that a page break occurs between the last two words, this is probably a hasty oversight on Mahler's part; Mildenburg was noted for her tallness (cf. HLG 2, p. 112; HLG 1, p. 339, and HLGF 1, p. 519, interpolate "bosom [*poitrine*]" for the missing word, without explanation).

[33] GMB2, no. 154 (GMBE, no. 145) [21 November 1895].

[34] NBL2, 180–181 (NBLE, 163–64), late December 1900; cf. also HLG 1, p. 339.

[35] HLG 1, p. 340.

from the *stürmisch* to the *heimisch*. Only certain aspects of this complex relationship are considered here, based upon a fresh review of the Mahler–Mildenburg correspondence.[36] Most significant are its two distinct yet intermingled trends: Mahler as lover, and Mahler as Pygmalion. For long after their affair had come to its prolonged and tortured coda – indeed, after he had used his power and magic as Pygmalion to bring about separation with honorable compensation – Mahler's artistic interest in Mildenburg continued, and they remained colleagues in music.

When Mahler met the twenty-three-year-old soprano, he was ripe for an intimate relationship. Now thirty-five and in his fifth Hamburg season, he no longer faced as many overwhelming family problems as he had in 1889; indeed, several had been resolved in ways beyond his control.[37] The emotional climax of the family saga occurred the previous February (1895), when his brother Otto committed suicide. Mahler's feelings about this tragedy were as sealed as the trunk containing Otto's personal effects, which Mahler could never bring himself to open. Nevertheless, the following summer had been a particularly productive one in which much of Mahler's Third Symphony had taken shape, and following his working holiday he and his sisters Justi and Emma moved into comfortable quarters in Hamburg's Parkallee. As far as we know, his previous relationships with women during the Hamburg years tended to be asexual. Adele Marcus, from whom he sublet an apartment when he first arrived in Hamburg in 1891, was a warm and artistically inclined widow, six years his senior, who introduced him to many of Hamburg's cultural elite. Natalie Bauer-Lechner, who first visited him in Budapest in 1890, soon became extended family; we shall return to their relationship shortly.

By the late autumn of 1895 Mahler and Mildenburg had become deeply involved – Mahler in his now characteristically tortured way. Usually aloof, often forbidding and intolerant, sarcastic at times, Mahler's behavior effectively masked his longing for an exclusive and all-encompassing closeness. And the revival of such early, infantile wishes for dependency and nurture from a maternal figure in the psyche of the dynamic, industrious adult Mahler of 1895 could be perilous in its intensity. Once he had become

---

[36] Vienna, Österreichisches Theatermuseum, Mildenburg Nachlaß.
[37] See Feder, "The Music of Fratricide" (n. 16 above).

involved, the emotional stakes were high: all or nothing. Disengagement or the slightest threat of it could be profoundly painful, with depression ever latent. But of course the cost of commitment was the threat of loss. During that first winter Mahler wrote to Anna of "what deep pain is bound with the blessedness of surrendering oneself entirely – 'with body and soul' – to a beloved person."[38] Although wishing for closeness, Mahler could be compared to a porcupine putting out protective spines. Interestingly, he perceived something of this in Anna: one of his own terms of endearment for her was "my quickly growing, magnificent fir tree with the delicate needles on which one pricks himself so bloodily ... Will you soon sting me again?"[39]

A letter to her perhaps dating from early in their relationship clearly reveals the vulnerability of Mahler's feelings: "Now – I say this to you frankly – I am going through something that I myself had not yet suspected one can endure. To lose the love of a being by whom one believed oneself loved, whose love was almost life itself – that is so terrible that you surely can't imagine it." The occasion was a letter from Anna containing an actual or perceived slight that upset Mahler "terribly": "Is it perhaps that I didn't write anything about myself? ... If I pass near you and don't seem to notice, don't take it the wrong way! ..."[40] Anna was distraught; she had her own fragile narcissism to protect. Mahler was "desperately worried." Whatever the event, doubtless of little significance in itself, the drama was taking place in the heightened emotional lives of the two sensitive participants. During the first winter of their affair, when Mahler was away in Berlin conducting his own works, he complained about her silence if he failed to hear

---

[38] Autograph letter probably written in January or February 1896: "Weißt Du es noch nicht, welch ein tiefer Schmerz mit der Seligkeit verbunden ist, sich ganz – 'mit Leib und Seele' – einem geliebten Menschen hinzugeben."

[39] Autograph letter dating from the winter of 1895–96 (probably January 1896): "mein aufgeschossener herrlicher Nadelbaum, mit den feinen Spitzen, an denen man sich so blütig sticht ... Wirst Du mich wieder bald stechen?"

[40] "Jetzt – ich sage es Ihnen offen – mache ich etwas durch, wovon ich selbst noch nicht geahnt habe, daß man es aushalten kann. – Die Liebe eines Menschen zu verlieren, von dem man sich geliebt glaubte, in dessen Liebe Einem das Leben beinahe war – das ist so furchtbar, daß Sie sicher es nicht ahnen können ... Vielleicht, daß ich nicht über mich geschrieben? ... – Wenn ich an Ihnen vorübergehe und es nicht merken laße – legen Sie es nicht falsch aus!" The top of this letter is marked "Herbst 1895" in Mildenburg's hand, but the date "1896" appears on the third page. Cf. also HLG 1, p. 341.

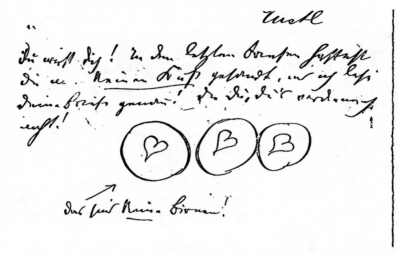

Plate 4.1   Mahler, autograph letter to Anna von Mildenburg dated 7 July 1896, closing with three encircled hearts: "Das sind *keine* Birnen! [Those are *not* pears!]"

from her regularly. But that summer (1896) it was she who appeared comparably anxious and jealous: separated from Mahler by the Alps (she in Malborghet, Italy, he busily composing in Steinbach), Anna now complained about the his coolness. By the following summer (1897) she was frankly suspicious.[41]

Mahler's sisters constantly hover in the wings as early as his first letters to Anna. In the distraught epistle cited above, he had forcibly explained to her that "I must drive myself terribly to make a living for my sisters and myself."[42] A recurring leitmotif is the figure of Justi as both helpmate and ongoing responsibility, and ultimately this was one of the factors leading to the termination of the relationship. Anna complained about Justi's behavior, and Mahler found himself mediating between the two women. Placating Anna in the fall of 1895, Mahler writes, "You indeed

[41]   See HLG 1, pp. 435–36.
[42]   "Ich muß furchtbar an mir arbeiten – um mir und meinen Schwestern das Leben zu ermöglichen."

know that I understand the human heart better, and am able to judge <u>yours</u> better, than a third party could. Don't hold it against Justine if she treats you unjustly, and believe me, she doesn't think badly of you."[43] At the heart of this triangle was the dilemma Mahler explicitly identified in a letter to Anna dating from the summer of 1896, when the conflict had become a source of depression:

> Do you really think, my beloved, that I can rejoice for even a moment in my "freedom"? How gladly I would give it up to be chained by your arms, if only I would not thereby turn <u>another's</u> life into a prison. See, my dear heart, it is indeed the same shadow that is always in the way of my wishes and hopes ... I worry terribly about it, and I still see no way out of the conflict. <u>I know</u> that through my own happiness I would forever destroy someone else's (you know who it is) ...[44]

The issue remained alive even into the next summer (1897), when indeed it was intensified by the guilt Mahler experienced as Justi nursed him through a serious illness. A letter from Mahler to Anna probably written on June 4 makes clear that "something is up" between the two women;[45] when pressed by his now-angry lover, Mahler can only reply lamely that "I still haven't talked with Justi about you at all. In the first place, I didn't get a chance to see her with this awful rush here. Secondly, I'm pretty much afraid of confronting her. She already left yesterday."[46]

Eventually détente was achieved. The incessant demands of Mahler's

---

[43] "Sie wissen doch, daß ich das menschliche Herz besser kenne, und daß ich besser <u>das Ihrige</u> beurtheile, als es ein dritter vermag. Rechnen Sie es Justine nicht an, wenn sie gegen Sie ungerecht ist und glauben Sie mir[,] sie denkt nicht schlecht von Ihnen."

[44] "– Glaubst du denn, meine Geliebte, daß ich mich nur einen Moment über meine 'Freiheit' freuen kann? Wie gerne gäbe ich sie für immer dahin, um von Deinen Armen gefesselt zu werden, wenn ich dadurch nur nicht einen <u>anderen</u> das Leben zu einem Gefängniß machte. – Siehst, mein liebes Herz, dies ist ja immer derselbe Schatten, der allen meinen Wünschen und Hoffnungen sich in den Weg stellt. Du kannst es mir vielleicht nicht nachfühlen, da Du noch nicht in einen ähnlichen Lage warst. – Es macht mir oft so furchtbaren Sorgen, und noch sehe ich nicht den Ausweg aus diesem Conflict. – <u>Ich weiß</u> <u>es</u>, daß ich durch mein Glück das einen Anderen (du weißt, wer es ist) für immer zerstöre ..." (19 June 1896)

[45] GMB2, no. 246 (GMBE, no. 232, severely abridged).

[46] GMB2, no. 247 (GMBE, no. 233, severely abridged), dated 12 June 1897.

dual career as composer and conductor, which increasingly entailed international tours, plus his constantly recurring physical symptoms[47] apparently persuaded the women who cared about him to cooperate. A real if ambivalent relationship eventually developed between Justi and Anna, although Mahler occasionally had to serve as moderator.

The foregoing picture of Mahler as lover does not attempt to convey the genuine affection or the warmly caring, even playful spontaneity of which his letters to Anna reveal him capable. Of particular importance, however, is his preoccupation with Mildenburg's physical health, which can be rationalized in part as the musical Pygmalion's well-informed, sensible concern for his singer's vulnerable vocal instrument. Mahler could also manifest a caring and tender attitude toward the well-being of his beloved. Beyond that, however, one senses in his concern the anxiety-ridden ruminations of the worrying parent. Reciprocally, he regularly reported to her the state of his own health (which was for Mahler a recurrent feature of his personal letters). The mutual sharing of such everyday matters, including family concerns on both sides, reveals a *heimisch* aspect of the relationship.

Interestingly, as in the case of Johanna Richter, Mahler once again used the occasion of a major move – this time to Vienna as director of the Court Opera – to end the relationship. According to Alma Mahler's account, Anna, crazily in love, "behaved like a madwoman." Feigning illness, she insisted that Mahler come to her; meanwhile she had also secretly summoned a Benedictine monk and, in operatic fashion, sought unsuccessfully to press both cleric and lover to proceed with a service of marriage.[48] Nothing in the extant Mahler-Mildenburg correspondence (which in any event begins to wind down in quantity and passion by this point) supports Alma's claim of such excesses and irrationality on Anna's part. Mahler did, to be sure, remark in a letter written that summer to Rosa

---

[47] Throughout this period Mahler was suffering from illnesses which were in part of psychosomatic origin – frequent and often prolonged migraine headaches as well as hemorrhoidal bleeding which was difficult to control. He also experienced periodic depression. Later, in June of 1897 following his move to Vienna, he suffered from dangerous and debilitating sore throats that finally required surgery for an abscess. Justi, as always, provided nursing care.

[48] AMML4, p. 12.

Papier, Mildenburg's former teacher in Vienna, that "the worries and humiliations of the last months in Hamburg are still very fresh in my memory," and Papier subsequently upbraided Mildenburg on grounds that "it was you who chose to advertise the whole affair in your usual way."[49] But on the whole, it appears Mahler sought to break things off quietly. The nature of Mahler's attachments was such that he needed some external closure as well as the reinforcement of geographical distance in order for him to separate. And even then the break was far from complete. In the last letter he sent Anna from Hamburg Mahler writes: "When you read these lines I will be on my way to Vienna . . . Good-bye my dear, dear Annie . . . The separation we will have to endure in the future shall only be a <u>physical</u> one. The bond that we have joined together shall never break. I am yours, my darling, and I remain faithful to you."[50] His subsequent letters from Vienna continue to comfort her.[51]

But the next two lines of Mahler's Hamburg farewell to Anna are striking: "I beg of you, my Anna, to live as though you always saw my eyes focused upon you! And never do anything important without consulting me in advance!"[52] The original Pygmalion aspect of the love affair continued to flourish, with Mahler actively involved in that part of Anna's life he now believed he had created: von Mildenburg the diva. Even as he foresaw the end of their personal liaison, Mahler continued to promote her career vigorously. In August of 1896, summoned by Cosima Wagner, Mahler attended her son Siegfried's conducting debut in the fourth *Ring* cycle of the Bayreuth Festival; his first letter to Mildenburg following this pilgrimage strongly suggests he seized the opportunity to urge that Cosima Wagner take the young singer under her wing.[53] That fall, concurrently with his

---

[49] See HLG 1, p. 437 (HLGF 1, pp. 667–68; HLG 2, pp. 40–41).

[50] Autograph letter of 25 April 1897: "Wenn Du diese Zeilen liest, bin ich auf dem Wege nach Wien . . . Auf Wiedersehen, mein theures, liebes Annerl! . . . unsere Trennung in der nächsten Zeit, die wir über uns ergehen lassen müssen, soll nur eine <u>leibliche</u> sein! Das Band, das wir geknüpft, soll nie zerreißen! Ich bin Dein, mein Lieb, und bleibe Dir treu!" [51] Cf. also HLG 1, p. 430.

[52] Autograph letter of 25 April 1897: "Ich bitte Dich, meine Anna, lebe so, als ob Du meine Augen immer auf Dich gerichtet sähst! Und thue nie etwas Wichtiges, ohne mich vorher zu befragen!" Cf. also HLG 1, p. 411.

[53] The fourth *Ring* cycle took place August 9–12; Mahler's letter to Anna, dated only "<u>Sonntag</u> [<u>Sunday</u>]," must have been written on the 16th: "<u>Der Moment</u>

political maneuvering for the Vienna appointment – which Cosima strongly opposed – he persisted in recommending Mildenburg to the heiress of Bayreuth, hoping to engage her in the "lofty mission" of rescuing this "still very young and *unspoiled* artist . . . from the corrupt influence of theatrical turmoil."[54] Cosima heard Mildenburg sing at Bayreuth that December, and was greatly impressed; Mildenburg's Festival debut took place the following summer (1897).

Meanwhile, the relationship between Mahler and Mildenburg gradually and miraculously shifted, eventually becoming confined to the professional arena where it had all begun. Mahler increasingly respected Mildenburg's musical maturity, in which he considered himself to have played no small part. In June of 1897, somewhat to his surprise, she was offered a guest appearance in Vienna for the fall, as a prelude to a permanent engagement at the Court Opera. Mildenburg's teacher Rosa Papier, mistress of the influential theater administrator Eduard Wlassak, was chiefly responsible for this invitation; in a letter to her written at the beginning of July, Mahler admitted that

> I cannot say our friend Wl. [Wlassack] is wrong. It would really be asking a lot to abandon the engagement of an artist of M.'s importance for purely personal reasons.
>
> . . . Anyway it is still a whole year yet [i.e., until the long-term contract]; and this will give me time to overcome the difficulties between M. and myself, which at present stand in the way of successful co-operation.[55]

Later that month Mahler addressed the matter openly and firmly in a letter to Anna, which she received just prior to her Bayreuth debut as Kundry in *Parsifal*:

> wird noch kommen, wo Du dort stehen wirst, und alle Deine Vorgängerinnen weit früher Dir zurück lassen wirst [The moment will yet come, when you will stand there, and will leave all of your predecessors far behind you]." Cf. also Eduard Reeser, "Gustav Mahler and Cosima Wagner," in *Mahler's Unknown Letters*, ed. Herta Blaukopf, trans. Richard Stokes (London, 1986), esp. pp. 203–05.
>
> [54] Letter to Cosima Wagner of 24 October 1896, *Mahler's Unknown Letters*, p. 218.
> [55] Letter to Rosa Papier dated 2 July 1897, KBD, p. 212; the German text is found in Herta and Kurt Blaukopf, comps. and eds., *Gustav Mahler: Leben und Werk in Zeugnissen der Zeit* (Stuttgart, 1994), pp. 124–25.

Dear Anna,

I am "battering down the door into your house" with an important question that I can no longer put off, even though I would rather spare you from it, since you have such a great event before you. I have smoothed the way for you in Vienna to such an extent that . . . you will soon receive a contract from there. But in the event that you accept it, it is <u>absolutely necessary</u> (now that I have a clear overview of the whole situation) that we should then restrict our personal relations to the very minimum, in order not to turn life into torment for both of us. The entire [Opera] staff are already on the alert because of the gossip from Hamburg, and the report of your engagement will burst like a bombshell. If we therefore gave even the slightest occasion for mistrust, etc., <u>my position</u> would quickly become an <u>impossible one</u>, and I would again have to pack my bags as in Hamburg. You, too, would again suffer just as much, even if it were not a question of life or death for you.

Now I ask you, dear Anna: do you sense in yourself the strength to be employed in Vienna together with me, and – at least during the first year – to renounce any personal relations and any show of favor from me? Hopefully you realize that it will be <u>no less difficult for me</u> than for you, and that only bitterest necessity brings me to pose this question. But it is too important, and I can and must not create any illusions about it, for either you or me. I ask of you, my dear Anna . . . answer me with a few lines, but be entirely <u>frank</u> and <u>honest</u>! – [56]

That December Mildenburg made a triumphant Viennese debut, singing three roles Mahler had previously taught her. (He, however, was not then on the podium, presumably for discretion's sake.) The following March she signed a five-year contract with the Court Opera.[57] In 1898 she gave her first performance under Mahler's baton in Vienna, and in 1900 she achieved tremendous success in her Viennese debut as Isolde, a role with which she was closely identified for the rest of her career.[58]

Mahler's final letter to Mildenburg was a very different kind of adieu from the one he sent her in Hamburg. In December 1907, after resigning his position in Vienna and just before departing for New York and the Metropolitan Opera, Mahler issued a printed letter of farewell to all members of the Vienna Court Opera; to Anna, however, he wrote separ-

---

[56] GMB2, no. 251 (not in GMBE), mid-July 1897; the entire letter is trans. in KBD, p. 213.   [57] HLG 2, pp. 79–81.   [58] HLG 2, pp. 222–23.

ately, realizing that "for me you stand entirely apart." "Dear Old Friend!" he addressed her, "I can only send you these few heartfelt words and press your hand in spirit. I shall always watch your progress with my previous affection and sympathy ... In any case, you know that even from afar I shall remain a friend on whom you can count ... May all go well with you, and be of good heart! Your old Gustav Mahler."[59]

Natalie Bauer-Lechner, 1889–1901

Although Mahler and Bauer-Lechner knew each other in passing during their conservatory days, it seems fitting that their relationship began to blossom in 1888 under "familial" circumstances when they met again at the Vienna home of Mahler's longtime friend Friedrich ("Fritz") Löhr. (As noted above, Fritz and his wife Uda were so much a part of Mahler's extended family that he depended upon them to help look after his younger siblings after the death of their parents the following year [1889].) During the Löhrs' gathering in 1888, Mahler, in an expansive mood, had invited everyone to visit him in Budapest, where he had just assumed the directorship of the Opera.

But the following year was one of turmoil for Mahler. In addition to the heavy demands of his new position, he had to become head of the family and provide for the remaining children. It was an equally difficult time for Natalie: her troubled marriage had ended in divorce in 1885, and in the fall of 1890, as she puts it, "I found myself at that time in the most confused and sorrowful condition, both inwardly and externally, and was very much in need of cheering up."[60] Both, then, were in a position of loneliness and need when Natalie decided to take up the casual invitation Mahler had issued a year and a half earlier. For his part, the thirty-year-old bachelor responded enthusiastically by clearing out his apartment and moving into a hotel, almost as though he were preparing for the arrival of a prospective fiancée.

But the possibility of engagement and marriage to Natalie, if ever seriously entertained by Mahler, was never to be realized. Notwithstanding, Natalie played an important role in Mahler's life for nearly eleven years,

---

[59] GMB2, no. 377 (GMBE, no. 355).
[60] NBL2, p. 21 (not in NBLE); see also HLGF 1, pp. 327–28.

and their relationship spanned a critical decade in his creative life. During that time his attitude and behavior toward her ranged widely. In September 1892, for example, he wrote to Fritz Löhr about cheerfully putting up with a rainy trip, "urged on by never failing impuls [sic] of our merry Natalie, who is such a dear [*unseres lustigen, lieben Kerls Natalie*]."[61] If nothing else, that characterization suggests that the possibility of an erotic attachment had already passed, which is amply confirmed in later years. Indeed, by 1894 Mahler was writing his sister Justine specifically *not* to invite Natalie to Steinbach for the summer, although she had by then become Justine's friend and a fixture in the family: "I cannot stand her constant mothering, advising, inspecting, and spying," Mahler declared.[62] Although Natalie did not join the Mahlers that particular year, she in fact spent all other summer holidays from 1893 through 1901 with them.

Mahler's appreciation of and respect for Natalie are evident from his numerous gifts of autograph manuscripts, and from the extent to which he shared with her both reflections on his professional activities and his private thoughts. Indeed, there developed between Mahler and Natalie a curious intimacy with regard to creative life on one hand and health matters on the other, including frank discussion of various bodily functions. Absent, however, were signs of any deeper attachment on his part that might correspond to her feelings for him. From this perspective, it seems Mahler largely took Natalie for granted as a fortunate fact of his life, whereas she remained singularly devoted to him. She soon became Mahler's Boswell and Eckermann, preserving each scrap and detail of their conversation as though it were a special treasure. As a result, her "Mahleriana," posthumously published in a considerably abridged version as *Erinnerungen an Gustav Mahler* (Vienna, 1923), is an indispensable source for the understanding of Mahler's creative life from 1890 to 1901. The book provides biographical data from earlier periods as well, but it is *par excellence* a chronicle of Mahler's "*Wunderhorn* years," just as Natalie was his *Wunderhorn* companion.

Something of Natalie's attitude toward female rivals can be gleaned from the fact that, although she certainly knew of Mahler's liaison with

---

[61] GMB2, no. 116 (GMBE, no. 108); the phrase "never failing impuls" is written in English.   [62] HLG 1, p. 303.

Anna von Mildenburg, Natalie's "Mahleriana" mention Anna solely in her professional capacity as a singer at the opera, in which case she conscientiously records Mahler's comments. As for Alma Schindler, it was Mahler's engagement to her that brought about the close of his relationship to Natalie, and therewith the end of her "Mahleriana." Although the original published edition of the *Erinnerungen* ends with a dutiful entry about the Vienna premiere of the Fourth Symphony on 12 January 1902 (which discussion, incidentally, fails to reveal Natalie's own intimate connection with this work), both the manuscript of the "Mahleriana" and the second German edition conclude thus: "Mahler became engaged to Alma Schindler six weeks ago. If I were to discuss this event, I would find myself in the position of a doctor obliged to treat, unto life or death, the person he loved most in the world. May the outcome of this rest with the Supreme and Eternal Master."[63]

Natalie's memoirs have been the cornerstone of Mahler biography for seventy-five years; nevertheless, our chief concern here is the *process* within the relationship between Mahler and Bauer-Lechner, which gave rise to the biographical memoirs. Natalie served an important function during the *Wunderhorn* years: she was the silent contributor and secret sharer within the creative process that produced the completion of the Second Symphony as well as the composition of the Third and Fourth Symphonies in their entirety. Like many creative artists, Mahler thrived upon interaction with a creative companion; Natalie served this role. An accomplished musician, she had studied violin at the Vienna Conservatory and had long been active as violist of the Soldat-Röger Women's String Quartet; thus, she knew a good deal of musical repertoire, and also understood the hurly-burly of professional life. She was a good and competent listener who could participate in whatever verbal exchanges and process of groping a composer might find useful in the organization of purely musical materials. As a result, she became privy to many details of how Mahler went about composing, despite his frequent claim that he disliked revealing details about works-in-progress. And it is noteworthy that, despite her idealization of Mahler and her careful rendering of his own philosophical viewpoints regarding the sources of inspiration, Natalie rarely lapses into

[63] NBL2, p. 204 (not in NBLE).

the mystical or emotionally "romantic" representation of inspiration that is frequently characteristic of the period when she was writing. Rather, she presents a fairly realistic picture of the artist at work: accounts of Mahler's internal struggles are balanced by his comments on more practical matters – overall musical form, sequence of ideas, specific technical details, problems of instrumentation, etc. – as well as broad aesthetic issues. Moreover, she appears sensitive to the pace at which creative work unfolds, which in Mahler's case could be very erratic indeed.

She was a good listener in another way as well, for natural aspects of friendship may verge upon psychotherapy. And her relationship with Mahler was in some respects a healing one for him; the "cure" was a cure-by-love that he was never to reciprocate. During the many hours they spent together at critical times in Mahler's life, the two of them walked endlessly, he talking, she listening. Mahler could thus ventilate the very considerable rage he harbored; he could also justify and even aggrandize himself, seek comfort for his many psychological wounds, and repair his chronically bruised self-esteem. Natalie would listen empathically, responding with assent, support, sympathy, and admiration. And it seems noteworthy that it was Natalie to whom Mahler revealed most of the few dreams he is known to have discussed with others.[64]

Finally, reading between the lines of Bauer-Lechner's *Erinnerungen*, one can detect something of the maternal role she uncomplainingly performed. During the summer months from 1895 through 1901, she was essentially "on call" for Mahler. Clearly, there was a reverse side to his earlier complaints about her "mothering": he accepted Natalie's (as well as his family's) attending to his needs as a matter of course. This emerges distinctly from an atypical passage of her chronicle for the summer of 1896, in which she is relieved that Mahler has gone away for a few days, almost as though she were the mother of a very demanding child: "When one lives in the same house with Mahler ... it's like being on a boat constantly pitched and tossed by the waves of the sea – one often feels the need to recover ..."[65] Natalie's sensitivity to Mahler's moods and her own need to comfort him characterized her loving. In this she could be excessive, and may thereby have made Mahler too conscious of his own vulnerability. In March of

---

[64] Cf. also HLG 2, pp. 340 and 716.   [65] NBL2, p. 61 (NBLE, p. 65), 6 July 1896.

1896, for example (during the midst of his affair with Mildenburg), Mahler was greatly dismayed by the disastrous reception of his First Symphony in Berlin; Natalie, who had come to hear the performance, sought to console him after they had gone their separate ways for the night, rather to his embarrassment:

> There [at the hotel] we all parted, and each with a heavy heart sought his own room. I alone stole a moment more at Gustav's door, and at his half-hearted "come in" I slipped into his room. I could not bear to go to bed without saying a word to him. Irresistibly I felt compelled to thank him, both for myself, and for the entire world, which caused him to suffer such malice. In a flash I seized his hand, bowed, and kissed it. And he could barely take it from me and exclaim, moved: "But Natalie, what are you doing!" when I had already hurried away to my room.
>
> Then the long built-up, powerfully suppressed agitation broke forth in a torrent of tears – and for Mahler as well; I saw it in his face the next morning.[66]

Nevertheless, the "Mahleriana" suggest Natalie was as much the confidante of the physical as of the spiritual – the confessor of belly and bowel, although evidently not of sex. Like the rest of Mahler's family, she was aware of the strain his affair with Mildenburg was costing him, especially at its height during 1896. And it is particularly interesting to note the two sides of Mahler revealed in his interactions with Bauer-Lechner and Mildenburg that summer. The anguish and passion he felt in relation to Anna had to be warded off and psychologically isolated so that he could concentrate on composing. Although Mahler missed her, their physical separation was helpful to him. She, however, inquired whether he ever thought of her while at work, and reproached him for his distractedness.[67] Engrossed in completing the Third Symphony, Mahler replied, "Don't you understand that it demands one's entire being, and to the extent that one delves into it, one is almost dead to the outer world."[68] It was, however,

---

[66] NBL2, p. 48 (not in NBLE); cf. also HLG 1, p. 355.
[67] GMB2, nos. 179 and 180 (first letter incomplete in GMBE, no. 173; the second is GMBE, no. 174).
[68] GMB2, no. 180, dated by the editor [28? June 1896] (GMBE, no. 174, mistakenly dated 18 July 1896); cf. also HLG 1, p. 368.

Natalie who understood this completely, and who was concurrently resigned to sharing the only world Mahler would share with her – or, indeed, needed to – with any passion. That summer she was involved in every aspect of the composition of the Third, all of which she recorded for us in minute detail. Nor does it appear Natalie was unhappy with this portion, even though she clearly longed for more. Anna, meanwhile, correctly if petulantly observed that her real rival was Mahler's work.[69]

The decade Natalie devoted to Mahler brought her into her forties. Whatever may have been her fantasies of a future with the man she loved, these were the last years in which she could reasonably expect to bear children. Instead, they were spent in creative midwifery, although she may well have considered them the happiest years of a sad life.[70] In what were perhaps her best days, Mahler himself acknowledged their creative partnership by proudly presenting her the sketches for the first movement of his Third Symphony, inscribed thus: "On 28 July 1896, a curious thing happened: I was able to present my dear friend Natalie with the seed of a tree that, nevertheless, is now grown to full size – flourishing and blossoming in the open air with a full complement of branches, leaves and fruit."[71] For some years following her alienation from Mahler, Natalie continued to perform with the Soldat-Röger Quartet; she also taught violin and wrote extensively, publishing a volume of *Fragmente* in 1907. Little is certain about her last years, except that she died in lonely poverty in 1921, almost precisely a decade after the death of Mahler.[72]

---

[69] GMB2, no. 183 (incomplete in GMBE, no. 171), 6 July 1896; cf. also HLG 1, p. 370.

[70] Natalie's will of 10 June 1918, cited in NBL2, p. 13, states: "That for which I most thank the Deity is that it permitted my life to encounter both of these great spirits, Lipiner and Mahler: to share their being, to follow their example – to the extent of one's own strength –, to be able to receive most inwardly and intimately their genius in word and creation, which soared above everything, and to serve them, was the highest and most exalting happiness of my being . . ."

[71] NBL2, 66 (NBLE, 67).

[72] See Herbert Killian's foreword to NBL2, as well as HLG 2, pp. 466–67. Killian (Natalie's great-nephew) claims that on account of an outspoken anti-war article probably published in 1918, Natalie was arrested, indicted for high treason, and given a long term of imprisonment. De La Grange, citing the unpublished diaries of Emma Adler (wife of the socialist politician Victor

The year 1901

If we are to take Bauer-Lechner's apparently lady-like farewell to Mahler literally – her claim of being "in the position of the doctor obliged to treat, unto life or death" – there can be little doubt that the "disease" was Alma. Mahler had met Alma on 7 November 1901 and they were engaged by Christmas. Like Natalie, she too kept a diary that turned into a book on Mahler, her well-known *Gustav Mahler: Memories and Letters*.[73] The pivotal year was 1901: as Natalie closed her book, Alma opened hers.

1901 was a watershed year for Mahler, arguably his most critical, during which changes became apparent in every sphere of his life. In February he suffered a life-threatening illness that jolted him out of any complacency he may have harbored regarding his own vulnerability; it was an episode that deeply affected his attitude toward the future.[74] Distinct stylistic changes immediately became apparent in his compositions.[75] The composing summer that year was a rich one as he began work on his Fifth Symphony, wrote his last *Wunderhorn* song, and made the transition to setting poetry by Friedrich Rückert, including three of the *Kindertotenlieder*. He played all of these new lieder for Natalie at the end of the summer and presented her with sketches for them "as a token of our perfect concord during this holiday" – fruits well-earned but

Adler [1852–1918]), states that Natalie was incapacitated by serious illness, then took up residence in a home for the elderly, and finally, suffering from a mental disorder, was committed to a lunatic asylum. In an unpublished letter to Anna Bahr-Mildenburg dated 7 April 1915, Natalie observes: "Es sind mir die Jahre, welche wir uns nicht sahen, nicht leicht geworden. Das Ärgste davon war die schwere Verdauungs-Nervenerkrankung, die mich vorigen Winter 3 Monate in Sanatorium – in einem Geisteszustand, den ich nie wieder erleben möchte – festhielt. [The years in which we haven't seen each other were not easy for me. The worst part was the difficult digestive-nervous illness, which kept me in the sanatorium last winter for three months, in a spiritual state that I never want to go through again.]" (Vienna, Theatermuseum, Mildenburg Nachlaß.)

73 *Gustav Mahler: Erinnerungen und Briefe* (Amsterdam, 1940).
74 See Stuart Feder, "Gustav Mahler um Mitternacht," *International Review of Psycho-Analysis* 7 (1980), 11–25.
75 For example, see the discussion by Donald Mitchell, MSSLD, pp. 55 ff.

destined shortly to be found bitter.[76] For Mahler, the *Wunderhorn* years were over.

As regards the problem of his sister Justine, the resolution could not have been more operatic. Soon after the two of them moved to Vienna, Justine met Arnold Rosé, concertmaster of the Vienna Court Opera. More than just a colleague of Mahler's, Rosé became a genuine supporter and friend; they read chamber music together and Rosé helped Mahler work out bowings for the string parts of his scores. Rosé rapidly became part of the small Mahler family, which included Natalie, and also joined the wider circle of Mahler's friends; frequently he accompanied Mahler on trips and vacations. On such occasions as well as at other social and professional events, Rosé and Justine together with Mahler and Natalie made up a foursome, at least half of which was celibate.

It was apparently during the spring of 1901 that Mahler discovered the nature of the bond between Justi and Arnold Rosé; if Natalie wrote anything about this, it has not come down to us.[77] According to Alma's version, when Gustav "discovered that his trust had met only with deceit he was so disconcerted that he refused to speak to Justine for weeks," and at length insisted that she should "either break with Rosé or marry him."[78] The result was a foregone conclusion, and it seems unlikely that Mahler, who rarely missed anything even if he was "dead to the world" when composing, was unaware of the growing closeness between the two. Although Gustav may have felt some sense of betrayal, as Alma suggests, in view of his years of inner conflict over Justine, he would very likely have felt a degree of relief as well.

Meanwhile, his sister Emma's future had already been secured. In August 1898, little more than a year after the family settled in Vienna, Emma married the cellist Eduard Rosé, Arnold's younger brother. According to

[76] NBL2, 193–95 (NBLE, abridged, pp. 173–74). According to NBL2, p. 195, "he gave me the sketches of all his recent lieder," but an inventory of Natalie's manuscripts entitled "Manuskript-Verzeichnisse der Natalie Bauer-Lechner Erben" dated 7 September 1925 (collection of Henry-Louis de La Grange, Paris) indicates that she owned autograph materials for four of the songs from the summer of 1901: "Der Tamboursg'sell," "Ich atmet' einen linden Duft," "Blicke mir nicht in die Lieder," and "Wenn dein Mütterlein."

[77] See HLG 1, pp. 618 and 938, n. 28, as well as HLG 2, pp. 340–41.

[78] AMML4, p. 13.

de La Grange, Alma claimed much later that "Justi and Arnold 'arranged' Emma's marriage so that they could see each other oftener."[79] Whether or not that was the case, Arnold did in fact spend the summer of 1898 with the Mahlers. The newlywed Rosés were soon to leave for America, where Eduard had been engaged by the Boston Symphony.

Justi could not have found a better oedipal substitute for her brother than the gifted and attractive Jewish musician Rosé; and Mahler could not have found a more agreeable and compatible brother-in-law if he had hand-picked Justine's husband (which, in any event, may well have been the case). For in Arnold Rosé, not only did Justine find a husband: Mahler also replaced a brother, having by then lost all three of his male siblings. His beloved Ernst had died during adolescence from terminal heart disease; Alois, mentally unstable, had vanished; and Otto had committed suicide six years earlier. Moreover, like the fine conductor he was – constantly anticipating, farther along in the score than any of the other musicians – Mahler was contemplating the future once again. In concluding his affairs with both Johanna Richter and Anna von Mildenburg, Mahler had ultimately managed to dovetail separation with the next progressive step in his life. Now his perception of changes in Justine's emotional life which might lead to marriage motivated Mahler to prepare for his own next move. Owing to his keen sense of the future as well as to his traumatic brush with death in February of 1901, Mahler was ready when the time came.[80] The two couples, Alma and Gustav, and Justine and Arnold, were married, respectively, on 9 and 10 March 1902.[81]

[79] HLG 1, p. 481, and HLG 2, pp. 110–11.
[80] See Feder, "Gustav Mahler um Mitternacht," esp. pp. 22–23.
[81] HLG 2, pp. 487–89.

5 Mahler and Smetana: significant influences or accidental parallels?

DONALD MITCHELL

Only comparatively recently – in 1991 during a visit to Prague – did I resume thinking about Mahler's musical relationships to those celebrated Bohemian composers, particularly Dvořák and Smetana, by whose works (especially operas) he was very likely influenced from time to time. Albeit in a rather random way, I touched upon this topic in the second volume of my Mahler studies,[1] drawing attention to the similarity between a passage from Smetana's overture to *The Bartered Bride* and the transition to the recapitulation in the finale of the First Symphony (fig. 45+8), a connection that still seems to me very telling. What I write now remains narrow in focus, but suggests that in assessing the Bohemian influences upon Mahler, we should be particularly mindful of Smetana.

To be sure, Mahler's preserved opinions of Smetana are not consistently enthusiastic. Nevertheless, his new production of *Dalibor* at the Vienna Opera, which opened on 4 October 1897, struck his friend and confidante Natalie Bauer-Lechner as something quite exceptional:

> He has been personally responsible for everything in it, having chosen and suggested the sets, costumes and lighting – not to mention his attention to the dramatic and musical aspects. In fact, he has even reworked the final section of the opera . . .
>
> Even apart from all this, I have perhaps never seen anything more perfect on the stage in every detail of performance and conception.
>
> Thus, although *Dalibor* had never been able to get a footing elsewhere, Mahler not only gave it a brilliant first night, but also assured it a genuine success.[2]

[1] MWY, p. 209 and pp. 291–92.
[2] NBLE, pp. 101–02 (NBL2, pp. 100 and 225, n. 113).

110

There can be no doubt about Bauer-Lechner's response to what was clearly a remarkable occasion; and to stage such an extraordinary event would have required, even of the hypercritical Mahler, a commitment and conviction based on the merits of Smetana's score (notwithstanding the fact that Mahler characteristically retouched and recomposed several passages of it).

Mahler conducted *Dalibor* a dozen times during 1897–98, but then only once or twice a season for the next six years.[3] Before the book was closed, so to say, he made one more comment to Bauer-Lechner, following the performance of 5 November 1901:

> You can't imagine how annoyed I was again today by the imperfection of this work, the work of so highly gifted an artist [*eines so hochbegabten Künstlers*]. He was defeated by his lack of technique and his Czech nationality (which hampered him even more effectively, and deprived him of the culture of the rest of Europe) . . . And when I'm conducting it I'm practically beside myself; there is a lot more I should like to cut and re-orchestrate, even re-compose – so unskillfully is it written, in spite of its many beautiful passages.[4]

This makes odd reading as our twentieth century comes to an end, when it is difficult for us to imagine that being Czech could be regarded as a cultural deprivation. But composers' views on other composers are frequently unreliable, and more often than not tell us more about the composer uttering the criticism than the composer who is criticized. As I hope to show, despite Mahler's highly qualified admiration, Smetana's music influenced him beyond the previously noted instance of *The Bartered Bride*, and in ways by no means negligible. Composers have always behaved thus, and Mahler was no exception.

Smetana's *The Bartered Bride* entered the repertoire in 1866, and was swiftly recognized as a masterpiece of comedy and lyricism: according to Loewenthal, there had been one hundred performances by 1882 and five hundred by 1909.[5] Thus, there is nothing surprising about the "quote" from

---

[3] Franz Willnauer, *Gustav Mahler und die Wiener Oper*, new edn. (Vienna, 1993), p. 232.   [4] NBLE, p. 180 (NBL2, pp. 199–200).

[5] Alfred Loewenthal, *Annals of Opera* (Cambridge, 1943), p. 1866. Reviews of Mahler's 1909 New York performance appear in Zoltan Roman's invaluable *Gustav Mahler's American Years 1907–1911: A Documentary History* (New York, 1989), pp. 220–23 and 238.

the opera's overture in Mahler's First Symphony: this was music with which he would have been thoroughly familiar.[6] A few years later (January 1894) Mahler introduced a highly successful production of the work at the Hamburg Opera, and in Vienna he conducted ten performances of it between 1899 and 1907.[7] Nor did he neglect the *The Bartered Bride* at the Metropolitan Opera: the New York première took place under his baton on 19 February 1909. By all accounts this was a brilliant production, splendidly performed, but one that also aroused adverse commentary owing to Mahler's characteristic (although creative!) textual infidelities – among them, it seems, playing the overture before the second act. Although the production was highly praised, it did not capture the enthusiasm of New York audiences.

Clearly it was the 1894 triumph of *The Bartered Bride* in Hamburg that led Mahler later the same year to revive Smetana's *Two Widows* – said to be Richard Strauss's favorite opera. (Did Strauss also find Smetana's technique wanting, I wonder?) This work had been previously performed at Hamburg in 1881 – which was the first time, indeed, that any opera of Smetana's had been staged in a German theatre. Mahler continued to bring Smetana to his listeners with the Hamburg première of *The Kiss* in February 1895; among the cast were two stars whose names loom large in any chronicle of Mahler's theatrical activity, Bertha Förster-Lauterer and Ernestine Schumann-Heink. Indeed, during the 1894–95 season Hamburg witnessed virtually a miniature festival of Smetana operas conducted by Mahler – a self-contained event that is surely worth attention in its own right, particularly as regards the reception of these operas by both public and critics.

The Kiss – *Hubička* in Czech – is probably one of the least familiar of Smetana's operas outside the Czech Republic. Although today not nearly so popular as either the *Bartered Bride* or *Two Widows*,[8] at its Prague première on 7 November 1876, *Hubička* "was the happiest and most successful of all of Smetana's operas and the work soon established itself as his most

---

[6] See also Henry-Louis de La Grange, "'Music about Music' in Mahler: Reminiscences, Allusions, or Quotations?," pp. 122–68 below.

[7] Willnauer, *Mahler und die Wiener Oper*, pp. 222 and 231.

[8] Perhaps now one ought to add *Dalibor* to the short list, staged successfully as it was for the first time in England by the English National Opera in 1976 and 1977.

Ex. 5.1   Smetana, *Hubička*, act I, scene 7, first lullaby

popular opera after *The Bartered Bride*."[9] Mahler would not have been long unaware of such a successful work. When the première of *Hubička* took place, he was a sixteen-year-old student at the Vienna Conservatoire, and he was twenty when the vocal score of the opera was first published in 1880 (to coincide, perhaps, with the production of *Hubička* presented at the Provisional Theatre in Prague in honor of Smetana's fiftieth year as a performing pianist).[10] Mahler conducted his first performance of *Hubička* in Hamburg on 20 February 1895. The foregoing assembly of dates and data provides a necessary context for what follows; and what follows derives, quite simply, from my chance encounter with *Hubička* in September 1991 at the Smetana Theatre in Prague.

In Act I, scene 7 of the opera, at the side of a cradle, Vendulka sings a lullaby – or rather, two lullabies. The first is a traditional one that begins (in F) as shown in Ex. 5.1. The second (in A), separated from the first by six bars of recitative, is Smetana's original composition. Two introductory bars establish the gently rocking motion of the slumber song, as shown in

[9]   John Tyrrell, "Kiss, The," *The New Grove Dictionary of Opera* (London and New York, 1992), vol. II, pp. 1000–02. Tyrrell's magisterial study *Czech Opera* (Cambridge, 1988) provides detailed statistical information about the number of performances of Smetana's operas given at the National Theatre, Prague, between 1883 and 1886, years which include the period Mahler spent there as second conductor at the German theatre. See also Brian Large, *Smetana* (London, 1970), pp. 289–316 and p. 348.

[10]   Two further operas succeeded *Hubička*: *The Secret* (1878) and *The Devil's Wall* (1879–82). Smetana left a fragment of an opera entitled *Viola* (based on Shakespeare's *Twelfth Night*) that he was working on up to his death in 1884.

Ex. 5.2 Smetana, *Hubička*, act I, scene 7, second lullaby

Ex. 5.3 Smetana, *Hubička*, act I, scene 7, ending of second lullaby

Ex. 5.2. Both these lullabies seemed to me sublime inspirations (if I may be forgiven that tired old adjective). But what gripped my attention – so much so that I almost exclaimed out loud – was how the second lullaby *ended* (see Ex. 5.3). Or, more precisely, how the lullaby did *not* end, but faded out, dissolved into the sleep that overtakes Vendulka. In short, she sings the child to sleep, and herself as well; Smetana graphically, almost magically, captures this lyric-dramatic vignette and sustains it for us.

114

Ex. 5.4   Mahler, "Der Schildwache Nachtlied," ending

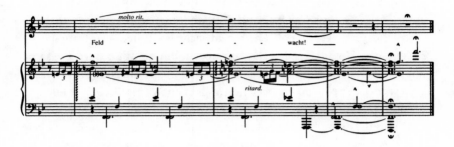

That unresolved dominant with its lingering pedal,[11] which leaves us suspended, like Vendulka, from the waking world of action, immediately brought back to my mind in an almost Proustian burst of memory the last bars of one of Mahler's orchestral *Wunderhorn* settings, "Der Schildwache Nachtlied": this is another *Nachtstück* that, if not exactly a lullaby, nonetheless brings us to the edge of dreams, whether through sleep or death (traditionally two closely associated states of being). And Mahler achieves the suspension of time and motion in the lyric-dramatic situation through virtually the same musical means as his Czech predecessor (see Ex. 5.4). We are left suspended on and over the dominant, another "still," frozen, cinematic like, in its frame, fading, along with the sentry, into some other world on the threshold of which we are left standing.[12]

---

[11]   Nor does Smetana resolve it in any orthodox sense. However, the immediately ensuing opening of scene 8, a lively Polka, is in F, the key of the first lullaby.

[12]   As I suggest above, whether the sentry drifts into dreams, sleep, or death remains to my mind an entirely open question: hence the unresolved dominant. The poem that Mahler set is surely enigmatic; although Deryck Cooke suggests without qualification that it tells of a sentry killed on duty while dreaming of his sweetheart, I am not sure that the text is not more ambiguous than this. (See Cooke, *Gustav Mahler: An Introduction to his Music* [London, 1980], p. 42.)

It is curious, moreover, that there has been very little comment on Mahler's audacious "dissolve" at the end of "Der Schildwache Nachtlied." To my knowledge, the first writer to draw attention to it was the perspicacious Ernst Decsey, who actually took the matter up with Mahler himself – only to be rebuffed for reading more into the treatment of the dominant than the composer was then prepared to concede. (Again, an altogether typical composer's response.) See Ernst Decsey, "Stunden mit Mahler," *Die Musik* 10/21 (1910/1911), 144–45, trans. in Norman Lebrecht, ed., *Mahler Remembered* (New York, 1987), p. 261.

Had "Der Schildwache Nachtlied" been composed after the Hamburg première of *Hubička*, there could be little question of Smetana's influence upon Mahler's *Wunderhorn* song. But we know with certainty that the voice-and-piano version of "Der Schildwache Nachtlied" was complete by 28 January 1892 (and the orchestral score followed by 26 April the same year), whereas *Hubička* was not staged in Hamburg until 20 February 1895. Yet it seems very probable indeed that Mahler knew *Hubička* before he came to conduct it himself in 1895. As noted above, the vocal score appeared in 1880 and the opera had become fairly popular. In addition, it seems likely that the famous lullaby (or lullabies) may have been performed independently in concert halls here and there, a point to which I shall return

Footnote 12 (*cont.*)

  An incomplete sketch for the song was once in the possession of Natalie Bauer-Lechner (now at the Library of Congress, Washington, D. C.; a photofacsimile of the first page is found in Emanuel Winternitz, *Musical Autographs from Monteverdi to Hindemith* [New York, 1965], vol. II, plate 163). In her memoirs (NBLE, pp. 170–71 [NBL2, p. 190]) Bauer-Lechner associates it with an operatic project of 1888, as follows:

  Mahler told me [in the summer of 1901] that in Leipzig, after finishing the *Pintos* with [Karl von] Weber [the composer's grandson], and at the request and urging of the latter's wife, he had wanted to write an opera of his own. He suggested the following subject to Weber for a libretto, outlining it in detail:

  A soldier on his way to the gallows is – according to medieval custom – spared the death penalty when a girl, whose deepest sympathy he inspires, claims him in marriage before the people and the judges. The mourning procession turns into one of jubilation, and everyone goes home rejoicing. But the stubborn young fellow cannot bear the shame of owing his life to the pity of a girl whom he, in turn, is beginning to love. His inner conflict becomes so intolerable that he rejects her gift of freedom and marriage, declaring that he would rather die. The last act was supposed to bring about the resolution of the matter with the girl's ardent pleading and confession of love.

  Weber, however, had immediately altered this simple story. He introduced an earlier love and sweetheart of the young man, running quite counter to Mahler's intentions, and leading him very soon to abandon the whole idea. "Der Schildwache Nachtlied" was salvaged from this attempt. To it, Mahler owed his renewed acquaintance with *Des Knaben Wunderhorn*, which was to become so significant for him.

  This has never seemed probable to me, and the description of the sketch sent me by Professor Edward R. Reilly, to whom I am much indebted, offers no evidence to support her attribution. However, what prompted my query to

below. More compelling, however, is the fact that Mahler spent the 1885–86 season in Prague, as temporary conductor at the Royal German Theater (Deutsches Landestheater). At Prague's newer Czech National Theater (Narodní divadlo), native works were presented in their original language, and it was here that Mahler came to know a number of Slavic operas, including those of Smetana, whose *Hubička* was performed at least four times during the first half of 1886.[13] Prior to his Prague engagement, however, Mahler had already signed a contract to become assistant conductor under Arthur Nikisch at the Leipzig Stadttheater for the 1886–87 season. In late June or early July he writes from Prague to the director of the Leipzig house, Max Staegemann, as follows:

Footnote 12 (*cont.*)

> Professor Reilly was my interest in the song's concluding bars: were they, I wondered, present in the sketch in the form that they appeared in the final version? Professor Reilly told me (private communications, April and June 1994) that they were not:
>
>> The Library of Congress sketch does not show the end of the song. It is clear from the manuscript that Mahler hit a snag at the equivalent of bar 97 [six bars after the beginning of the song's closing 6/4]. The vocal line for [the words] "Verlorne Feldwacht" differs from the final form, and four further bars of unharmonized vocal line are cancelled. So we don't know how he would have ended it at this stage. Most interesting, however, is the fact that although the sketch begins in B flat, as in the final form of the song, the passage beginning at bar 92 is in G, and in fact at bar 94 is marked "G dur." The last three bars look as if they move in the direction of E minor.
>
> It would have been fascinating, of course, for us to have had an early sketch from Mahler of a conclusion for the song. It is almost more fascinating to know that at the stage of this sketch he clearly didn't know himself how to end it.
>
> As for the "opera," it is difficult indeed to envisage a whole evening in the theatre emerging from the outline Bauer-Lechner gives. Perhaps Weber and Mahler talked over the kernel of an idea, but did not pursue it. Is it then not likely that Mahler's memory of the "project" of 1888 came back to mind when he was selecting *Wunderhorn* texts for setting in the 1890s and helped determine his choice of "Der Schildwache Nachtlied" – i.e., that Mahler found the "opera" had already been written for him in the shape of a poem?

13 See František Bartoš, ed., *Mahler: Dopisy*, trans. František and Maríe Bartoš (Prague, 1962), p. 185 [a valuably annotated edition of Mahler's letters, especially with regard to the years up to his appointment to the Opera at Vienna]. Cf. also HLGF 1, pp. 203–04 and 226, n. 81, as well as KBD, pp. 174–75 and plates 61–69. According to Josef Bohuslav Foerster, *Der Pilger: Erinnerungen eines Musikers*, trans. Pavel Eisner (Prague, 1955), p. 374, *Hubička* (*Der Kuß* in German) was indeed among the operas Mahler heard during the 1885–86 season in Prague.

Incidentally, I have several times been to the Bohemian National Theatre here and have heard a number of works by *Smetana* [Mahler's emphasis], Glinka, Dvořák, etc., and I must confess that Smetana in particular strikes me as very remarkable.

Even if his operas will certainly never form part of the repertory in German, it would be worth while presenting such an entirely original and individual composer to audiences as cultivated as those in Leipzig.[14]

"An entirely original and individual composer": rather different words and tone from the judgment Mahler would later pronounce upon *Dalibor* when he was director of the Vienna Court Opera! But that apart, it seems reasonable to assume that what Mahler had in mind in writing so persuasively to Staegemann was precisely the sort of mini-Smetana-festival that he finally brought to the boards in Hamburg during the 1894–95 season, comprising *The Bartered Bride, Two Widows,* and *Hubička.* Thus, although the evidence is not completely conclusive, it seems legitimate to me to suggest that the impact *Hubička* (or at any rate its lullabies) made on Mahler during his year in Prague became a significant influence upon "Der Schildwache Nachtlied" in 1892. It was not, I believe, a conscious influence, but a subconscious recollection that served him as a poetic and technical model for the concluding, or rather *in*concluding, bars of the sentry's *Nachtlied.* I find it not at all surprising that Mahler's preternaturally sensitive and all-consuming ear would have stored away a memory of Smetana's masterly little inspiration for future use.

The apparent connection between Smetana's lullabies and Mahler's song strikes me as a most telling and fascinating example of a creative legacy, inherited by Mahler from his great Bohemian predecessor, that transcended the bounds and boundaries of nationalism. But at least one further passage of *Hubička* made an uncanny impression upon me when I heard it in Prague in 1991. It was, as it happens, yet another *Nachtstück,* but of a quite different character: not a lullaby, but a night patrol through a deep forest. The music in question is a chorus of smugglers, which John Tyrrell aptly characterizes as "an atmospheric piece with a Baroque crotchet tread and hushed voices above."[15] I don't quarrel with any of that. Yet it was not an association with the baroque that floated into my mind,

---

[14] GMBE, no. 44 (GMB2, no. 48).   [15] Tyrrell, "Kiss, The," p. 1001.

Ex. 5.5 Smetana, *Hubička*, act II, scene 1, chorus of smugglers
(vocal parts omitted)

but rather a distinct evocation of a passage from the development in the first movement of Mahler's Second Symphony – the first version of which, entitled "Todtenfeier," was completed in September 1888, in Prague. (Thus Mahler would already have heard the Smetana operas he mentioned to Staegemann in the letter of 1886 cited above.) Example 5.5 illustrates the nature of Smetana's nocturnal scene; undoubtedly it was the combination of the ostinato plus a tapestry of winds (bassoons, horns, clarinets, flutes and oboes) projected above the insistent bass tread that once again brought me, so to say, face to face with Mahler – and very much the Mahler of the 1880s. To make the point as clear as possible I have omitted from Ex. 5.5 all the vocal parts, which in themselves are of only secondary musical significance. The parallel passage in Mahler, which is easily accessible, is from fig. **16** to bar 270 in the score of the Second

Symphony.[16] It is, I repeat, the character of the Smetana example that seems so embryonically yet authentically Mahlerian, together with its texture, its lay-out, and the color of it. Was this once again music that Mahler had absorbed which resurfaced just below the threshold of consciousness when he found himself working on his own dark processional in the "Todtenfeier" movement of the Second?

Although I cannot pretend to know all the answers to the questions that my own first faltering steps in this field have generated, it is clear to me that there is between Mahler and Smetana a creative relationship of potential significance which has not yet been thoroughly explored. Brian Large, in his voluminous work on Smetana,[17] makes only two very brief mentions of Mahler, in one of which he states that "Mahler knew and loved *Má Vlast*, and *Tábor* and *Blanik* may well have inspired parts of the Sixth Symphony." True or false? It seems to me that there is work to be done as regards *Má Vlast*. And what about *Dalibor*? Has anyone seriously examined the opera to discern what ignited Mahler's enthusiasm, qualified though it was? (His editing and retouching might tell us something as well.) As I write, moreover, additional correspondences occur to me. Of course all lullabies tend to have features in common, but in the sublime slumber song that closes the *Kindertotenlieder*, particularly in its gently ululating figuration, might there be a distant trace of Vendulka's second lullaby?

That possibility returns us to *Hubička*, and therewith to the last piece in this jigsaw puzzle, which comes from the very last year of Mahler's life. On 20 November 1910 at the Brooklyn Academy of Music Mahler conducted the New York Philharmonic in a program (twice repeated at Carnegie Hall) that included Dvořák's "Carnival" overture and two pieces by Smetana – one of which (with soloist Alma Gluck) was none other than the "Böhmisches Wiegenlied aus *Hubička*."[18]

---

[16] In the "Todtenfeier" full score published as Supplement Band I of KG, this passage runs from fig. **18** to **19**.

[17] Large, *Smetana* (London, 1970), p. 185.

[18] See Knud Martner, *Gustav Mahler im Konzertsaal, 1870–1911* (Copenhagen, 1985), p. 139. A review of Mahler's 1910 performance is to be found in Roman, *Mahler's American Years*, p. 408. The "arrangement" was made by Kurt Schindler; and it was no doubt in this shape that the excerpts from the opera had enjoyed some sort of independent life on the concert circuit. I have not been able to locate this particular arrangement, but it must have found a way

round the second lullaby's expiring on the dominant (which would not make much sense outside the theatre), while even the first lullaby is not rounded off but leads into the brief recitative that acts as bridge between the two. Or perhaps Mahler came up with a solution of his own? A possibly relevant piece of evidence is a 1937 78 r.p.m. shellac disc of the lullaby made by Elisabeth Schumann with an anonymous conductor and orchestra. The very existence of the recording indicates that the lullaby was performed independently from the opera. As for the concluding bars, the arranger replaces Smetana's poetic open end with a conventional resolution. In all other respects, however, the performance is faithful to the text, and Schumann sings (in German, of course) with incomparable charm. The recording has been re-issued on CD on the Beulah label, 2PDH ("78 classics, Volume Two").

6 Music about music in Mahler: reminiscences, allusions, or quotations?

HENRY-LOUIS DE LA GRANGE

If music critics could consign to oblivion music they considered unworthy of survival, Mahler's music would have been finally forgotten long ago, for the "infernal judges" of his time were almost unanimous in finding him guilty of unforgivable faults. Their verdict was delivered in tones ranging from the most sarcastic irony to violent indignation, but the substance was always the same: such "Kapellmeistermusik," consisting exclusively of "banalities" and "reminiscences" of the past, was clearly fated to be soon forgotten, since its author revealed in it nothing so much as a total lack of melodic imagination. The severest judges went so far as to call Mahler's symphonies "gigantic pots-pourris."[1] Whether it was possible to identify the origin of all these borrowings – intentional or unintentional – was quite irrelevant as far as they were concerned.

At the end of the nineteenth century, originality of thematic material was fully enshrined as the first principle for a work of art, rather as though nothing had changed since German classical literature had reached its zenith, when Friedrich Schlegel in 1797 could declare: "originality is the supreme goal of the artist, the ultimate criterion of the connoisseur."[2] Romanticism, on the other hand, had not been so categorical. Thirty-five years after Schlegel's observation, when the new aesthetic had conquered the whole of Europe, the idealist philosopher Hegel, whose aesthetic theories profoundly influenced German art and thought throughout the nine-

---

[1] Quoted by Arnold Schoenberg in his "Prager Rede," in *Gustav Mahler* by Arnold Schoenberg, Ernst Bloch, Otto Klemperer, Hans Mayer, Dieter Schnebel, Theodor W. Adorno (Tübingen, 1966), p. 38.

[2] Friedrich Schlegel, "Über das Studium der Griechischen Poesie," in *Schriften zur Literatur (1795–1797)*, (Munich, 1972), p. 108.

teenth century, stated flatly in 1832 that an authentic work of art had to "produce itself spontaneously in strict coherence and in a single out-pouring." In his opinion, the source "of any true originality" must be "the identity of the artist's subjectivity with the authentic objectivity of the presentation [*Darstellung*]."[3] For the young Robert Schumann, the notion of originality had been even less restrictive. On 6 August 1828 he wrote in his diary: "Just as no man resembles another, so everyone carries within himself the stamp of originality and spiritual strength ... The person who goes looking for originality has to a certain extent lost it ..."[4]

Seventy years later, however, the music critics of Germany and Austria considered Mahler's music far from unique and personal; on the contrary, they regarded it as a jumble of borrowings and reminiscences. In their view it did not satisfy the fundamental criterion of "internal coher-ence [*in sich Geschlossenheit*]" to which all artistic creativity had to conform; Mahler had simply attempted to "produce superficial effects [*Effekten*]" with material he had collected from all over the place. The German word *Effekt* has a pejorative flavor, unlike *Wirkung* – the force which captivates because it comes from within and is produced by the quality of the musical ideas and the thematic development. Mahler himself was perfectly aware of the difference between *Effekt* and *Wirkung*, and firmly rejected the charge of plagiarism. He was highly aware of his own originality, and considered that quality equally significant in appraising the work of his contemporaries. Two passages from Natalie Bauer-Lechner's *Erinnerungen* illustrate this: in the first, Mahler (rather surprisingly) accuses Alexander von Zemlinsky of having had a very bad memory because he had failed to eliminate some obvious thematic reminiscences from his opera *Es war einmal*;[5] in the second he criticizes himself, in the presence of his friend and confidante, for having unconsciously introduced reminiscences of Beethoven and Brahms into his Fourth Symphony.[6]

The heterogeneity of style for which he was constantly reproached

---

[3] Georg Wilhelm Friedrich Hegel, *Vorlesungen über die Aesthetik* (1832), vol. I, in the *Suhrkamp Werkausgabe*, vol. XIII (Frankfurt, 1970), pp. 376 and 383.

[4] Robert Schumann, *Tagebücher 1827–1838*, vol. I (Leipzig, 1971), p. 104.

[5] Natalie Bauer-Lechner, "Mahleriana" (unpublished manuscript, Bibliothèque musicale Gustav Mahler, Paris), cited in HLG 2, p. 221 (HLGF 1, p. 841).

[6] NBL2, p. 64; cf. also HLG 2, p. 276 (HLGF 1, p. 898).

was also a characteristic of which Mahler was fully aware: in a letter written to Bruno Walter in June of 1896 he ironically alludes to the "trivialities" that his favorite disciple would not fail to discover in the Third Symphony.[7] Nevertheless, Mahler's confidence in himself and in his destiny as a composer was never seriously shaken by the critics' reproaches. Only on one occasion did he apparently consider the intrusions of plebeian music into his works to be a genuine weakness. That was in Holland, in August 1910, during his celebrated interview with Freud in Leiden.[8] Mahler told Freud of an incident in his childhood, when he had witnessed a violent quarrel between his father and mother; when he could stand it no longer, he fled outside into the street and heard a barrel organ playing a well-known folksong, "Ach, du lieber Augustin." The incident was so traumatic that it was continually reflected in his compositions, with the result that, as Freud later recounted, "his music had always been prevented from achieving the highest rank through the noblest passages, those inspired by the most profound emotions, being spoilt by the intrusion of some commonplace melody."[9] In my opinion this single moment of doubt should not be given too much prominence, and that for three quite distinct reasons. First, composers themselves are rarely the best judges of their own music; second, Freud recalled this incident many years after the fact when speaking to his disciple Marie Bonaparte, and may not have remembered Mahler's exact words; and third, when Mahler went to see Freud he was still suffering from the most painful crisis of his entire life: his discovery of Alma's affair with the young Walter Gropius. This left him feeling deeply pessimistic both about his previous achievements and about his future.

The crime of *lèse-majesté* against the symphony

The fact remains – and no one would dream of denying it today – that the thematic material of Mahler's symphonies is certainly heterogeneous, and replete with what seem to be quotations. As Adorno observes, his music "has absolutely nothing in common with the idea of originality as this has

[7] GMB2, no. 182 (GMBE, no. 170), 2 July 1896.
[8] See AMML4, p. 175, and HLGF 3, pp. 769 ff., esp. p. 772.
[9] Ernest Jones, *The Life and Work of Sigmund Freud*, 3 vols. (New York, 1953–57), vol. II, p. 88.

been formulated ever since the early romantics, if not earlier."[10] Of course "quotations" and self-quotations in the works of many earlier composers have long been recognized,[11] but no one before Mahler had dared to introduce music that was frankly popular, and even plebeian, into the elevated genre of the symphony. One might object that Schubert's dances and lieder, Chopin's mazurkas and *Chants polonais*, and Brahms's *Hungarian Dances* and *Volkslieder* also derive their inspiration from folk music. But while these composers draw upon folk idiom in songs, dances, and character pieces, they do so relatively rarely in large-scale works such as symphonies. To be sure, such stylistic interpolations were permissible in scherzos, but were generally avoided in sonata-form movements. The great symphonic tradition, initiated by Haydn and Mozart, to which Beethoven contributed nine supreme models for posterity, had been largely maintained in the work of Brahms and Bruckner. Faithful to the criteria of romanticism and the legacy of Beethoven, nineteenth-century symphonists aspired to the universal by means of abstraction, whereby their first movements and finales were expected to preserve both purity of style and unity of inspiration.

For Mahler's contemporaries those were the two conditions *sine qua non* of symphonic composition; therefore in 1902 it must have shocked them to hear in the opening movement of his Third Symphony the constant alternation between two violently contrasting moods: the tragic, as it were telluric, grandeur of the introduction, and the plebeian insolence of the marches, in which "the inferior music bursts in upon the superior music with Jacobin violence," as Adorno so aptly puts it.[12] How could these brutal contrasts and the snatches of band music be regarded as anything but a profanation of the symphonic genre? How could the juxtaposition of two such disparate styles be accepted if one did not, as we do today, recognize that Mahler would henceforth refuse to admit the traditional distinction between the inferior and superior "spheres" of music, and that he had

[10] Theodor Adorno, "Mahler: Centenary Address, Vienna 1960," in *Quasi una Fantasia: Essays on Modern Music*, trans. Rodney Livingstone (London, 1992), p. 84 (Adorno, *Gesammelte Schriften*, vol. XVI: *Musikalische Schriften I-III* [Frankfurt, 1978], p. 326).

[11] See Günther von Noé, "Das musikalische Zitat," *Neue Zeitschrift für Musik* 124 (1963), 134–37, and Charles Rosen, "Influence: Plagiarism and Inspiration," *19th Century Music* 4 (1980), 87–100.   [12] TAM, p. 53 (TAME, p. 35).

concluded, as Adorno observes, a "provocative alliance with vulgar music," such that "ill-dressed, unmannerly people romp in a ceremonial chamber, the absolutistic imago of which bourgeois music continues to delineate"?[13] For the first time in history, Mahler's symphonies "shamelessly flaunt what rang in all ears, scraps of melody from great music, shallow popular songs, street ballads, hits."[14]

In countless passages of Mahler's music the grotesque mingles with the sublime. The contrasts are all the more marked because Mahler presents the popular material "for the first time in its original dress"[15] – that is to say, in timbres characteristic of village and military bands or "spa" music (whereas "nationalist" composers who adopted folkish elements had carefully eliminated any trace of such uncouthness from their symphonies). A prime case in point is the grotesque funeral march in the First Symphony, an amazing collage of quotations, self-quotations, and allusions, among which "Frère Jacques" ("Bruder Martin" in German), the simplest and most familiar of nursery tunes, functions as a refrain. Brusque shifts of mood occur constantly throughout Mahler's music; sometimes the intrusion of new material is underlined by an abrupt change of tempo,[16] while in another instance the very theme which surprised us with its apparent banality changes into a solemn, mysterious chorale tune.[17] The most obvious of these metamorphoses occurs in the finale of the Fifth Symphony, wherein a fragment of the Adagietto, one of the loveliest lyrical melodies Mahler ever wrote, is parodied and accelerated into a brisk round.[18] This process is reversed when Mahler interrupts the cruel travesty of the Ninth's "Rondo-Burleske" to insert a moment of pure emotion.[19] Even more shocking and unconventional is the Rondo-Finale of the Seventh Symphony, a movement that still embarrasses many convinced

13 TAME, pp. 35 and 37 (TAM, pp. 52 and 55).
14 TAME, p. 35 (TAM, pp. 52–53).
15 Robert P. Morgan, "Ives and Mahler: Mutual Responses at the End of an Era," *19th Century Music* 2 (1978), 74–81.
16 E.g., Fourth Symphony, third mvt., bars 282–83; Fifth Symphony, first mvt., bars 154–55, and second mvt., bars 287–89; Sixth Symphony, first mvt., bars 250–52 and 381–82; Seventh Symphony, first mvt., bars 265–66.
17 Seventh Symphony, first mvt., cf. bars 19–26 and 258–65.
18 Fifth Symphony, finale, bars 191–231, 373–414, and 643–86.
19 Ninth Symphony, third mvt., bars 347–442.

Mahlerians: the sudden breaks are more brutal and more provoking than anywhere else in his music.[20]

Upon closer examination, two characteristics can be distinguished in Mahler's use of heterogeneous material and *objets trouvés* ("found items," to use a term currently applied to music since the 1960s): first, it is neither habitual nor systematic, and second, these intrusions can be classified into a number of different categories according to their nature, origin, and function in context. In my view, the main categories to be distinguished are (1) reminiscences, which are in principle unintentional, and (2) allusions or quotations, which are intentional. One can then inquire into the origin and significance of particular *objets trouvés*. Recently some German and Austrian musicologists have tried to define the various categories of "music about music" in Mahler and have proposed the following terms: *Zitat* (quotation), *Gedächtniszitat* (quotation from memory), *Selbstszitat* (self-quotation), *Paraphrase*, *Anspielung* (allusion), *Anlehnung* (taking something as a model), *Entlehnung* (borrowing), *Anklang* (echo or reminiscence), *Ähnlichkeit* (similarity), and *Huldigung* (homage).[21] Yet the musicologists in question seldom agree about the nature of these various procedures, or the reasons for them. Perhaps the time has arrived to look squarely at a subject about which so much has already been written, and try to answer a few fundamental questions such as the following:

(1) Was Mahler ever guilty of the flagrant plagiarisms for which his contemporaries so often reproached him? Is his "eclecticism" real or merely apparent?

(2) To what extent can the materials in question be classified as *objets trouvés*, quotations, allusions, or reminiscences? Are they deliberate or unconscious?

(3) Which composers and what sort of music did Mahler most often "quote"?

---

[20] Seventh Symphony, finale, bars 52–53, 86–87, 201–02, and especially 516–17.

[21] See Monika Tibbe, *Lieder und Liedelemente in instrumentalen Symphoniesätzen Gustav Mahlers* (Munich, 1971), p. 103; Marius Flothuis, "Kapellmeistermusik," in Rudolf Stephan, ed., *Mahler-Interpretation: Aspekte zum Werk und Wirken von Gustav Mahler* (Mainz, 1985) pp. 9–16; Reinhard Kapp, "Schumann Reminiszenzen bei Mahler," in Heinz-Klaus Metzger and Rainer Riehn, eds., *Musik-Konzepte: Sonderband Gustav Mahler* (Munich, 1989), pp. 325–61. On the subject of musical quotation, see von Noé, "Das musikalische Zitat."

(4) In the case of apparently intentional quotations, can any precise significance be attributed to them?

(5) Is Mahler comparable (or not) to those of his predecessors who also borrowed some of their material and wrote "music about music"? To what extent is his activity similar to that of the neoclassicists in the 1920s and 30s?

The countryside and forests of childhood days

Before speaking of "plagiarisms," it must first be stressed that while Mahler's use of heterogeneous material seems beyond dispute, his borrowings were not limited to music of the past. Most obvious of all were those Nature supplied him, which he termed *Naturlaute* (sounds of nature). Bird songs are the most common of these; striking examples are the cuckoo in the introduction to the First Symphony, and in the Second, the nightingale that Mahler called "the bird of death," whose song echoes on in the emptiness and desolation following the end of the world like a "last terrestrial sound."[22] Bird songs are to be found in most of Mahler's symphonies; they grow increasingly stylized across the span of his oeuvre, yet always remain recognizable, right up to *Das Lied von der Erde* and the Ninth.[23] We should note here as well that the *Naturlaut* episodes, like the military fanfares, recur as distant memories; they are, therefore, both "reminiscences" and "quotations." Nor is that surprising, given Mahler's admission to Natalie Bauer-Lechner that "Composition can be compared to a game of bricks, in which with the same bricks one keeps making new buildings. But the bricks are already there, trimmed and dressed since one's childhood, the only period in life for collecting and preparing them."[24]

Then there are the "trivial snatches," the reminiscences of popular music already mentioned above. There was nothing furtive or unacknowledged about Mahler's love of street music, as two incidents amply illustrate:

---

[22] See NBL2, p. 40 (NBLE, pp. 43–44) and AMML4, pp. 213–14.

[23] *Das Lied von der Erde*, fifth movement, bars 37–44, and sixth movement, bars 137–45; Ninth Symphony, first movement, bars 376–91.

[24] NBL2, p. 138 (NBLE, p. 131), July 1899.

Alma tells of his delight in the sound of an Italian barrel organ coming through the window in New York,[25] and Natalie Bauer-Lechner records his pleasure in the sounds of two barrel organs softened and mingled with the strains of a brass band, all of which wafted across the Wörthersee during a walk in Maiernigg.[26] As regards reminiscences from classical and romantic music, a fairly comprehensive list of those identified to date, by myself and by many others, appears as the appendix to this essay. But the search continues – an ongoing game for those who have a taste for it, among whom I include myself.

Music about music before Mahler

Composers of all epochs have been borrowers to various degrees. One need only think of the Renaissance, when imitative music, countless transcriptions and adaptations, and "parody" masses abounded. The custom continued in various forms right through the baroque period, culminating in Handel's copious borrowings from many composers, including himself. Bach did it less often than Handel, but did not hesitate to transcribe and adapt a large number of scores from various sources. In addition, he introduced into the last of the Goldberg Variations a cantus-firmus "Quodlibet" made up of two different popular tunes.

The Viennese classical composers, however, proved much more touchy about the use of borrowed material, at least in symphonies. One is nevertheless struck when listening to Haydn, the "disciplined revolutionary," by the detachment with which he treats his material, and the way in which he occasionally appears to be making fun of the conventions of the time,[27] or seems to take pleasure, as Mahler later would, in surprising his listeners with unexpected tricks. (More could be written, I think, on "music about music" in Haydn.) Mozart's transcriptions of Bach, Beethoven's use of Russian tunes in his "Razumovsky" Quartets and of an aria from *Don Giovanni* in one of the *Diabelli Variations* (no. 22), Schubert's self-quotations from his songs in his instrumental music, and his adoption of the Italian style in two of his overtures – all these examples are perhaps no more

[25] AMML4, p. 135 (cf. also HLGF 3, p. 244).

[26] NBL2, p. 165 (NBLE, p. 155), 5 August 1900 (cf. also HLG 2, p. 280).

[27] E.g., Symphony No. 60, "Il distratto."

129

than exceptions to the rule. In Schubert's music, however, the frontier between the trivial and the sublime has already become less distinct, and one can already perceive on the horizon the intimate mixture of the two spheres that would much later characterize Mahler's music.

Wagner certainly did not like to be reminded of the themes by Liszt he had appropriated for the *Ring*. He may perhaps have considered that borrowing within the family was acceptable, especially since his treatment of the borrowed material was infinitely more elaborate than Liszt's. But it is in *Die Meistersinger* that one finds, besides a very significant quotation of *Tristan*, the most interesting and novel form of neoclassicism – a half-affectionate, half-humorous imitation of the "scholarly" style attributed to the eponymous Masters. In this case Wagner's attitude in reinventing the past is strangely similar to Mahler's own alienation from his "models"; and it should be recalled in passing that Mahler would quote the *Meistersinger* Overture quite explicitly near the opening of the Finale in his Seventh Symphony (bars 15–23), which he thus placed, as it were, under the patronage of *Die Meistersinger*.

In Bruckner's symphonies the popular sources are obvious, but only in the ländler-form scherzos; his sonata movements preserve an irreproachable "purity" of style, such that the two spheres of music remain quite distinct. Karl Michael Komma has drawn attention to both the temporal proximity and thematic similarity of two well-known scherzos – that of Bruckner's Fourth (1874–81) and Mahler's Second (1888–94). Since the Mahler passage bears the indication "mit Humor" ("humorously"), Komma concludes that between the completion of the two works, any possibility of introducing folk elements into "serious" music without offense had disappeared.[28] Mahler himself, moreover, in the program he drew up for the Second, gave a "negative" interpretation of the whole of this Scherzo. For him it expressed a "profound disgust" at the absurdity of human existence.[29]

Komma rightly speculates about the stringency of criteria for "banality" and "vulgarity" outside Germany, and asks whether, for example, the

[28] Bruckner, Fourth Symphony, scherzo, opening; Mahler, Second Symphony, third mvt., bars 42–48. See Karl Michael Komma, "Vom Ursprung und Wesen des Trivialen im Werk Gustav Mahlers," *Musik und Bildung* 5(64)/11 (November 1973), 573–77, and Ex. 6.40 below.　　[29] See n. 22 above.

main melody of the Andante from Tchaikovsky's Fifth Symphony sounds as trivial to a Russian as it did to Theodor Adorno.[30] However that may be, two of Tchaikovsky's works, the suite entitled *Mozartiana* (1887) and the pastorale in the second act of *The Queen of Spades* (1890) are among the earliest manifestations of deliberate neoclassicism. As regards the relativity of such criteria, some critics have condemned as excessively facile Rossini's deliberate use of clichés and melodic formulae that would seem banal coming from a less sophisticated writer; yet in his hands, they yield an amazing range of comic effects. Only Offenbach was able to follow and occasionally equal him in this respect.

Dialogues with the past

The term "neoclassicism" emerged at the beginning of the nineteenth century in the fields of poetry and painting. No one then foresaw that it would be extended to music, and would later flourish vigorously in both practice and discussion of the art. Certainly there were plenty of precursory signs, both in Germany and elsewhere, of general historical awareness in music. At the beginning of the twentieth century, Max Reger (1873–1916) was already engaged in a "return to Bach" as an antidote to Wagnerian style. But although many works demonstrate Reger's preference for the organ and solo violin as well as for moto perpetuos, dense polyphony, and old forms, his rich and complex harmony, which very often oversteps the limits of classical tonality, places Reger among Wagner's descendants. Overall, his approach to composition is substantially different from Mahler's, who in any case always refused to take the music of Reger seriously.

Richard Strauss also showed marked awareness of the past from early in his career (one need think only of the F minor Symphony and First Horn Concerto, two of the works that brought him the support of Hans von Bülow, who was by then a staunch conservative). Strauss's musical language verges upon expressionism in *Salome* (1905) and *Elektra* (1908), but *Der Rosenkavalier* of 1910 marks a turning point in his career: two years later the

---

[30] Adorno, "Commodity Music Analysed," *Quasi una fantasia*, trans. Livingstone, pp. 41–42. Comparing this theme with the Adagietto of Mahler's Fifth Symphony, Komma (p. 577) points out the difference between a genuinely banal and trivial theme and that invented and developed by a truly great symphonist.

first version of *Ariadne auf Naxos* (then a one-act opera performed in conjunction with a condensed translation of Molière's *Bourgeois gentil-homme*) established itself as the first work of musical neoclassicism properly speaking, in that the entire flavor of the score derives from the confrontation between past and present. The stylization and deformation of the historical material often produced entertaining results, although that was not the work's central feature. Apart from this early venture into neoclassicism, Strauss's "music about music" deploys one device perhaps more than any other composer's: quotation, particularly self-quotation. Often it is used to evoke irony or humor, while sometimes it is apparently done for the simple pleasure of making the allusion; in any case, it seems that Strauss always quotes with complete awareness.[31]

The neoclassical temptation

It was, however, in France that, in keeping with tradition dating back to Rameau and Couperin, composers very soon discovered the pleasures of allusion and reference, of alienation and stylization, and also the joys of erudite memory games. While their detached treatment of the old models did not include systematic distortion (such as Stravinsky's), they nevertheless treated inherited material with extreme freedom, modernizing its musical language. The twentieth century had not yet arrived when Ravel wrote his "Menuet antique" in 1895; six years later, Debussy followed suit with his suite *Pour le piano*, consisting of a Prelude, a Sarabande and a Toccata. Later he, too, frequently took his inspiration from the past, either in serious mode, as in *Hommage à Rameau*, or in ironic vein, as in *Children's Corner*. Throughout his life Ravel also composed works cast in classical molds, such as the *Sonatine* (1905), *Valses nobles et sentimentales* (1911), *Le tombeau de Couperin* (1917), and *La Valse* (1920), and neoclassical characteristics continued to predominate right up to his last concertos in the 1930s.

---

[31] See Günther von Noé, "Das Zitat bei Richard Strauss," *Neue Zeitschrift für Musik* 125 (1964), 234–38. In *Das Heldenleben* alone, von Noé lists no fewer than eighteen quotations.

The case of Stravinsky

But it is to the music of Stravinsky written just after World War I that Mahler's play on style must be compared, since it is generally agreed that the composer of *Le Sacre* is also, if not the inventor, at least the foremost representative of twentieth-century neoclassicism. In 1918 *L'Histoire du Soldat* already established some central features of his future style: abandonment of the pre-war Russian manner, satirical wit, sardonic, almost cruel stylization (in the two chorales and the dance rhythms), and use of an extended tonality often concealed behind chords that, although relatively simple, were spiced with aggressive discords. Two years later, *Pulcinella* marked the beginning of a new period in Stravinsky's music, which Boris de Schloezer has called "musique au second degré" ("music at second remove"), an "art d'après l'art" ("art based upon art"). Henceforth Stravinsky would treat the historical models with the greatest freedom, like simple objects or "conscious stylistic references." Later he declared that he both "loved" his models and felt a desire to "possess" and expropriate them for himself – a sort of kleptomania that was sometimes affectionate, sometimes disrespectful and even aggressive. Yet in every case Stravinsky imposes an unmistakably personal style and an extreme sophistication through distortion, exaggeration, reinterpretation, fragmentation, etc.

All of these works, which are at least ostensibly a return to the past, provide the listener with the twofold pleasure of both recognizing the model and appreciating the composer's transformation of it. The "original" diatonic harmony is irrevocably corrupted by a corrosive irony, or what one might call imaginary quotation marks. In this respect Stravinsky's attitude toward the quoted material is not unlike Mahler's. But in any comparison of the two composers the dissimilarities are clearly as numerous as the similarities, if only because Stravinsky largely abandons both sonata form and the developmental procedures of the classical tradition, whereas Mahler never dispensed with them, even though he transformed them considerably.

Theodor Adorno used all the resources of his hermetic but infinitely rich and subtle language to condemn what he regards as "montages of dead material" in Stravinsky.[32] Nevertheless (perhaps owing to his obsession with Schoenberg and his unshakable faith in the serial principle), Adorno fails to point out that the borrowings in Stravinsky are often as vague and ambiguous as they are in Mahler. Rather than pastiches, deformations, and stylizations, Stravinsky gives us his impressions, his feelings, his opinions of the past. Curious though it may seem, his approach is in this respect more modern than that of Schoenberg and his pupils: as we shall see, the permanence of their heritage and its traditional forms became an obsession with them, whereas Stravinsky never tries to resuscitate, prolong, or transform historical material. Rather, he is content to touch up a preexistent style with modern "features"; his essential theme is not borrowed from the past, but is, quite simply, the past itself.

The many ways of returning to the past

Twentieth-century music as a whole, particularly during the thirty years just reviewed, has been marked by an almost universal determination to refer to previous models. There are, of course, some rare exceptions, such as the "nationalist" composer Janáček who, starting from folk material, could forge his own original language with little dependence upon the past. But everywhere else in Europe and even in the United States, one finds traces of neoclassicism. It is omnipresent in the works of the two great Russians, Sergei Prokofiev (whose *Symphonie classique* dates from 1917) and Dimitri Shostakovich. In music of the Hungarian Béla Bartók, neoclassicism is deprived of its usual irony and associated with a rediscovery of national folklore, comparable to Janáček's. Elsewhere in Europe, returning to the past finally became the natural thing to do, rather than a conscious play on style; notable composers in point are the Pole Karel Szymanowski, the Spaniard Manuel de Falla, the Italians Gianfrancesco Malipiero, Alfredo Casella, and Ottorino Respighi, and the American Aaron Copland. In the mid-1920s the German Paul Hindemith developed a style "explicitly and almost defiantly anti-romantic" that "drew strength from the gestures and aesthetic of the high Baroque."[33]

---

[32] *Quasi una fantasia*, trans. Livingstone, p. 147 (*Gesammelte Schriften*, vol. XVI, p. 383).

[33] *The New Grove*, s.v. "Hindemith, Paul" by Ian Kemp, p. 578.

With all these composers Mahler has very little in common. At the most, one might compare him with Bartók or Janáček in his recreation of a true folkloric style, without ornaments or transpositions – a style that, viewed in the context of the great nationalist upsurges reaching their peak at the end of the nineteenth century, seems like a genuine return to original sources. In his attitude toward the past and his frequent use of quotations, Mahler has also been compared to Charles Ives.[34] But it was above all Shostakovich who later purposefully prolonged some of the most characteristic features of Mahler's music, in particular his habit of quotation and self-quotation, his detachment from the material quoted, and his corrosive irony. The main difference, perhaps, is that Mahler's irony was usually directed at the *Alltag*, the mediocrity of everyday life, whereas Shostakovich's target was bureaucratic petty-mindedness and the oppression of a tyrannical regime.

It remains for us to take note of the neoclassicism practiced by Mahler's direct descendants, Schoenberg and his pupils; this had little to do with the procedures followed by Stravinsky (who considered their form merely more "concealed" than his own). Anxious to prolong a secular tradition to which he saw himself faithful heir, Schoenberg adopted the forms of the past. It was only natural that he should do this when, having perfected the serial system during the early 1920s (in the Serenade, Op. 24 and the two Suites, Opp. 25 and 29), he abandoned the post-romanticism of his earlier years and attempted to go back beyond the nineteenth century to the forms and disciplines of the eighteenth. At the start of his career as a composer, Mahler, too, had been preoccupied with a desire to take his place in a time-honored tradition. On one occasion, indeed, he congratulated himself for having used, without thinking about it, the classical musical forms invented by Mozart and Haydn – sonata form as well as the traditional adagio, rondo, minuet, etc., with the same "old structure" and "familiar periods," and "in which deep, eternal laws are inherent."[35] This same concern would later become an obsession of Alban Berg's when he revived classical and traditional forms in his two operas. Similarly, Webern wanted

---

[34] See Carl E. Schorske, "Mahler et Ives: Archaïsme populiste et innovation musicale," in *Colloque international Gustav Mahler, 25. 26. 27. janvier 1985* (Paris, 1986), pp. 87–97, and Morgan, "Ives and Mahler."

[35] NBL2, p. 64 (NBLE, p. 66), 27 July 1896 (see also HLG 1, p. 376).

to reappropriate the monothematicism of the baroque period by trying to develop whole pieces from a single initial cell – an ideal that, curiously enough, Mahler had formulated in Webern's presence in 1905.[36] On the other hand, Berg's quotations of a Carinthian tune and a Bach chorale in his Violin Concerto (1935),[37] and of *Tristan und Isolde* as well as Zemlinsky's *Lyrische Symphonie* in his *Lyric Suite* (1925–26), are autobiographical in character and in no way neoclassical. Thus, they have nothing in common with Mahler's procedures as defined below; only the cabaret music played on an out-of-tune piano in the second act of *Wozzeck* (third tableau) falls into the same category.

Mahler and the past: reminiscences and quotations, homages and sarcasm

In Mahler one often encounters music that merits the description "neoclassical before its time," since it comes so close to the aesthetic of the 1920s. The initial movement of the Fourth Symphony, with its almost continuous semiquavers and its naively diatonic melodies, can hardly be thought of as anything but a homage to Haydn and Viennese classicism. Robert Hirschfeld, the witty critic of the *Wiener Abendpost*, was not altogether mistaken when, after the first Vienna performance, he declared that it conjured up visions of "Papa Haydn rattling past in a motorcar enveloped in a cloud of gasoline fumes."[38] Elsewhere, the same neoclassical spirit is manifest in the fugatos of the Scherzo and Finale of the Fifth: here "old" style is both imitated and parodied, as in *Die Meistersinger*. The bitter-sweet serenade of the Seventh (fourth movement) offers another reference to the past, as does the Rondo-Finale of the same symphony, with its dotted

---

[36] See Hans Moldenhauer (with Rosaleen Moldenhauer), *Anton von Webern: A Chronicle of His Life and Work* (London, 1978), p. 75; cf. also HLGF 2, p. 576.

[37] According to Douglas Jarman, "Alban Berg, Wilhem Fliess and the Secret Programme of the Violin Concerto," *International Alban Berg Society Newsletter* (Fall–Winter 1982), 5 f., the Carinthian melody in Berg's Violin Concerto alludes to the young Carinthian girl, Maria Scheuchel, with whom he had an affair and a child in his youth. The Bach chorale introduces a quiet meditation on the subject of death, inspired by that of Alma Mahler's young daughter, Manon Gropius, to whom the work is dedicated.

[38] Cited in HLG 2, pp. 474–75 (HLGF 2, p. 214).

rhythms and grotesque minuets. On the other hand, the first movement of the Eighth also evokes a far-off epoch, yet in quite another manner and without a shade of irony. Indeed, this symphony as a whole can be considered an attempt to synthesize all historical forms (symphony, cantata, oratorio, motet, song cycle) as well as all manner of styles (from homophonic to elaborately contrapuntal). Finally, the Eighth can be deemed the crossroads of all techniques of tonal composition, from the strictest to the freest.[39] In Mahler's last completed symphony, the Ninth, the harsh caricature of the scherzo, the parodistic fugatos, the ironic canons, and the quasiperpetual movement of rapid quavers in the Rondo-Burleske may be considered "music about music," and even "critical music," to use another of Adorno's favorite terms. Most of these strikingly modern features would not be out of place in a score of the 1920s, and it is not surprising that commentators who view Mahler as a direct precursor of Schoenberg and his students invariably point to the Ninth.[40]

Of course Mahler never composed from a preexistent model (as Stravinsky certainly did in works such as *Pulcinella*), nor can one say that his musical thought was fertilized by the past in the way that Stravinsky's was; nevertheless, the play upon allusions and reminiscences is a fundamental feature of Mahler's style. The presence of heterogeneous material in his music can be at least partly explained by his living in an infinitely rich, polyglot, multiracial, multicultural, and multinational society, the Vienna of 1900.

As noted above, a compilation of "reminiscences" already identified in Mahler's music accompanies this essay. Not all of them are convincing, of course, but a large number of them are entirely so. The fragments quoted are of very diverse origins. One could, of course, find allusions and quotations like these in works of many composers active at the end of the nineteenth century.[41] The weight of the past was then steadily growing, and

---

[39] Cf. Henry-Louis de La Grange, "The Eighth: Exception or Crowning Achievement?" in Eveline Nikkels and Robert Becqué, eds., *A "Mass" for the Masses: Proceedings of the Mahler VIII Symposium, Amsterdam 1988* (Rijswijk, 1992), esp. pp. 135–39.

[40] E.g., Adorno, *Quasi una fantasia*, trans. Livingstone, p. 92; Dieter Schnebel, "Das Spätwerk als Neue Musik," in *Gustav Mahler* (n. 1 above), pp. 169–71.

[41] See n. 11 above.

Mahler's life-long experience as a conductor gave him an acute awareness of music history. Among the predecessors Mahler quotes, Schubert's name occurs many times; this is understandable given that Julius Epstein, Mahler's professor of piano at the Vienna Conservatory, had edited piano music for the complete Schubert edition then underway, and that Mahler had studied with Epstein several of the sonatas which were then still practically unknown. Numerous souvenirs of Schumann in Mahler's music have been cited by Reinhard Kapp, who demonstrates convincingly that the resemblances concern not only the melodic content, but also the formal arrangement. Indeed, Mahler's Schumann reminiscences often occur at points analogous to the structural moment of the Schumann work he is recalling.[42] Kapp accordingly suggests that, in his search for new approaches to symphonic composition, Mahler probably studied the Schumann symphonies, and that his borrowings were therefore conscious and deliberate.

Folk song as a new leaven for the symphony

Much more significant than the classical reminiscences in Mahler are the many fragments borrowed from a folklore that was more "imaginary" than real. As already noted, even in his First Symphony Mahler refused to make any distinction between the superior and inferior spheres of music; like Charles Ives after him, he would "reinstate plebeian music, hitherto excluded, as a legitimate constituent of the 'most elevated' musical forms."[43] Although many other composers, such as Dvořák, Rimsky-Korsakov, and Sibelius, had used or were then using folk themes and rhythms in their symphonies, they raised them to the level of "great music" by incorporating this homespun material into the musical logic of the classical ideal. Mahler went much further, introducing into his symphonies military music (fanfares and marches), *Kurpark* ("spa") music, ländler, waltzes, simple ditties, and so forth, always presented in their "original clothing," and often made the highlight of a large section or even an entire movement. Many essential characteristics of Mahler's oeuvre are, of

---

[42] Kapp, "Schumann Reminiszenzen," p. 343.
[43] Schorske, "Mahler et Ives," p. 87.

course, obvious legacies from romanticism – his aspirations toward the universal and metaphysical, his wish to address humanity as a whole, his long meditative Adagios, and even his proclivity toward strong contrasts. But Mahler's direct allusions to the music of the people – trivial, banal, and of an almost Brechtian realism – strike us very often as being essentially anti-romantic.[44] Mahler needed this plebeian element to further intensify contrasts and conflicts: the banal to bring out the sublime, and vice-versa.[45]

Thanks to these intrusions of the popular, his symphonies emerge as a faithful reflection of a world alienated and broken, which was never to regain its former unity and coherence.[46] The popular or pseudo-popular elements carry within them strong emotional and social connotations, which enable Mahler to combine and juxtapose laughter and compassion, tenderness and terror, death and mockery, coarseness and refinement. Introduced "as a leaven into noble music,"[47] these allusions to the "inferior" sphere create tensions and shock effects that are already modern. Ceaselessly torn between mockery and nostalgia, these episodes also reflect the multicolored spectacle of everyday experience, of its ambiguities and contradictions – a true image of life in all its heterogeneity.

A reinvented folklore

At several points I have drawn attention to "quotations of style" rather than "quotations of substance": this is because the extensive research of Bohemian and Viennese folk music undertaken to identify Mahler's sources has produced only scanty results. Above all, it has confirmed what one already suspected: namely, that Mahler invented most of the pseudo-popular melodies contained in his symphonies.[48] His

---

[44] A good example is the *Wunderhorn* lied "Revelge," in which the sound of the orchestra, predominantly woodwinds and brass, deliberately imitates a military band. Its cruel realism anticipates that of, say, *L'histoire du soldat.*

[45] One of Mahler's earliest surviving letters, written in 1879 to Josef Steiner, is fraught with similar switches of mood (GMB2, no. 5 [GMBE, no. 2]).

[46] See Mahler's letter of December 1909 written to Bruno Walter just after he introduced his First Symphony in New York (GMB2, no. 429 [GMBE, no. 407]).

[47] TAM, p. 54 (TAME, p. 36).

[48] See Vladimir Karbusicky, *Gustav Mahler und seine Umwelt* (Darmstadt, 1978).

"synthetic re-creation, based on certain types of music" that are familiar[49] refers to genres (marches, ländler) or styles (Bohemian or German folk music), but almost never to actual, individual models. In addition to the rearrangement of the popular material, the "known and recognizable objects" are as it were "defamiliarized," "neutralized," "reactivated by the new context, by unexpected intervals and by complex and ambiguous relationships between the phrases."[50]

As the Israeli musicologist Talia Pecker has observed, this distancing of himself, this detachment, can be attributed without any doubt to Mahler's origin as a central European Jew, an eternal "stranger" ("homeless three times over"), someone living in a multinational empire that was really for him a "no man's land." Such a situation inevitably developed in a great Jewish artist the faculty of observation, and engendered a freedom of choice, a freedom of thought, a rejection of any kind of conformism, a refusal of any kind of comfort. It incited Mahler to create each of his works as "a closed world . . . decipherable only by means of a code inherent in the work itself."[51] And that is also the reason why the style, the particular "tone" of Mahler's music, defies all attempts to define it. His "quotation" is often a response to a nostalgic longing, a yearning for a better world, for that "age of innocence" that the Fourth Symphony, for instance, endeavors to revive. As the Roman critic Fidele d'Amico observes,

> Mahler uses his so-to-speak "banal" motives . . . like the words of another world, like objects of nostalgia, symbols of an innocence lost and longed for. When he uses them, it is precisely in the difference of level that exists between their original nature and their [subsequent] arrangement and elaboration that the music takes on its meaning.[52]

The only compositions in which Mahler drew his inspiration directly from authentic popular models are the *Wunderhorn* lieder: in certain of them, the original songs can often be recognized, although profoundly transformed. Mahler also modifies the texts of the poems, sometimes

[49] Morgan, "Ives and Mahler," p. 75.
[50] Ibid.
[51] Talia Pecker-Berio, "Radici ebraiche in Mahler," in Agostino Ziino, ed., *Musica senza aggettivi: Studi per Fedele d'Amico* (Florence, 1991), vol. II, p. 482.
[52] Fidele d'Amico, "Mahler 1860–1960," in *I Casi della musica* (Milan, 1982), p. 402.

significantly so. On first hearing these songs, one is first and foremost impressed by their folkloric simplicity, but closer acquaintance reveals the refined technique of a highly sophisticated artist. Indeed, the compositional procedures are just as complex in the Fourth Symphony and the most intricate of the *Wunderhorn* lieder as in a monumental work like the Eighth Symphony. Nevertheless, Mahler's refinement never detracts from the apparent spontaneity of his pseudo-popular music. Were the characteristic folkish tone not so faithfully preserved, one could speak of serious music masquerading as folk art.

Yet the spontaneity and freshness that the present-day listener immediately perceives in Mahler's *Wunderhorn* songs seemed highly suspect to his contemporaries. Nationalist musicologists such as the Munich critic Rudolf Louis accused him of "speaking German with the accent of an oriental Jew."[53] They saw in his fondness for the *Wunderhorn* no more than a desperate attempt, quite unsuccessful moreover, at assimilation. But Mahler had been steeped in such music throughout his childhood, and he was simply going back to his roots; far from wishing to recreate an artificial folkloric style, he was rediscovering in memory the tone and rhythms of his early years. The nationalist critics were entirely mistaken as to his intentions. Moreover, Mahler was able to compose imaginary folksongs without the self-consciousness of such nationalist musicians as the members of the Wandervogel and Bacchanten movements, who did their best in the early 1900s to revive the lost naïveté of the good old days.[54] No better proof of this is needed than the little *Tanzlied*, "Hans und Grete," which he composed at the age of nineteen, in March of 1880. Much of Mahler's youthful music is already imbued with the spirit of the

---

[53] See HLGF 3, pp. 384–86 (quote from p. 385) and p. 819.

[54] The collections of German folk songs published in Berlin in 1903 and 1908 at the behest of the German Emperor contain nothing by Mahler. On the other hand, two composers as far removed from folk music as Richard Strauss and Max Reger felt compelled to compose songs in folk style at this time: Strauss's Op. 49 (1900–01) contains three, and Reger's sixty *Schlichte Weisen* were all written between 1903 and 1912. Cf. also Mahler's letter to Ludwig Karpath of 2 March 1905, written shortly after seven of the *Wunderhorn* songs were first performed in Vienna (GMB2, no. 341 [GMBE, no. 319]), as well as Edward F. Kravitt's article, "The Trend towards the Folklike, Nationalism, and Their Expression by Mahler and His Contemporaries in the Lied," *Chord and Discord* 2/10 (1963), 40–56.

Wunderhorn, which he did not yet know.[55] The dividing line between humor and irony is all the more difficult to establish because Mahler constantly takes mischievous pleasure in playing on that very ambiguity. But it can also happen that his "quotations" are entirely free of irony, that they express instead a poignant nostalgia for an earlier epoch. On these occasions his stylistic re-creation is just as convincing, as for instance in the trumpet solo of the Second Symphony's Scherzo, and the unforgettable posthorn solo in the Third.[56] The stark despair of the "soldier songs," such as "Zu Straßburg auf der Schanz" and "Der Tamboursg'sell" carries the same conviction. But Mahler also wrote at least one piece in which nostalgia and derision are intimately mingled – namely, the second *Nachtmusik* in the Seventh Symphony mentioned above. Here the style evoked is far removed from the popular, but the seemingly detached view Mahler takes of the material is so disquieting that it makes one acutely uneasy, if only because the few emotional outbursts are always quickly broken off by a return to the stubborn rhythm of the serenade.[57]

From self-quotations to thematic metamorphoses

One last type of borrowing remains to be mentioned: Mahler's self-quotations. Many composers have, of course, quoted themselves, but not as often as he. In any case, no one before Mahler had thought of transforming preexistent lieder into symphonic movements, which Mahler did repeatedly.[58] But although these borrowings constitute an important feature of Mahler's compositional practice, they fall outside the framework of this paper, which focuses upon the various procedures Mahler employed for "music about music." Suffice it to say, however, that the lieder are intro-

---

55 Mahler himself told Richard Specht that he became acquainted with the anthology only in 1888, in Leipzig, while visiting his friends Karl and Marion von Weber (see Specht, *Gustav Mahler* [Berlin, 1913], p. 18). There is no reason to doubt what is obviously a first-hand statement.
56 Second Symphony, third mvt., bars 271–323; Third Symphony, third mvt., bars 256–309, 321–46 and 485–528.
57 Seventh Symphony, fourth mvt., bars 211–15, 247–57, and 319–26.
58 First Symphony, first, second, and third movements; Second Symphony, third and fourth movements; Third Symphony, fifth movement; Fourth Symphony, fourth movement.

duced into the symphonies in such a way as to form an "organic" whole, and that, furthermore, they almost always take on a broader meaning in the symphonic context. Thus "Urlicht" in the Second announces the principal message of the finale, while "Das himmlische Leben" as the finale of the Fourth becomes the culminating point that explains and justifies the whole work.

The "Ewigkeitmotiv." One particularly striking facet of Mahler's self-quotation, however, deserves a word here. Throughout the whole of Mahler's music there recurs a characteristic thematic "kernel" now known as the *Ewigkeitmotiv* ("eternity motive") because it is borrowed from the third act of Wagner's *Siegfried* (the love duet, Brünnhilde's monologue, etc.), where it is associated with the text "Ewig, ewig." Since Mahler frequently conducted both *Siegfried* and the *Siegfried Idyll* (in which this motive is prominent from the beginning), it is difficult to imagine that such a borrowing could have been unconscious. The *Ewigkeitmotiv* begins with a descending fifth, continues with a rising scale and frequently ends with a disjunct interval, rising a third or a fourth (typically to an appoggiatura). Philip T. Barford, apparently the first to draw attention to it more than thirty years ago, located the motive (and its inversion) in the great majority of Mahler's works; the German musicologist Constantin Floros has discussed its appearance in the Second, Fourth, and Eighth Symphonies.[59] The list of its main recurrences is included in the appendix to this article. In the Finale of the Second Symphony it is incorporated into the climactic "Resurrection" theme,[60] which has already been anticipated in the fourth movement, "Urlicht."[61] In the Fourth Symphony, it comes at the end of the Adagio and prepares the way for the ascent into paradise, or at least into the "heavenly life" of the Finale.[62] Appearances of the "Ewigkeit" motive in the

[59] Barford, "Mahler: A Thematic Archetype," *The Music Review* 21 (1960), 297–316, and Floros, *Gustav Mahler*, vol. II: *Mahler und die Symphonik des 19. Jahrhunderts in neuer Deutung* (Wiesbaden, 1977), pp. 259–60 and 408 (Table 58). It has also been studied by the American musicologist James L. Zychowicz, who points out that the theme comes almost always when Mahler is alluding to heaven, to life eternal, or more generally to some form of transcendence ("Quotation and Assimilation: The Ewigkeit Motive in the Music of Mahler," unpublished article, sent to me by the author).

[60] Bars 421–40, 672–76, and 696–702.   [61] Bars 3–5, 27–29, and 63–64.

[62] Bars 45–47, 66–68, 299–303, and 326–32.

Eighth are directly linked to the text: in the first movement it comes in the passage "Accende lumen sensibus" ("Illuminate our senses"), and in the second it is specifically associated with the moment of Faust's final redemption.[63]

In "Ich bin der Welt abhanden gekommen" and in the Adagietto of the Fifth,[64] two pieces whose close thematic affinity has often been pointed out, the *Ewigkeitmotiv* is not so easily explained, unless one assumes that, for the artist, the blissful isolation described in the poem opens the way toward transcendence ("in meinem Himmel, in meinem Lieben, in meinem Lied [in my heaven, in my love, in my song]"). On the other hand, its presence in two of the *Kindertotenlieder*[65] alludes perhaps to the promise, expressed on several occasions in Rückert's poems, of survival after death. The last and most important appearance of the *Ewigkeitmotiv* occurs, appropriately, at the end of *Das Lied von der Erde*. Here, too, the explanation is to be found in the poem: the theme appears first at the crucial moment when the two friends are bidding each other an eternal farewell. Later, it dominates the last pages of the work, as the consoling thought emerges that nature blossoms anew every springtime.[66] While the frequency of this motive in Mahler's music is a unique phenomenon, his choice of a rising motive to symbolize transcendence is thoroughly traditional: already in the Renaissance and baroque eras such symbolic meaning was attributed to similar melodic patterns.

"The lion consists of all the lambs it has devoured"

After such a lengthy discussion of reminiscences and quotations in Mahler, it may seem surprising if I draw to a close by suggesting that, in my opinion, they really do not matter all that much. Yet that is the conclusion I propose. We observed in passing that Mahler's music, despite its allusions to various folk styles, does not subscribe to any "nationalist" conception of art. But neither is it "trans-national" in the sense of being a polyglot mixture. Its elements are fused and merged into a perfectly coherent whole

---

[63] Eighth Symphony, first mvt., bars 263–64 and 565–66; second mvt., bars 221–25, 270–71, 385–89, 396–99, 1414–17, 1467–75.

[64] Fifth Symphony, fourth movement, bars 2–6, 50–52, etc.

[65] No. 2, bars 5–6, 29–30, 43–44, and 65–66.

[66] "Der Abschied," bars 202–6 and 464–67.

144

– so coherent, indeed, that I doubt whether Mahler, at heart, could have felt as guilty about the heterogeneity of his *objets trouvés* as he himself pretended, at least during his consultation with Freud. In any case, the melodic material in his music loses much of its original value because of the variety and flexibility of the development to which he subjects it. Thus, whether it is "borrowed" or not is of little importance. Valéry's well-known phrase, which Hans Keller applied to Stravinsky's music, may also be apropos of Mahler's: "The lion consists of the lambs he has devoured."[67] And the French musicologist Dominique Jameux imagines Mahler saying:"from an external given, and by means of technique, to produce *my* honey."[68]

To the Berlin critic Max Marschalk, himself a composer, Mahler one day explained his aesthetic principles thus:

> *Mood*-music [*Stimmungsmusik*] is dangerous ground. Believe me: for the moment nothing has changed: *Themes* – clear and *plastic,* so that one easily recognizes them in each transformation and further development – and then a *varied* presentation, gripping above all because of the logical *development* of the inner idea – and on the other hand, because of the *genuine opposition* of the conflicting motives.[69]

"Thought-out" music

Because "logical development" and thematic elaboration were for him the twin pillars of all composition, Mahler criticized composers such as Verdi, Tchaikovsky, Johann Strauss, and even Schubert, to whom melodic inspiration came easily, for not knowing what to do with the treasures supplied by their imagination. Surprisingly, he included Brahms in the same category as well.[70] What matters in Mahler's music is less the nature of the material than its treatment, because his inspiration is always subjected to a thorough compositional process, regardless of its origin.

---

[67] Hans Keller (and Milein Cosman), *Stravinsky Seen and Heard* (London, 1982), p. 10.

[68] "d'un donné extérieur, et via une technique, produire *mon* miel." Dominique Jameux, "Gustav Mahler et Pierre Boulez: Parallélisme/Divergences," in *Colloque international Gustav Mahler* (n. 34 above), p. 79.

[69] GMB2, no. 169 (GMBE, no. 160), 12 April 1896; cf. also HLG 1, pp. 358–59.

[70] See Mahler's three letters to Alma from June 1904 in AMML4, pp. 238–40 as well as the postscript on p. 236, and also HLG 2, pp. 707–8.

Even the *Naturlaute* undergo such treatment. In the opening of the First Symphony, for example, the cuckoo song has its characteristic interval of a third transformed into a fourth, and that becomes the parent cell of the entire first movement. Later, Mahler subjected bird song to even more astonishing transformations in the Seventh and Ninth Symphonies, and in *Das Lied von der Erde* (see above, p. 128).

Mahler knew, perhaps better than any other composer, how to avoid platitudes and constantly renew interest through technical procedures of which he was a master.[71] The technique of the "variant," ever-present in his symphonies, is analyzed by Theodor Adorno: not only are the melodic elements ceaselessly transformed, but their places and functions themselves constantly vary. Erwin Stein, writing about the first movement of the Fourth Symphony, strikingly compares the various motives to a pack of playing cards that the player shuffles continuously.[72] In his analysis of Mahler's compositional procedures, the German musicologist Reinhard Kapp observes that none of his themes is ever "given," but rather always "composed," in the original sense of the word – i.e., put together of elements that are meant to be varied, developed and transformed.[73] Luciano Berio, whose *Sinfonia* composed sixty years after Mahler's death is a fascinating commentary on the Second Symphony's Scherzo, noted that the Mahlerian melody was formed of

> elements of a banal nature which scatter, dilate, turn upside down, disappear, change one another reciprocally because they exchange their specific characters.
>
> . . .
>
> . . . One cannot speak of a true melody, but of a melodic process characterized in its turn on the level not of totality and finality, but of details which confer on that totality a new, hitherto unheard musical meaning.

[71] In 1906 Alma writes to Mahler, who is then conducting Mozart's *Figaro* in Salzburg, and inserts in the letter a short quotation from the second movement of the Eighth Symphony, which Mahler obviously played for her on the piano before leaving Maiernigg. In his reply, he expresses amazement that she should have remembered so much after a single hearing and attempts to correct the end of the quotation. But he cannot remember what he himself had written, and adds: "It continues in every possible way but not this one, which would make it a very ordinary sequence!" (Bibliothèque musicale Gustav Mahler, Paris).

[72] Erwin Stein, *Orpheus in New Guises* (London, 1953), p. 7.

[73] Kapp, "Schumann Reminiszenzen," p. 330.

The details emerge from a plan of construction that produces ineluctable events.[74]

A singular unity

In spite of appearances, therefore, Mahler does not refer to the past, nor to folk music, but rather assimilates them and integrates them into a discourse entirely his own. What makes him already a twentieth-century composer is his manner of distancing himself from his material, whether borrowed or recreated from models, and his extreme stylization of it. His music is unlike all other music in that it is both composite and strictly unitary. One must be careful therefore, to my mind, not to over-interpret most of his "allusions," especially in a work like the Seventh Symphony, where they are particularly numerous. In the second movement, for example, fragments of military music (urban music par excellence) are directly mingled with bird song (evoking the countryside and nature). The same birds are heard at the end of the Ninth Symphony's initial Andante, in a stylized "cadence" wherein melodic lines, as if suspended in space, pursue their individual ways, wholly independent of each other in pitch, rhythm, and note-values. The original *Naturlaut* is no more than a distant reference in this passage, yet the music itself, in its apparent freedom and spontaneity, still takes its inspiration from nature. On the other hand, in the Finale of the Seventh, the various elements seem impossible to synthesize into a whole, unless one invokes the Joycean notion of "stream of consciousness." Sudden breaks, constant mood changes, irony travestied as jubilation, or

---

[74] "des éléments de nature banale qui s'éparpillent, se dilatent, retournent sur eux-mêmes, disparaissent, s'altèrent réciproquement parce qu'ils échangent leurs caractères spécifiques.

. . .

. . . Il ne s'agit pas d'une véritable mélodie mais d'un processus mélodique constitué d'éléments extrêmement caractérisés. Processus mélodique à son tour caractérisé non pas au plan de la totalité et de la finalité mais des détails qui confèrent à cette totalité un sens musical jamais entendu auparavant. Les détails se détachent d'un plan de construction producteur d'événements inéluctables." Berio, "Une mélodie de Gustav Mahler," in *Colloque international Gustav Mahler* (n. 34 above), p. 111. Contrary to Berio, Theodor Adorno considers that Mahler's forms are not laid out in advance, but emerge, so to speak, spontaneously as the "symphonic novel" unfolds.

vice versa, create from the beginning a feeling of uneasiness further heightened by the already mentioned quotation from *Die Meistersinger* that, heard so early in the movement, immediately catches the ear. Yet the allusion is doubly ambiguous, because Wagner's own procedures marked the beginning of a new ambiguity between "scholarly" and "comic." And this ambiguity is subsequently prolonged by the minuet episodes of the Seventh's finale, which keep recurring when one least expects them.

For us today these intrusions, allusions, sudden halts, these changes of mood and tone, are among the most characteristic features of Mahler's style, features that make his music immediately recognizable. Nevertheless, any systematic interpretation of these "second degree" procedures is pointless, and even dangerous, since it could lead to wrong conclusions. The search might then go on indefinitely, since Mahler, not content to change his mood, does not hesitate to interrupt the flow of the music, sometimes to insert a fragment that is utterly out of context. The truth is that he remains completely himself and always uses an original, inimitable, infinitely varied, and interesting language; his characteristic "tone" could never for a moment be mistaken for anyone else's. Irony, tragedy, nostalgia: one might attempt to sum up Mahler in those three moods, since they are combined in his music as in that of no other composer. But those are only the three most recognizable facets of the prism that refracts his whole conception of the world and of life.

Mahler's borrowings from all sides express not only his "rebellion against the constraints placed on music by private bourgeois conventionality," as Adorno has written.[75] They are above all indispensable to his universal message. Adorno has found a particularly apt metaphor to express this: "With the freedom of a man not entirely overwhelmed by culture, in his musical vagrancy he picks up the fragment of glass that he finds on the road and holds it up to the sun so that all its colors are refracted."[76] And he concludes: "Every bar in Mahler's music opens wide its arms."[77] By quoting all styles, by introducing street music into the symphony, Mahler has indeed succeeded, as he himself put it, in "constructing a universe."[78]

---

[75] Adorno, *Quasi una fantasia*, trans. Livingstone, pp. 84–85 (*Gesammelte Schriften*, vol. XVI, p. 326).   [76] TAM, p. 54 (TAME, p. 36).
[77] TAM, p. 57 (TAME, p. 38).   [78] NBL2, p. 35 (NBLE, p. 40).

APPENDIX: MUSICAL EXAMPLES

Roman numerals indicate the number of a symphony; a virgule followed by an arabic numeral indicates the number of a movement within a work (e.g., "Mahler, V/2" means Mahler's Fifth Symphony, second movement).

Ex. 6.1 (a) Mozart, Symphony no. 36 in C, K. 425 ("Linz") /2; (b) Mahler, I/2, trio

Ex. 6.2 (a) Beethoven, Quartet no. 16 in F, op. 135 /3; (b) Mahler, III/6

Ex. 6.3 (a) Beethoven, IV/1; (b) Mahler, I/1

Ex. 6.4   (a) Beethoven, IX/3; (b) Mahler, II/1

Ex. 6.5   (a) Beethoven, VIII/2; (b) Mahler, III/3

Ex. 6.6   (a) Beethoven, Fourth Piano Concerto in G, op. 58 /1; (b) and (c) Mahler, IV/1

150

Ex. 6.7 (a) Beethoven, *Fidelio*, act I, no. 3; (b) Mahler, IV/3

Ex. 6.8 (a) Schubert, "Mainacht," D. 194; (b) Mahler, *Lieder eines fahrenden Gesellen*, no. 1

Ex. 6.9 (a) Schubert, Piano Sonata in E♭, D. 568 /1; (b) Mahler, IV/1

Ex. 6.10 (a) Schubert, Piano Sonata in A minor, D. 784 /1; (b) Mahler, I/1

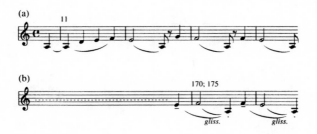

Ex. 6.11 (a) Schubert, Piano Sonata in G, D. 894 /4; (b) Mahler, "Lob des hohen Verstandes"

Ex. 6.12 (a) Schubert, Piano Sonata in G, D. 894 /3; (b) Mahler, "Rheinlegendchen"

Ex. 6.13 (a) Schubert, Piano Sonata in D, D. 850 /4; (b) Mahler, IV/4

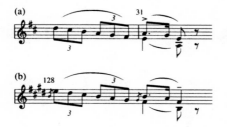

Ex. 6.14 (a) Schubert, Impromptu no. 1 in C minor, op. 90, D. 899; (b) Mahler, VII/2

Ex. 6.15 (a) Schumann, II/4; (b) Mahler, VII/5

Ex. 6.16 (a) Schumann, III/1; (b) Mahler, VIII/1

Ex. 6.17 (a) Schumann, III/3; (b) Mahler, II/2

Ex. 6.18 (a) Schumann, III/5; (b) Mahler, I/4

Ex. 6.19 (a) Schumann, III/5; (b) Mahler, I/4

Ex. 6.20   (a) Schumann, III/5; (b) Mahler, I/1

Ex. 6.21   (a) Schumann, IV/1; (b) Mahler, I/4

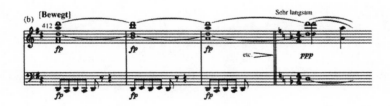

Ex. 6.22   (a) Schumann, *Dichterliebe*, op. 48, no. 9, "Das ist ein Flöten und Geigen"; (b) Mahler, II/3

155

Ex. 6.23   (a) Schumann, *Kinderszenen*, op. 15, no. 7; (b) Mahler, VII/4

Ex. 6.24   (a) Schumann, II/3; (b) Mahler, *Das Lied von der Erde*, no. 6, "Der Abschied"

Ex. 6.25 (a) Schumann, *Manfred Overture*, op. 115; (b) Mahler, VI/1

Ex. 6.26 (a) Schumann, Piano Quintet in E♭, op. 44 /2; (b) Mahler, V/1

157

Ex. 6.27 (a) Chopin, Ballade No. 1 in G minor, op. 23; (b) Mahler, V/2

Ex. 6.28 (a) Chopin, Nocturne in E, op. 62, no. 2; (b) Mahler, I/4

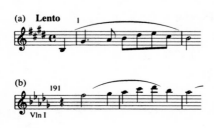

Ex. 6.29 (a) Liszt, Piano Concerto no. 1 in E♭; (b) Mahler, VI/1

Ex. 6.30 (a) Liszt, *Rhapsodie espagnole* for piano; (b) Mahler, III/3

Ex. 6.31   (a) Bizet, *Carmen*, act III, scene 19; (b) Mahler, VII/2

Ex. 6.32   (a) Bizet, *Carmen*, act III, scene 19; (b) Mahler, VII/2

Ex. 6.33   (a) Bizet, *Carmen*, act II, scene 14; (b) Mahler, VII/2

Ex. 6.34   (a) Bizet, *Carmen*, act I, prelude; (b) Mahler, VII/2

Ex. 6.35   (a) Bizet, *L'Arlésienne* Suite no. 1/3, Adagietto; (b) Mahler, V/4, Adagietto (harp arpeggiations omitted)

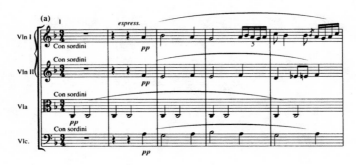

160

Ex. 6.36   (a) Musorgsky, *Boris Godunov*, act I, scene 1; (b) Mahler, *Das Lied von der Erde*, no. 2, "Der Einsame im Herbst"

Ex. 6.37   (a) Wagner, *Die Walküre*, act I, scene 2 (Hunding's entrance); (b) Mahler, II/1

Ex. 6.38   (a) Wagner, *Götterdämmerung*, act II, scene 5 (Brünnhilde);
(b) Mahler, *Das klagende Lied*, part III, "Hochzeitsstück"; (c) Mahler, *Lieder eines fahrenden Gesellen*, no. 3

Ex. 6.39   (a) Smetana, Overture to *The Bartered Bride*; (b) Mahler, I/4

Ex. 6.40   (a) Bruckner, IV/3 (Trio); (b) Mahler, II/3 (also "Des Antonius von Padua Fischpredigt")

Ex. 6.41   (a) Bruckner, IX/3; (b) Mahler, X/1

(a) **Langsam, feierlich**

(b) **Adagio**

Ex. 6.42   (a) Brahms, Piano Concerto no. 2 in B♭, op. 83/1; (b) Mahler, I/1

(a)

(b)

Ex. 6.43   (a) Beethoven, IX/4; (b) Brahms, I/4; (c) Mahler, III/1

(a)

(b)

(c)

163

Ex. 6.44   (a) Brahms, I/3; (b) Mahler, IV/1

Ex. 6.45   (a) Brahms, II/1; (b) Mahler, V/3

Ex. 6.46   (a) Brahms, II/4; (b) Mahler, I/1

164

Ex. 6.47 (a) Brahms, *German Requiem*, op. 45 /1; (b) Mahler, II/5

Ex. 6.48 (a) Brahms, *German Requiem*, op. 45 /3; (b) Mahler, III/1

Ex. 6.49 (a) Weber, *Oberon*, act I, scene 2; (b) Mahler, *Lieder eines fahrenden Gesellen*, no. 3

Ex. 6.50   (a) Lehár, *The Merry Widow*, finale (no. 16); (b) Mahler, IX/3; (c) Mahler, VII/5

Ex. 6.51   (a) Wagner, *Tristan und Isolde*, prelude ("suffering" motive); (b) Tristan, prelude ("gaze" motive); (c) Mahler, *Kindertotenlieder*, no. 2, "Nun seh' ich wohl, warum so dunkle Flammen"

166

The "Ewigkeit" motive in Mahler's oeuvre

Ex. 6.52   (a) Wagner, *Siegfried*, act III, scene 3 (Brünnhilde); (b) Mahler, II/5

Ex. 6.53   Mahler, II/5

Ex. 6.54   Mahler, IV/3

Ex. 6.55   Mahler, "Ich bin der Welt abhanden gekommen"

Ex. 6.56   Mahler, V/4

Ex. 6.57 Mahler, *Kindertotenlieder*, no. 2, "Nun seh' ich wohl, warum so dunkle Flammen"

be - reits zur Heim-kehr schik-ke

Ex. 6.58 Mahler, VIII/1

ff Ac -cen - de,   ac - cen-de lu - men sen-si-bus

Ex. 6.59 Mahler, VIII/2

Ge - ret - tet   ist das ed - le Glied   der Geis-ter - welt vom Bö - sen:

Ex. 6.60 Mahler, VIII/2

zieht uns hin-an,___   zieht uns hin-an,___   zieht uns hin-an,___

Ex. 6.61 (a) and (b): Mahler, *Das Lied von der Erde*, no. 6, "Der Abschied"

(a)

O   Freund, an   dei - ner   Sei   -   te

(b)

all   ü - - ber - - all ___

7 "*Ihm in die Lieder zu blicken*": Mahler's Seventh Symphony sketchbook

STEPHEN E. HEFLING

For Edward R. Reilly, with gratitude, in honor of his retirement.

Blicke mir nicht in die Lieder!	*Do not look at my songs!*
Deine Neugier ist Verrat, ist Verrat!	*Your curiosity is betrayal, betrayal!*
Bienen, wenn sie Zellen bauen,	*Bees, when they build their cells,*
lassen auch nicht zu sich schauen . . .	*likewise do not let themselves be watched . . .*

Mahler / Rückert, "Blicke mir nicht in die Lieder" (1901)

The text of "Blicke mir nicht in die Lieder" is as characteristic of Mahler
as if he himself had written the poem. Natalie Bauer-Lechner, August 1901[1]

It has long been known that, especially from about 1900 on, Mahler made use of pocket sketchbooks to preserve musical ideas for immediate or future use. But studies of these notebooks, which are among the earliest stages in Mahler's compositional process, have been considerably limited,

Research for this study was conducted during several visits to Vienna that were variously supported by a Martha Baird Rockefeller Grant-in-Aid for Musicology, a Morse Fellowship for Junior Faculty at Yale University, a Griswold Grant for research abroad from Yale University, and a Research Grant from the American Philosophical Society. I am also grateful to the late Anna Mahler for permission to obtain a microfilm of the sketchbook, as well as to Frau Dr. Christine Gruber of the Theatersammlung in the Österreichische Nationalbibliothek, Hofrat Dr. Oskar Pausch, director of the Österreichisches Theatermuseum, and especially Frau Jarmila Weissenböck of the Theatermuseum, for their kind assistance in providing access to the autograph manuscript and permission to publish portions of it.

[1] NBL2, p. 194 (NBLE, p. 174). Cf. also Mahler's comments from the summer of 1893 about eavesdropping while his works were in progress: "To me it is as if a mother would undress herself and expose to the world the child in the womb before it is born" (NBL2, 34 [NBLE, 39]).

and that for two reasons. First, only two are known to survive, and even these have probably come down to us by accident. In August of 1901 Natalie Bauer-Lechner recorded the following conversation with Mahler in her diary:

> G[ustav] spoke of his sketchbooks and sketch sheets: "For God's sake, that they aren't preserved and don't outlive me – I will see to that and will destroy everything that is unfinished. For they only give rise to misunderstandings. What have they divined from Beethoven's! That, for instance, he supposedly worked simultaneously on compositions which are completely different from each other ... That's nothing! ... Or they say that the completed work signifies such progress beyond the sketched draft; meanwhile, they have no notion of what entirely different things could have come from such a first inkling in his hands!"[2]

Of course Mahler did not destroy everything unfinished; he in fact gave a number of important sketches and drafts to Natalie, who, as he must have known, had quietly assumed the role of his Eckermann and Boswell. The two extant pocket sketchbooks were not in Natalie's collection; they have, however, long been inaccessible – the second reason why this stage of the compositional process has not been studied. The later of the booklets, which contains material for the Ninth Symphony plus ideas not associated with any of Mahler's known oeuvre, was in a private collection until 1994.[3] The earlier, pertaining to the Seventh Symphony (and also containing unused material), was until recently restricted according to

---

[2] Natalie Bauer-Lechner, "Mahleriana" (unpublished manuscript, Bibliothèque musicale Gustav Mahler, Paris); the German text will be found in my "'Variations in nuce': A Study of Mahler Sketches and a Comment on Sketch Studies," *Beiträge '79–80 der Österreichischen Gesellschaft für Musik: Gustav Mahler Kolloquium 1979* (Kassel, 1981), p. 125, n. 13. Cf. also HLG 2, p. 362.

[3] This notebook was long in the possession of Hannah Adler, widow of the conductor F. Charles Adler, who willed it to the musicologist H. C. Robbins Landon; in 1994 it was acquired by the Musiksammlung of the Österreichische Nationalbibliothek in Vienna (Mus. Hs. 41.634). I am grateful to Prof. Landon, and especially to Hofrat Dr. Günter Brosche, director of the Musiksammlung, for their kind efforts in helping me to examine this sketchbook. It has been transcribed from photocopies (without regard to original pagination) in Colin Matthews, *Mahler at Work: Aspects of the Creative Process* (D.Phil thesis, University of Sussex, 1977; repr. New York, 1989), pp. 105–24; a more detailed study by the present author is in progress.

provisions of the Anna Bahr-Mildenburg Nachlaß, which is in the Österreichisches Theatermuseum; with grateful acknowledgment to that institution, the present essay undertakes the first detailed examination of it.

A bibliographic description of the sketchbook and an inventory of its
contents are given in the table below. In brief, it is an oblong booklet
approximately 3 × 5 inches in size that contains thirty leaves (originally
thirty-two), on each side of which six staves are printed; the binding is
black imitation leather, with "Skizzen" ("Sketches") embossed near the
upper-right corner. (The "Ninth Symphony" sketchbook is of identical
manufacture.) Slipped over the cover is a paper sleeve that bears the following dramatic inscription in the handwriting of Anna Bahr-Mildenburg, the
famous Wagnerian soprano with whom Mahler had a passionate affair in
Hamburg (1895–97), and who later sang at the Vienna Court Opera under
Mahler's direction:

> Gustav Mahler's last sketchbook. It lay on his breast when he died. His
> father-in-law Moll kept it and gave it to me today, 25 January 1943, when
> he visited me. I also gave him letters from Gustav Mahler to read.[4]

Karl Moll, Alma Mahler's stepfather, was in fact present in the hospital
room when Mahler expired, and it was he who took the well-known death
mask of the composer. But for several days before he died Mahler's condition had been such that he could scarcely move, let alone compose.
Moreover, it had been his habit for nearly twenty years to reserve the task of
composing new music "from scratch" for his summer holidays, when the
peace of the Austrian countryside afforded him the necessary relaxation
and concentration to follow his muse. Thus it seems altogether unlikely that
he kept a sketchbook at hand in hospital; nor does any among the several
fairly detailed accounts of his final days even hint that the dying composer
continued to work until the last.[5] As we shall see, both the content and the
ordering of material in this notebook suggest that Mahler used it chiefly
(perhaps exclusively) during the summer of 1905, when he composed the
first, third, and fifth movements of his Seventh Symphony. Whether Moll or
Mildenburg is chiefly responsible for the "last sketchbook" myth, and how

---

[4] The German text is given in Table 7.1.
[5] See AMML4, pp. 191–201, and HLGF 3, pp. 965–85.

Moll came to possess the notebook in the first place, are questions that must remain unanswered, at least for the moment.[6]

Mahler's use of sketchbooks

The memoirs of both Natalie Bauer-Lechner and Alma Mahler mention Mahler's use of sketchbooks during composing holidays, which provides us with some notion of the contexts in which the notebooks came into play. As usual, Natalie is the more substantive reporter; her several journal entries seem to indicate that Mahler carried such booklets in his youth, and also during the composition of the Third and Fourth Symphonies. In his younger days Mahler apparently made no systematic effort to preserve inspirations that were not immediately needed for the work at hand. During the summer of 1893, for example, he was making no progress toward the finale of the Second Symphony because instead of ideas in 4/4 time (the meter he needed), only 3/4 themes came into his mind; Natalie then asked him, "What do you do with these uninvited tones? Surely you don't let them go entirely, but save them up?" To which Mahler responded:

> No, they are nothing, nothing but unborn thoughts, expressions that were able to arise under conditions favorable to them, and therefore they arose.

[6] To judge from Alma Mahler's memoirs – *And the Bridge is Love* (New York, 1958) and *Mein Leben* (Frankfurt am Main, 1960) – she had scant regard for her stepfather Moll. Indeed, Alma claims that after she and Werfel fled Austria in 1937, Moll and his son-in-law (both Nazis) plundered her Vienna home (*Mein Leben*, pp. 261 and 366–67); and it is well known that Moll transferred Alma's collection of paintings, including three by her father Emil Schindler, to the Österreichische Galerie, from which she never recovered them (see Andrew Decker, "A Legacy of Shame: Nazi Art Loot in Austria," *Art News* 83/10 [December 1984], 54 ff., esp. 64–65). When Alma returned briefly to Austria in 1947, she found that both Mahler's and Werfel's writing desks "with their irreplaceable treasure of letters and manuscripts" had been destroyed by an Allied bomb; "all I recovered was a couple of the small notebooks Mahler used to carry with him" (*Mein Leben*, p. 366; *And the Bridge is Love*, pp. 299–300). Apparently, then, more of Mahler's sketchbooks did survive until the last days of World War II. It is therefore not out of the question that Moll acquired the Seventh Symphony notebook by less than honest means, and that, not knowing what it actually contained, he himself made up the "last sketchbook" story when he presented it to Mildenburg in 1943. The Ninth Symphony sketchbook (n. 3 above) may be one of those that Alma recovered in 1947; the late Mrs. F. Charles Adler told me she thought her husband had obtained it from Alma after the war.

Table 7.1. *Description and contents of the sketchbook*

Mahler, Gustav, 1860–1911

> Letztes Skizzenbuch. [n.p.: n.d., 1905?]
>
> score (64 pp.) 8 × 12.7 cm.

> Holograph.
>
> Cover title: Skizzen.
>
> Composed at Maiernigg, Austria, 1905(?).
>
> Leaves [3–4], part of Symphony No. 7 sketches,
>
> torn out at different times.
>
> Inside front cover: Gustav Mahler / letztes Skizzenbuch; in the hand of
> Anna Bahr-Mildenburg
>
> Detachable sleeve: Gustav Mahlers' letztes Skizzenbuch. Es lag als er
> gestorben war auf seiner Brust. Sein Schwiegervater Moll nahm es an sich u.
> schenkte es mir heute am 25 Janner 1943 als er mich besuchte. Ich gab ihm
> auch Briefe von Gustav Mahler zu lesen; in the hand of Anna Bahr-
> Mildenburg.
>
> In original binding: full imitation leather (black oil cloth).
>
> Stamped on inside back cover: J. Mayr & A. Fessler [stationery store,
> Kärntnerstraße, Vienna].

> The booklet comprises four sewn signatures of four bifolios (= 8 leaves
> [16 pages] per signature). Each page contains six printed staves. Folio
> numbers in an unknown hand were added from the back of notebook
> (inverted), after leaves [3–4] were removed. The sketches are in pencil with
> (very few) corrections in ink; diagonal lines in blue crayon through entire
> pages indicate their use in the Seventh Symphony.
>
> Colophon: N°. 80. / Jos. Eberle & C°. Musikaliendruckerei Wien, VII;
> appears in left or right margin of eight pages. Watermark: J. E. & Co / WIEN;
> fragments visible in leaves numbered 10, 21, and 22.

Contents

(Folio numbers in boldface preceded by asterisks indicate materials adopted
in the Seventh Symphony. FV = "Final Version," ed. Erwin Ratz, Kritische
Gesamtausgabe, vol. VII [Berlin, 1960].)

Table 7.1 (*cont.*)

Folio	Meter	Tonality	Description
1r	3/4	a	Two brief fragments on separate systems, of 3 and 4 bars' duration respectively; no continuity from either.
1v	4/4	D, a	Three brief fragments on separate systems: 4 bars (D major), 2 bars (tonality uncertain), 2 bars (a minor); no continuity from any of them.
2r	4/4	C	6 continuous bars on 2 systems; no continuity from end of this sketch
2v	3/4	C to g	7 continuous bars on 2 systems; no continuity from end of this sketch
3r	4/4	C, shifting	14 continuous bars on 3 systems; recurring progression of I–V–deception (= ♭VI, ♮VI major); bars 13–14 seem related to the finale of Mahler's Sixth Symphony, bars 192–94 (and related spots). Sketch continues onto fol. 3v.
3v	4/4	C, ending in D	11½ continuous bars on 3 systems, proceeding on from fol. 3r. Encircled D major bar on second system may be related to encircled bar at top of fol. 4r; otherwise, no direct continuity from end of this sketch.
4r	4/4	C	One encircled bar perhaps related to fol. 3v (see above); then two C major fragments on separate systems, of 5 and 9 bars' duration respectively. Second fragment introduces motive of open-string ostinato accompaniment (here

174

Table 7.1 (*cont.*)

Folio	Meter	Tonality	Description
			C/g/d, "pizz", and d/a, "Celli"), which is also prominent on fols. 5v–6v. No direct continuity from this sketch, which appears generally related to material following on fol. 4v.
4v	4/4	C	Two generally related sketches of 7 bars (1 system) and 11 bars (2 systems). First system provisionally linked by arrow to second system of fol. 5r. Direct continuity to fol. 5r; last two bars of second system encircled, provisionally to be replaced by opening bars of fol. 5r.
5r	4/4	C	9 continuous bars on 2 systems; bass line of last 3 bars = opening motive of fol. 4v. No direct continuity from this page.
5v	4/4	C	Three related fragments on 3 systems, each 4 bars in length; variants and incipient development of ideas on fols. 4v–5r (including recurrence of open-string ostinato, G/d/a). No direct continuity from this page.
6r	4/4	C, modulating	22 continuous bars on 3 systems; material closely related to fols. 4r and ff., esp. open-string ostinato accompaniment, which yields harmonies that at times seem polytonal; basic tonal scheme = C (4½ bars), a (7 bars), d (10½ bars). Sketch continues directly onto fol. 6v.

Table 7.1 (*cont.*)

Folio	Meter	Tonality	Description
6v	4/4	d to C	9 bars on 2 systems of 3 lines each, continuing from fol. 6r. Open-string ostinato continues to yield quasi-polytonal sonorities. No direct continuity from this sketch.
7r	4/4	A, c♯	Three related sketches on 3 systems, of 5, 4, and 8 bars' duration respectively. First 2 systems begin in A and modulate; third system, which contains main motive of fols. 3r–3v, begins in c♯, apparently modulating to d. No direct continuity from this page.
7v	4/4	D, modulating	11 continuous bars of new material on 3 systems. Bars 1–2 and 9–10 distinctly related to finale of Mahler's Ninth Symphony, bars 3–4 and 7–8 (plus similar spots). No direct continuity from this sketch.
8r	4/4	modulating	Three related fragments on 3 systems of 3, 5, and 3 bars' duration respectively. Bars 1–2 distinctly related to finale of Mahler's Ninth Symphony, bars 126–27; bars 8 and 11 distinctly related to first movement of the Ninth, bar 33. No direct continuity from this page.
8v	3/4	a	12 bars of continuous scherzo-like material on two systems; continues directly onto fol. 9r. Cue marking "Seite X" ("Page X") indicates further sketching of scherzo material on fol. 12v.

Table 7.1 (*cont.*)

Folio	Meter	Tonality	Description
9r	3/4	a	17 bars on 3 systems continuing scherzo from fol. 8v. No direct continuity from this sketch.
9v	3/4	D, modulating	16 bars on 3 systems similar in some respects to material on fols. 8v–9r; perhaps a D major trio for the A minor scherzo. Continues directly onto fol. 10r.
10r	3/4	D	9 bars on 2 systems; opening idea from fol. 9v recurs in bars 3 ff., rounding off sketch with 7 bars (plus anacrusis) concluding in D. No direct continuity from this sketch.
*10v	"3/2"	e	11 bars on 3 systems, closely corresponding to bars 495–500 and 502–04 of Seventh Symphony, first movement (recapitulation, high point of movement). Two bars not found in FV precede the equivalent of bar 502. Continues directly onto fol. 11r.
*11r	3/2	e	10 bars on 3 systems, closely corresponding to bars 505–11 of Seventh Symphony, first movement. First system (2 bars plus anacrusis) = preliminary melodic sketch for bars 505–6. One bar (encircled) not found in FV precedes equivalent of bar 510. Continues directly onto fol. 11v.
*11v	3/2	e	12 bars on 3 systems, closely corresponding to bars 512–22 of Seventh Symphony, first

Table 7.1 (*cont.*)

Folio	Meter	Tonality	Description
			movement (= just prior to final coda). One bar (encircled) not found in FV precedes equivalent of bar 514. No direct continuity from this sketch.
*12r	"2/2"	e	17 bars on 3 systems. First 6 bars on first system correspond closely to Seventh Symphony, first movement, bars 50–55 (= first presentation of main theme in FV). Remainder of page melodically related to this material, but not found in FV. No direct continuity from this page.
12v	3/4	a	6 bars on 2 systems, related to scherzo material on fols. 8v–9r, as also indicated by the cue "X" that heads the sheet. No direct continuity from this page.
13r	3/4	modulating	6 bars on 2 systems, related to scherzo material on fols. 8v–9r and 12v. No direct continuity from this page.
13v–27r	—	—	BLANK

[Sketchbook inverted; folio numbering now reads backward. Folio "30v" is the first page in this segment of the book; "30r" plus "29v" constitute an opening; etc.]

*30v	4/4	b (3 ♯s)	7 bars on 3 systems; preliminary ideas for bars 2–3, 4–5, and 9 of Seventh Symphony, first movement. No direct continuity from this page.

Table 7.1 (*cont.*)

Folio	Meter	Tonality	Description
*30r	4/4	F	11 bars on 3 systems, closely corresponding to bars 118–28 of Seventh Symphony, first movement (= the third subject in FV, but there in C major). Continues directly onto fol. 29v.
*29v	4/4	(F) modulating	4 bars on 2 systems, closely corresponding to bars 129–31 of Seventh Symphony, first movement. First system = preliminary melodic sketch for bar 129. Horizontal line across entire page beneath second system, plus annotation "Es-dur probieren" ("try E♭"). No direct continuity from this page.
*29r	"3/2", "2/2"	C	9½ bars on 3 systems, closely corresponding to bars 87–95 of Seventh Symphony, finale. Appears to have continued on next page, now missing; no direct continuity to other pages currently included in this sketchbook.

[Two leaves torn out (before folios were numbered)]

Folio	Meter	Tonality	Description
*28v	3/2, 4/4	(B), (G)	13 bars on 3 systems. The first 8 correspond closely to bars 436–49 of Seventh Symphony, first movement (= recapitulation of second theme, but meter in FV = ¢). This material leads directly into a transitional passage, beginning in G major, found in bars 136–40 of FV; continues directly onto fol. 28r.

179

Table 7.1 (*cont.*)

Folio	Meter	Tonality	Description
*28r	4/4, "3/2"	to e	8 bars on 2 systems, closely corresponding to bars 141–48 of first movement (145 ff. = modified return of main theme in E minor). Appears to continue for one additional bar onto fol. 27v.
*27v	4/4	(e), b, B	6½ bars on two systems. The first bar on the first system appears to be a tentative continuation from fol. 28r, which is not found in FV. Next, marked "Anfang" ("Beginning"), is a melodic sketch in B minor of bars 2–4 (tenor horn solo) of the first movement, while the second system is a melodic sketch in B major corresponding to bars 79–83 (second theme). No direct continuity from this sketch.

Little by little they form the material that lies latent in one; it emerges again in the course of working if one merely knocks, and it always allows one to draw freely on lavish resources. Often such thoughts occur years later, at the right time and the right place. As a result, it often seems as though one is being unoriginal, since, as things go in composing, one comes up with so much that is familiar, already one's own. In the lied that I wrote this afternoon, there is a turn of phrase that rattled about in my head three years ago, and which I hadn't thought of since.[7]

But by 1899, when Mahler was nearly forty, the situation had changed somewhat. Owing in large measure to the pressures of his position as direc-

[7] NBL2, p. 28 (not in NBLE); the lied Mahler refers to is "Rheinlegendchen," dated 9 August 1893 in the piano-vocal autograph (Berlin, Staatsbibliothek Preußischer Kulturbesitz, Mus. ms. Autogr. Mahler 1), and 10 August in the orchestral score (New York, Pierpont Morgan Library, Lehman Deposit). See also NBL2, pp. 58 and 61 (NBLE, pp. 61 and 64–65) (29 June–5 July 1896) for additional references to sketchbook usage.

tor of the Vienna Court Opera, he had composed but little during the vacations of 1897 and 98. And the entire month of June 1899 apparently brought forth only the *Wunderhorn* lied "Revelge" (spontaneously composed during an emergency trip to the commode, when Mahler happened to have a sketchbook at hand).[8] He had begun to fear that his creative spring was drying up: "it trickles a little, but that is all."[9] Then, well into July, he was seized by inspiration for the Fourth Symphony; Natalie describes the inception of the work as follows:

> So it really is his Fourth Symphony that has fallen into Mahler's lap at the eleventh hour! . . . God knows what he has succeeded in salvaging during the ten-day respite remaining to him . . . He worked in spite of all hindrances, wherever he could, even when out walking (alone, or often with us, in which case he lagged behind), something he hadn't done since *Das klagende Lied* [1880].[10]

She continues in the unpublished portion of her diary with additional remarks Mahler made at this time:

> when an idea came to me on a walk and I glimpsed a modification to incorporate into my composition, I would tell myself that I would write it down as soon as I returned. But now, when I arrive at home, the idea has already fled and I've forgotten everything. It's the same with everything else. If I've read something, or something has occurred to me, and I want to recount it later, I realize that I no longer know anything about it. It often seems to me that I am like someone whose digestion is too good, and whose organism immediately rejects or accepts various foods: absorbed or not, they no longer exist.[11]

Despite difficulties getting underway that summer, Mahler could claim at the end of his vacation that while in previous years his inventiveness had often come to a standstill during the sketching process, "this time it flowed and swelled through me so richly that I utterly did not know how to catch everything, and was almost embarrassed about how to dispose of it all properly."[12] Similarly, in the summer of 1900 he could not immediately

---

[8] See NBL2, p. 135 (not in NBLE), as well as HLG 1, pp. 522–23 (HLGF 1, pp. 798–99). [9] NBL2, p. 138 (NBLE, pp. 130–31).

[10] NBL2, pp. 138–39 (NBLE, p. 132, which is based on the first edition of NBL [Leipzig, 1923], presents this passage in the present tense).

[11] Bauer-Lechner, "Mahleriana" (n. 2 above), cited in HLGF 1, p. 802 (HLG 2, p.180). [12] NBL2, p. 143 (NBLE, p. 135).

resume work on the Fourth, which was only half-finished, and again he feared that his muse had vanished.[13] But when the creative process was again underway after a week of stalling, Mahler once more found that there simply was not enough time to record all his musical ideas and complete a large work as well, which left him grumbling about the accursed Opera and the general inhumanity of this life. Natalie reports that

> when he is fully engaged in working, the number of ideas that come to him in great torrents is staggering. It would take even him an entire year to capture and collect everything. Thus, everything that doesn't fit with the work in progress and isn't integrated into it actually has to be let go. How sad to think of that![14]

By the summer of 1901, however, Mahler was apparently making at least selective efforts to save up musical capital for the future. According to Natalie,

> Mahler is now beginning to write down much of what occurs to him in music, and regrets that he had not long since done this, so that if the flowing richness of invention should perhaps diminish, this or that from the warehouse could be turned to advantage and worked up. "What a superhuman expenditure of work and strength it is to have to create everything for the first time in an inkling, without anything in stock, any collection [Sammlung] (in the true meaning of the word). On the other hand, if one let nothing be wasted during the summertime, but instead harvested it all and laid it up, later on one would only have to reach out to find exactly what one needed. Just so did Beethoven in his later days often latch onto and utilize themes from times long past."[15]

The following March (1902) he married Alma; her book on Mahler includes an amusing recollection of the frequent interruptions in their walks during their first summer together:

---

[13] NBL2, p. 157 (NBLE, p. 145).

[14] Bauer-Lechner, "Mahleriana," cited in HLGF 1, 899–900 (HLG 2, p. 278), 26 July 1900.

[15] NBL2, 189–90 (NBLE, 170); cf. also "Natalie Bauer-Lechner. / Mahleriana. / Erinnerungen an Gustav Mahler. / Vorläufiger Auszug: Über die erste bis fünfte Symphonie," typescript, Vienna, Österreichische Nationalbibliothek, Musiksammlung, Mus. Hs. 38.578, p. 106 (17 June 1901).

Often and often he stood still, the sun beat down on his hatless head, he drew out his little musical sketchbook and wrote and meditated and wrote; sometimes he beat time in the air and wrote further. This often lasted an hour or more. In the meanwhile I sat at some distance in the grass or against a tree trunk and tried not to watch him [which he detested, as Bauer-Lechner also reports]. Then sometimes he smiled over to me, when he was pleased with an inspiration. He knew that nothing in the world brought me greater joy. Then we went on or else turned back if, as often happened, he felt compelled to get home quickly and into his workroom.[16]

The nature of Mahler's surviving sketchbooks

Taken together, the accounts just cited seem to indicate that Mahler's method of processing his initial ideas gradually changed between the period of the first three symphonies, when he apparently allowed unused material to lie fallow, and the time of the Fourth and Fifth Symphonies, when he began to rely upon notebooks both as an aid to memory for the current work in progress and as a means of selectively storing up ideas for the future. The two surviving pocket sketchbooks are, of course, from later years – most probably 1905 and 1909 respectively – yet the nature of their content seems largely congruent with the purposes for notebooks suggested by the memoirs of Bauer-Lechner and Alma Mahler. The substantial majority of their pages is devoted to ideas that, although apparently not used in any of his surviving works, Mahler felt worth preserving for possible future deployment (cf. Table 7.1 above). But a number of the little leaves – about a third of those in the Seventh Symphony sketchbook, and rather less in that for the Ninth – are distinctly related to those works, and were almost certainly conceived for immediate use. Many of these pages, especially in the Seventh sketchbook, have been "cancelled" with diagonal slashes in blue pencil, evidently to set them apart from the unused ideas that might be incorporated into a new work.

Most of the notebook sketches are in pencil (although half-a-dozen in the Ninth Symphony booklet are in ink); they range from very rough ideas of a few bars' duration to longer segments of twenty to thirty bars. The

---

[16] Alma Mahler, *Gustav Mahler: Erinnerungen und Briefe*, 2nd edn. (Amsterdam, 1949), p. 63 (AMML4, pp. 46–47).

more primitive material rarely extends beyond a single page, but some of the more developed ideas may continue for two or three pages; as we shall see, several such sketches in the Seventh Symphony notebook correspond very closely to passages of the completed work. Indications of instrumentation are quite rare at this stage. The features of the sketchbooks just noted are also apparent in a number of full-size preliminary sketch sheets surviving from the genesis of earlier works (e.g., the Second, Third, and Fourth Symphonies).[17] So, too, are two additional characteristics of the compositional process. First, Mahler rarely writes more than a few bars without immediately making revisions; the kernels of his inspiration begin to branch forth at once, and not always in particularly obvious ways. Secondly, he makes purely melodic sketches rather rarely; while it is clear that the melody is the leading voice in most of Mahler's "first ideas," the bass line is almost always present as well. Occasionally chord progressions are notated in simple rhythms beneath the melodic material, but more often than not the bass is already developing contrapuntally. In a few instances figured-bass numerals are used to indicate the most essential components of harmony and voice leading.[18]

Thus Mahler's initial conceptions are based on the traditional structural polarity of soprano and bass voices. Michael Kennedy has suggested that "the fundamental principle in Mahler's technique of composition was two-part counterpoint,"[19] and many surviving sketches indicate that it indeed was. Just such an initial two-part conception was characteristic of

[17] See Stephen E. Hefling, "The Making of Mahler's 'Todtenfeier': A Documentary and Analytical Study," 3 vols. (Ph.D. diss., Yale University, 1985), and "Content and Context of the Sketches," in *Mahler: The Resurrection Chorale*, ed. Gilbert E. Kaplan (New York, 1994), pp. 13–35 (incl. color facsimiles); Morten Solvik Olsen, "Culture and the Creative Imagination: The Genesis of Gustav Mahler's Third Symphony" (Ph.D. diss., University of Pennsylvania, 1992), pp. 394 ff. and 582–628; James L. Zychowicz, "Sketches and Drafts of Gustav Mahler, 1892–1901" (Ph.D. diss., University of Cincinnati, 1988); and Hefling, "'Variations *in nuce.*'"

[18] As Robert Wason has shown in *Viennese Harmonic Theory from Albrechtsberger to Schenker and Schoenberg*, Studies in Musicology, no. 80 (Ann Arbor, 1985), Rameau's notions of chord inversion never really replaced figured bass and counterpoint as the foundation of music theory and practical training in nineteenth-century Vienna (see also n. 33 below).

[19] Michael Kennedy, *Mahler*, rev. edn. (New York, 1990), p. 106.

Richard Wagner's compositional procedure from the time of *Tristan* on, as Robert Bailey has observed.[20] Whether Mahler knew anything of Wagner's working methods remains uncertain, but it seems beyond doubt that years of studying and performing Wagner's scores made clear to him the underlying structure of their often complex textures.

Content of the Seventh Symphony sketchbook

The composition of the Seventh Symphony was unusual in two respects. As a rule, Mahler concentrated upon one symphony at a time; yet evidently during the summer of 1904, while still at work on the Sixth, he drafted two complete movements of the Seventh. These were, moreover, the two *Nachtmusik* interludes – two self-sufficient character pieces, yet related in tone such that one could scarcely imagine their following one another. To be used in a single work of typical Mahlerian shape, they would need to be sandwiched between a symphonic first movement and finale, with something else separating them; a scherzo would seem the likely choice. That this is how things stood is strongly suggested by Alma Mahler's report that "'architect's drawings [Bauskizzen],' as he called them" were made for the work as a whole in the summer of 1904:[21] these very likely included one or more lists of movements such as those that survive for the Third, Fourth, and Eighth Symphonies.[22] In a letter to Alma from 1910 Mahler describes

[20] Robert Bailey, "The Evolution of Wagner's Compositional Process after Lohengrin," *International Musicological Society: Report of the Eleventh Congress, Copenhagen, 1972*, ed. Henrik Glahn, Søren Sørenson, and Peter Ryom (Copenhagen, 1974), vol. I, pp. 240–41; see also idem, "The Method of Composition," in *The Wagner Companion*, ed. Peter Burbidge and Richard Sutton (London, 1979), pp. 272–73 and passim.

[21] Alma Mahler, *Erinnerungen*, p. 115 (AMML4, p. 89).

[22] See, e.g., HLGF 1, pp. 1038–39; GMB 2, nos. 145 and 146 (GMBE, nos. 136 and 137); Paul Bekker, *Gustav Mahlers Sinfonien* (Berlin, 1921), pp. 145 and 273; HLGF 3, pp. 1079–80. Donald Mitchell, in his essay "Chronology" for *Gustav Mahler: Facsimile Edition of the Seventh Symphony* (Amsterdam, 1995), p. 23, insists that Mahler's "architectural drawings" from 1904 must have comprised "*extensive* compositional sketching" (his italics) for the outer movements of the symphony. But as we shall see from the content of the sketchbook, it appears unlikely that much, if any, of the first movement had been sketched at that point.

Plate 7.1 fol. 30v

Transcription of fol. 30v (bracketed bar numbers correspond to FV; corrections = boldface

the rather tricky task he faced in the summer of 1905 (and to complicate matters further, he had once again experienced difficulty getting down to work that year):

> One summer before that [i.e., in 1905] I made up my mind to finish the Seventh, both Andantes of which were there on my table. I plagued myself for two weeks until I sank into gloom, as you well remember; then I tore off to the Dolomites. There I was led the same dance, and at last gave it up and returned home, convinced that the whole summer was lost. You were not at Krumpendorf to meet me, because I had not let you know the time of my arrival. I got into the boat to be rowed across. At the first stroke of the oars the theme (or rather the rhythm and character) of the introduction to the first movement came into my head – and in four weeks the first, third and fifth movements were done. Do you remember?[23]

What may well be the sketch Mahler made on the boat (or shortly after stepping off) is shown in Plate 7.1: this rudimentary but energetically sketched fragment for the opening bars of the first movement is found on the first page inside the cover bearing the title "Skizzen" (fol. 30v).[24] The jagged arpeggiations and highly characteristic half-diminished seventh chord of the tenor horn solo (FV, bars 2–3) are readily apparent in the first bar of sketching; the second and third bars on the first system are melodically less certain, but the harmonic progression to another half-diminished seventh ($c\sharp$, $a\sharp$, e^1, $g\sharp^1$) is quite clear (cf. FV, bars 3–4).[25] Depending upon the local context (spacing and registration, progression to the next chord, etc.), these sonorities may also be heard as minor triads with added sixths; they are thus close cousins of both the famous "Tristan" chord and the pentatonic added-sixth sonority on which *Das Lied von der Erde* would conclude three years later (c–e–g–a). As example 7.1a shows, both a perfect

---

[23] Letter to Alma Mahler of [8 June] 1910, in AMML4, p. 328.

[24] That this was Mahler's first sketch during or after the boat ride has already been suggested by Colin Matthews (n. 3 above), p. 124. Donald Mitchell raises doubts about this in "Chronology," pp. 22–23, n. 14; as we shall see, however, detailed consideration of the notebook's content indicates that this is quite plausibly Mahler's first idea for the movement's opening.

[25] The abbreviation "FV" ("Final Version") refers to KG, vol. VII, ed. Erwin Ratz (Berlin, 1960).

Ex. 7.1   Fourths and tritone in (a) half-diminished seventh chord, and
(b) added-sixth chord

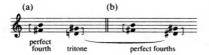

fourth and a tritone are contained within the chord when it is in closed
position; the tendency of the tritone to resolve into a fourth yields another
added-sixth chord, as shown in Ex. 7.1b: this is a major triad with added
sixth, and as the brackets indicate, it comprises two perfect fourths. Out of
these two sonorities and their constituent intervals grows much of the
characteristic musical language of the Seventh's first movement, including
the quartal harmonies that seem to anticipate slightly later developments in
Schoenberg's music.[26]

At the beginning of the second system the second of the half-diminished chords (c♯, a♯, e¹, g♯¹) resolves to a B minor triad, thereby articulating
what will be the tonal center of the movement's introduction (cf. bar 5 of
FV). It seems most likely that Mahler now sketches the melodic idea found
on the left-hand side of the third system (the five sharps clearly indicate that
B has been chosen as tonic, and also that modal mixture will be an issue in
this music). Although the melodic contour is slightly changed, the rhythm
and nervous trills of this bar are taken over into bar 10 of FV. Overall, what
Mahler has sketched here are kernels (to use a term he frequently

---

[26]   The best discussion of this issue to date is Christopher Alan Williams's
unpublished paper, "Mahler's Seventh Symphony and the Emergence of a Post-
tonal Harmonic Vocabulary" presented at the 1994 annual meeting of the
American Musicological Society, Minneapolis. As Williams observes, in the
Seventh's first movement the interval of a fourth "comes to pervade the texture
progressively, through the kind of vegetative motivic growth Schoenberg would
later term 'developing variation' . . . the movement's quartal harmony is more a
product of the incremental proliferation and unfolding of the main theme's
single descending fourth than an assertion of a complex non-diatonic sonority
per se . . . Mahler's quartal harmonies are primarily motivic rather than
harmonic in origin" (typescript, pp. 12, 15, and 16).

employed) – fragments that, although as yet rather disjointed, are charged with potential for expansion and development. There is no direct continuity from this page to any other; as we shall see, however, another brief sketch in this portion of the booklet (fol. 27v) clarifies the rhythm of the introductory melodic idea.

But before proceeding with further detailed exploration of the individual sketches, it will be useful to take stock of the notebook as a whole. Table 7.1 above provides an overview of the contents, in which those folios containing material actually used in the Seventh are printed boldface and marked with asterisks. As previously noted, Mahler wrote from both ends of the notebook, turning it "upside-down" when working on the opposite side, such that the binding was always on the left and the leaves could be turned normally, recto to verso.[27] (The only feature distinguishing obverse of the black binding from reverse is the imprint "Skizzen" on the front.) Twenty-eight pages in the middle portion of the book are blank; effectively, it is as though Mahler had two shorter sketchbooks, which probably made it easier for him to find a given item when needed. The folio numbering is not Mahler's, but will serve adequately so long as we keep his "double-sketch-book" scheme in mind. Accordingly, Table 7.1 first inventories folios 1r through 13r – the "back" portion of the booklet in relation to its binding. Then, following the hiatus of blank pages, the table proceeds in retrograde motion from folio 30v through 27v. (Folio 30v, as noted above, is the first page beneath the cover stamped "Skizzen.") Although it seems plausible that Mahler began at the "front" of the book with the sketch for the introduction shown above (fol. 30v, Plate 7.1), there are no decisive clues on this issue, and once underway, he may have gone back and forth between the two sections. While both contain material for the first movement of the Seventh, most of the sketches for that movement are in the "front" section of the notebook (fols. 30v–27v) – which indeed contains only one page pertaining to anything else: an important sketch in C major for the finale appears on fol. 29r, reproduced below as Plate 7.7. That conjunction – a C major sketch in close proximity to B and E minor ideas – suggests that

---

[27] Such is also the case in the Ninth Symphony sketchbook, although only one page from the back section of that booklet has been used.

Mahler is already contemplating the rather unusual tonal plan ultimately manifest in the symphony as a whole; indeed, this would likely have been a feature of his "architect's drawings" (see also below).

The twenty-five inscribed pages in the "back" portion of the sketchbook fall into three distinct groups. (1) Four pertain to the first movement (fols. 10v–12r, in E minor). (2) Eight contain scherzo- or ländler-like material not used in the symphony (fols. 1r, 2v, 8v–9r, 9v, 10r, 12v, and 13r); four of these pages are in A minor, one is unstable, one is centered on C and G major, and two are in D major (and are perhaps ideas for a trio). (3) Thirteen pages of 4/4 (or possibly ¢) material, generally bold and buoyant in character, but ultimately not incorporated into the work (fols. 1v, 2r, 3r–3v, 4r, 4v–5r, 5v, 6r, 6v, 7r, 7v, and 8r). Nearly two-thirds of these sketches (eight, to be precise) are in C major, while the others explore various modulations; of the latter, three are thematically related to the C major sketching (the other two will be discussed presently). In addition, it will be observed that the first-movement material in this portion of the notebook (fols. 10v–12r) falls in between sketches of the other two types, and in particular that scherzo-like material straddles the first-movement sketches: the cue sign of an "X" leads from A minor music in 3/4 on folio 8v to related material on folio 12v.[28]

Thus the contents of this sketchbook strongly suggest that Mahler was searching for just the sort of material he would have needed to round out the Seventh Symphony in the summer of 1905: a first movement (B minor/E minor), a scherzo (A minor, perhaps with a trio in D major), and a finale (C major), all of which would have to complement the two *Nachtmusik* interludes already drafted. In the event, he adopted none of the scherzo sketching and only one of the C major ideas in the finale; nevertheless, he found this surplus material worth preserving. More detailed

---

[28] Edward R. Reilly's essay "The Manuscripts of the Seventh Symphony" for *Facsimile Edition of the Seventh Symphony* (n. 22 above) mistakenly suggests that "The Sketches for the Seventh are all found on the opposite sides of the pages of the later group [i.e., materials not used in the Seventh] and are upside-down in relation to the latter" (pp. 75–77). This leads Reilly to tentatively accept the "last sketchbook" designation, which, as noted above and below, seems unlikely given the nature and disposition of material in the notebook.

examination of it must await another occasion, since our principal focus here is the sketches pertaining directly to the Seventh Symphony. But two facets of the "unused" music are too noteworthy to overlook. First, embedded within it are kernels that would grow to major dimensions in Mahler's last completed work, the Ninth Symphony. These are found on folios 7v and 8r, two pages of 4/4 material not related to the C major material in that meter, which are reproduced in Plates 7.2 and 7.3, with relevant bars transcribed in Exx. 7.2a–d (p. 194). The first two bars of folio 7v contain two prominent gestures from the Ninth's finale: the often repeated "motto progression" (I–V–♭VI, etc., which crops up in the second and third movements as well),[29] and the close juxtaposition of D♭ major and D major that constitutes a crucial element of the movement's tonal drama. The second and third bars in the third system of this page (Ex. 7.2b) are a variant upon this idea: here we find the turn figure that becomes ubiquitous in the Ninth, especially in the finale, as well as a veiled allusion to Mahler's song "Urlicht" that is taken over into bar 8 of the Ninth's finale. At the top of folio 8r is another variant (Ex. 7.2c), beginning and ending in D major, that extends the "motto" progression in a manner resembling bars 126–27 of the same movement. This is encircled, which is Mahler's usual marking that an idea is to be kept and possibly reconsidered; ultimately he did both in extenso. Finally, at the end of the second system on this page is a gesture that finds its way into the D minor second subject of the Ninth's first movement at bar 33 (cf. Ex. 7.2d). Apparently, then, such turns of phrase could indeed "rattle about" in Mahler's mind for several years until the right occasion for their use emerged.[30]

The second bout of sketching unrelated to the Seventh that calls for brief mention here is especially striking on account of its harmonic content. Several of the pages containing C major material in 4/4 (presumably for possible use in the finale) show indications of an ostinato

---

[29] E.g., second movement, bars 261–64; third movement, bars 109–11.

[30] The presence of these Ninth Symphony motives also suggests that this booklet probably was not Mahler's "last sketchbook"; it is difficult to suppose that during his last hours the composer would seek to rework – commencing with such simplistic, exploratory sketching – material he had developed so extensively and eloquently in the completed Ninth.

Plate 7.2   fol. 7v

accompaniment in open fifths derived from the open strings of the cellos
and violins (C–G–d–a, g–d^1–a^1–e^2, etc.). The most intriguing and fully
notated of these passages occurs on folio 6r, reproduced as Plate 7.4. Here
the rustic-sounding, almost polytonal sonorities that result from these
heaped-up fifths are extraordinary indeed; one can only wonder what sort
of movement further development of this idea might have yielded.

The remaining Seventh Symphony sketches (i): folios 30r–27v

As we have seen, Mahler revealed that it was the inspiration for the
first movement's introduction (fol. 30v, Plate 7.1) which released the creative process leading to the completion of the Seventh, although we have
no decisive data about the subsequent order of events in that process.
Clearly he was working rapidly, and the fragmentary jottings in this sole

Plate 7.3   fol. 8r

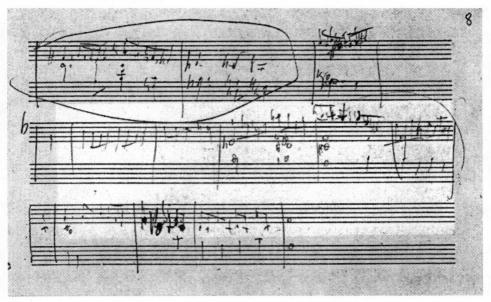

surviving notebook must have been supplemented by extensive sketching done on full-size worksheets in the *Häuschen* at Maiernigg. Accordingly, it will be convenient to examine the remainder of the sketchbook directly related to the Seventh by continuing through the "front" portion of it, recommencing with what immediately follows the "rhythm and charac-ter" sketch (fol. 30v) for the introduction discussed above. Somewhat surprisingly, what we find on folios 30r–29v is the ardently lyrical episode that will become the first movement's third subject (bars 118 ff.); but here it is in F major (rather than C), with an annotation "Es dur probieren" ("try E♭") (see Plates 7.5 and 7.6, plus accompanying transcriptions). Both melody and harmony are very nearly what they will be in the finished work, up to the point at which it abruptly abandons this material (bars 132 ff.). However, both the original key of the sketch (F) and the note to try E♭ suggest that the tonal architecture of the first movement is not yet clear to

193

Ex. 7.2 (a) fol. 7v, bars 1–2; (b) fol. 7v, bars 9–10; (c) fol. 8r, bars 1–2; (d) fol. 8r, bar 8

(a)

[etc.]

(b)

[etc.]

(c)

(d)

194

Plate 7.4   fol. 6r

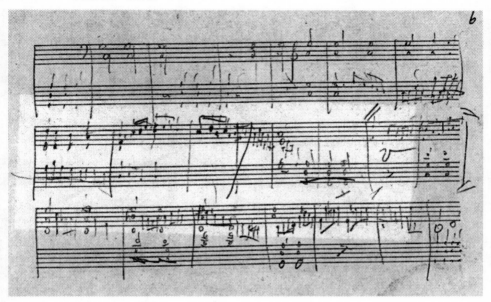

Mahler; nor is that surprising, for as we shall see, he had probably not yet composed the main theme.

Folio 29r is the single page of C major sketching that was adopted in the finale of the Seventh (Plate 7.7). Curiously reminiscent of the concluding C major chorus of Janissaries in Mozart's *Die Entführung aus dem Serail*, this idea appears in bars 87–95 of the finale very nearly as sketched in the notebook. Evidently, then, it first occurred to Mahler in the energetic eighth-note motion of that passage, although its basic melodic contour informs a number of motives in the finale, most notably the *pesante* figure shown in Ex. 7.3. This "augmentation" of that contour is already present as counterpoint in the third and fourth full bars of the sketch's third system (f^2–g^2–e^2–f^2–d^2). There, however, the rhythm originally consisted of even quarters; the characteristic dotted values (cf. transcription of fol. 29r) were added only later as one of the few ink corrections found in the sketchbook.

195

Plate 7.5   fol. 30r

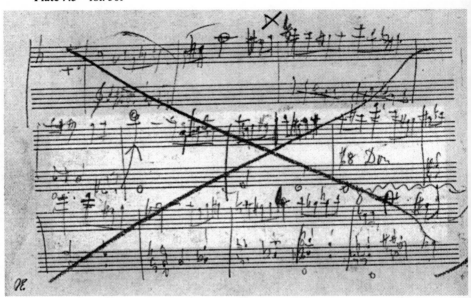

Transcription of fol. 30r

Plate 7.6   fol. 29v

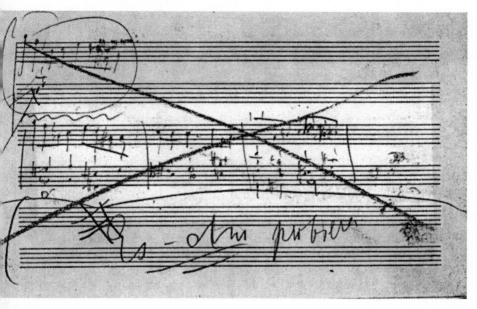

Transcription of fol. 29v

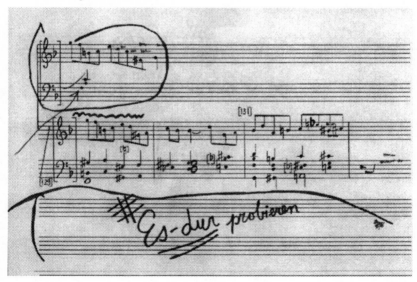

Plate 7.7   fol. 29r

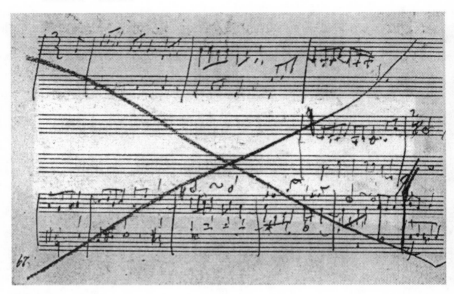

Transcription of fol. 29r

Plate 7.8   fol. 28v

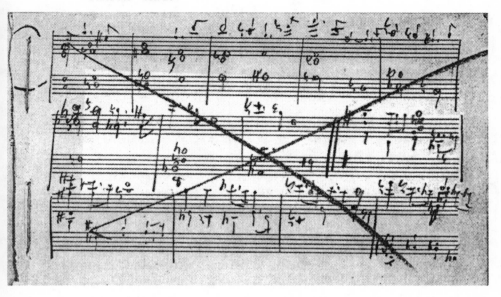

Transcription of fol. 28v

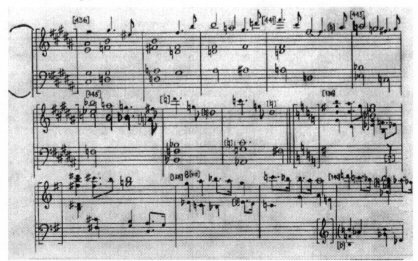

Ex. 7.3   Seventh Symphony, finale, bars 23–24

The presence of this single C major finale sketch in the midst of material for the first movement makes one wonder whether Mahler were already entertaining the possibility of cyclical connections between the two (cf. especially bars 455 ff. and 492 ff. of the finale in FV); but in the completed work these links are based upon recurrence of the first movement's main theme, which, as noted above, may well not yet have been formulated (see below, pp. 211–12).

At this juncture the stubs of two torn-out leaves are found in the gutter of the booklet. Since there is no break in the folio numbering, the missing material must have been removed prior to the notebook's pagination (which was probably done by librarians of the Österreichische Nationalbibliothek). Karl Moll and Anna Bahr-Mildenburg are unlikely to have vandalized what they apparently thought to be Mahler's last sketchbook; given that a few single leaves detached from other sketchbooks are known to have survived Mahler's campaign to destroy them,[31] one wonders whether he himself may have torn out these sheets for some practical purpose. In any case, on the next surviving page in this section of the notebook, folio 28v, we find ourselves in mid-phrase of the first movement's second subject as it occurs in the recapitulation at bars 436 ff. (see Plate 7.8 and transcription; the curved lines in the gutter opposite the first system are almost certainly a cue linking these bars to something sketched on the now-missing opposite page). The relatively finished state of this material suggests that the beginning of the theme (now missing) was probably very

---

[31]   E.g., a leaf pertaining to the finale of the Ninth Symphony now located in the Jewish National and University Library, Schwadron Collection, Gustav Mahler File. According to Zychowicz, "Sketches and Drafts," pp. 188–89, several such single leaves are among the holdings of the Bibliothèque musicale Gustav Mahler in Paris; judging from the dimensions he provides, however, none of them belonged to the Seventh Symphony notebook.

close to bars 427–35 – i.e., just over nine bars of music, which could easily have been sketched on a single preceding page of the notebook. It should be noted as well that the sketch for the finale on folio 29r breaks off in medias res, whereas in the finished movement this passage continues for another eleven measures (before it is interrupted by a new event): this continuation, or material related to it, could well have occupied another single side of the two missing leaves. Thus, our hypothetical inventory would indicate that there must have been at least two pages of material quite possibly unrelated either to folio 29r or to 28v of the current numbering; it may be that Mahler decided to rip them out, either during the completion of the Seventh, or (more likely) while composing a later work.

Folios 28v and 28r (Plates 7.8 and 7.9) are the most extensive continuous sketch in this "front" portion of the notebook, and the nature of the handwriting suggests that it was composed "of a piece" in one short session. The first eight bars are very close in melodic and harmonic structure to bars 436–49 of the completed work; particularly noteworthy are the prominent motivic fourths as well as the frequent half-diminished and added-sixth sonorities (e.g., the first, second, seventh, and eighth bars of the sketch). The main difference from the finished movement is the meter: here the familiar second subject of the movement is in 3/2, whereas in both exposition and recapitulation of the final version it is in ¢. We do not know how often Mahler may have transformed musical material wholesale from triple to duple meter during the gestation of his works, but to judge from the sum of the preliminary sketches that have come down to us, such a change is rare.[32] However, metric ambiguity and the transformation of duple-time music to triple are indeed to play a role in the Seventh's first movement, specifically in the varied treatment of the primary thematic material, and presently we shall see hints of this emerging in the sketchbook. Also missing from this sketch of the second subject is any hint of the descending chromatic inner-voice figure that animates the sustained phrase endings of the

[32] More common is Mahler's uncertainty as to whether a duple/quadruple passage should be notated in e or ¢; prominent instances crop up in sketching for both the slow movement of the Fourth Symphony and the Rückert lied "Ich bin der Welt abhanden gekommen" (see Hefling, "'Variations in nuce,'" pp. 108 and 114, and "The Composition of Mahler's 'Ich bin der Welt abhanden gekommen,'" in *Gustav Mahler*, ed. Hermann Danuser, Wege der Forschung, vol. 653 [Darmstadt, 1992], passim).

Plate 7.9 fol. 28r

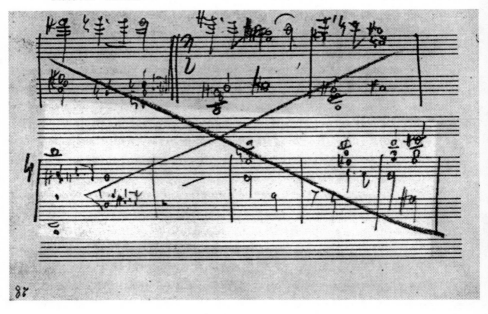

Transcription of fol. 28r

Plate 7.10   fol. 27v

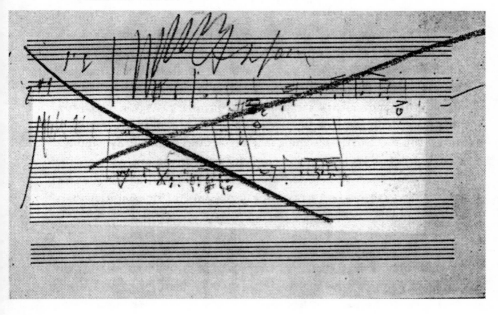

Transcription of fol. 27v

melody (e.g., bars 437–38); but as we shall see, Mahler will hit upon this idea very shortly.

In the printed score, the equivalent of the eighth bar in this sketch (bar 450/fig. **56** and ff.) is followed by an interruptive episode of main-theme material. But as the transcription of fol. 28v shows, at the change of key indicated in the ninth bar the music shifts to what we know as bars 136 ff. in the first movement – a transitional, sequential passage in march-like rhythms initially based on the progression I–V–♭VI (which progression is also encountered in the sketching that foreshadows the Ninth Symphony's finale – see above, p. 191). In the completed work this passage occurs in the introduction (bars 19 ff.) and, augmented by two additional bars at the beginning, serves as a link between the third subject of the exposition (bars 118–33) and the opening of the development (bars 145 ff.). Thus, as previously, Mahler is here composing "building blocks" that, as he put it, would fit together as pieces of a puzzle only later (see below, pp. 213–14). More interesting, however, is the thematic substance of the last three bars on folio 28r (Plate 7.9): this is our first glimpse of the movement's principal subject, in its principal tonality of E minor. Presently we shall see that, curious though it seems, the "back" portion of the notebook suggests Mahler actually did not sketch the main theme in its first presentation until after he had worked out the climactic version of it that would ultimately occupy the latter part of the recapitulation (bars 495 ff.; see below).

The first-theme material continues for one additional bar onto folio 27v (Plate 7.10). Then, following a scribble, we find the word "Anfang" ("beginning"): here is notated the precise outline of the introduction's initial melodic idea. Present only as kernels and "mood" on folio 30v (see above, pp. 186–89), this opening motive has now taken on the dotted rhythm of the second subject, which had just been worked out on the preceding pages. On the second system of folio 27v we find the first two gestures of the second subject – both boldly quartal in intervallic content. As noted above, this music must already have appeared on one of the torn-out leaves; in all likelihood, the new feature in this abbreviated sketch is the sliding chromatic accompaniment on the lower staff – which is missing from the texture of folio 28v at the spot analogous to bars 437–48 in FV, but which is adumbrated by the melodic activity in the bars of the sketch corresponding to bars 445–46 of FV. Through such motivic linkages (which, owing to their close proximity, seem readily apparent in the sketches) the work takes on subtle subcutaneous coherence.

The remaining Seventh Symphony sketches (ii): folios 10v–12r

As already indicated, the "back" portion of the notebook begins with some nineteen pages of material, apparently for the projected scherzo and finale, that was not ultimately used in the Seventh Symphony. The next item of sketching that *was* incorporated into it occupies folios 10v–11v (Plates 7.11 through 7.13): this is the long climactic episode of principal-theme material corresponding to bars 495–522 in FV – a passage that, in the completed movement, leads directly to the final coda. While we cannot be altogether certain about the chronology of ideas, this sketch provides a strong hint that it was composed after the first jottings for the movement's introduction: the jagged arpeggiating accompaniment outlined here, although subsequently to be modified, clearly imitates the contours and dotted rhythms of the initial idea found on folios 30v and 27v (cf. FV, bars 2 ff., tenor horn).

This is the longest passage in the entire notebook, and once again it appears that Mahler is working in one sweep, all the way to the juncture that we know as the closing stretto of the movement (bar 523) on folio 11v (Plate 7.13). Many details will be refined in these twenty-eight bars – yet it is utterly striking how much of their essence is already present in this preliminary sketch, as comparison of the transcription to FV quickly reveals. The encircled bars (which follow those in the sketch corresponding to bars 499, 509, and 513 of FV) are the spots where Mahler is least certain of precisely what he wants; but even here he ultimately departs only slightly from his initial inspirations. While the first eight-bar phrase opens as we know it (bars 495–502),[33] the harmonic fluctuations of its second half were initially less complex than what we find in FV; Ex. 7.4 provides a comparative analytical sketch of the two versions (cf. also Plates 7.11 through 7.13 plus

---

[33] Noteworthy in bars 497–98 is Mahler's use of figured bass, which crops up occasionally in the two surviving notebooks; cf. Wason, *Viennese Harmonic Theory*. Mahler's sketches provide concrete evidence that the concept of polyphony he inherited from the Viennese tradition influenced even his latest compositions.

Plate 7.11   fol. 10v

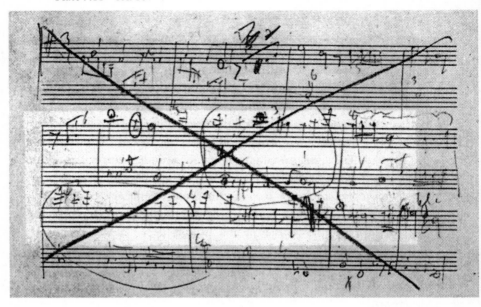

Transcription of fol. 10v

Plate 7.12 fol. 11r

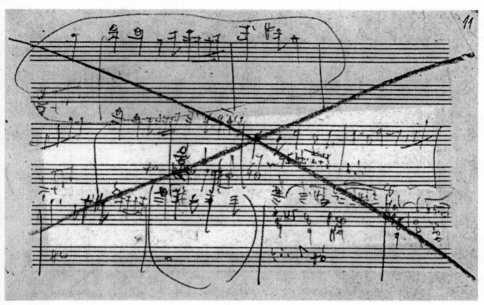

Transcription of fol. 11r

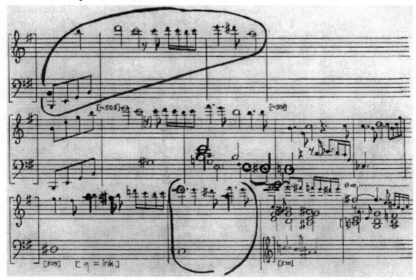

Plate 7.13   fol. 11v

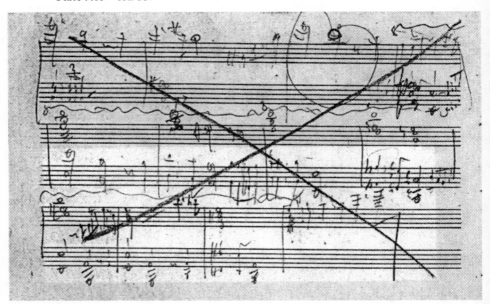

Transcription of fol. 11v

Plate 7.14 fol. 12r

Transcription of fol. 12r

Ex. 7.4 Comparative analysis of (a) Seventh Symphony, 1st mvt., bars 495–512, and (b) sketching for the passage on fols. 10v–11v

transcriptions). In the last two bars of folio 10v, the beginning of the second phrase (bars 503 ff.) is clear, both in melodic contour and in harmonic focus on the dominant.

Mahler continues the melody onto folio 11r, only to encircle it before having provided either bar lines or bass support. A revision is written immediately below, and it would appear that he proceeds from here through the remainder of the page. Once again the harmonic scheme of the sketch is slightly simpler than the finished product, although the chromatic bass descent toward D in bar 506 is already present. Less certain is whether a D pedal (not specifically indicated) is intended for bars 507–09, as in FV. This seems likely, since otherwise the role of e♭ in 508 (and, to some extent, d♯ in 509) is unclear. But the upper voice lacks the striking downward fourths familiar from the violin part of FV: although we do not know just when Mahler decided to highlight this prominent motive in the present passage, the sketch provides us with a glimpse of its derivation from more commonplace linear activity. If we assume the pedal D in bars 507–08, then the upper voice as sketched is a simple passing motion, which can be summed up in figured-bass numerals as 6–7–8. Dropping the c^2 and d^2 half notes of these bars down an octave provides the characteristic seventh-spans of the completed movement (b^1–c^1, c^2–d^1), and adding a neighbor-note f♯^{1} in 507 plus its resolution to g^1 in 508 yields its famous fourths.

The encircled bar that follows 509 seems clearly to have been a false start, since it is more disjunctive and less developed than the music surrounding it. The next two bars, however, contain all structural essentials of the approach to the dominant pedal that we find in bars 510–11 of FV. And that pedal arrives, complete with a hint of the accompanying rhythm, on the top of folio 11v (Plate 7.13). There is another false start at bar 514, and its replacement appears to resolve on the tonic one bar earlier than will FV. But bars 515 to the end of the segment are composed straightaway, with very few corrections.

At this juncture the completed work bursts into the final stretto. What we find on folio 12r (Plate 7.14) of the sketchbook, however, is the first clear annotation of the main theme, in 2/2 meter, the first six bars of which are nearly identical to the theme's first full appearance at figure **6** of the score. (Especially striking is the harmonic overlay of tonic elements onto the Neapolitan, present even at this stage, in the bars corresponding to 54–55.) Perhaps Mahler was already thinking of a quick duple-time chaser to the passage of broad 3/2 material just sketched – which of course is the plan we find in FV (bars 523 ff.). If so, "ma fin est mon commencement" aptly describes the genesis of the movement's principal subject. In any case, the melodic content of folio 12r clearly derives from material contained in the three preceding pages (cf. esp. bars 495–98, 503–04, 512, and 515–16). And what follows the first six bars on this page is more like a groping first sketch than an effort to elaborate ideas already spawned. The semicircles isolating the last bar of the first system and the first bar of the second reveal uncertainty about how to continue. Then in the middle of the second system we find a relative rarity in Mahler's sketches: harmonic and melodic ideas that, apparently, do not belong together. Here the encircled material in what had been the bass staff is a coherent if colorfully unusual progression from the relative (G) to the tonic major (E); the attempted melodic line above, however, requires different harmonies. Another effort to continue from the first system appears on the third, where melody and bass are once again coordinated: these bars progress easily, if rather prosaically, from the Neapolitan underpinnings of bars 54–55 back to the tonic (major) by way of secondary dominant.

The sketchbook as document of compositional process

At the end of the third system on folio 12r Mahler's writing becomes quite tentative, and the ensuing two sheets of the booklet bear no direct relation to the completed Seventh Symphony. We can only wonder just how the movement progressed from this point forth, for no manuscript material prior to the orchestral draft score is known to survive (save for one sheet of *Particell* spliced into the orchestral draft).[34] Did Mahler take up another sketchbook, or was he able to proceed directly from the rich yet fragmentary ideas scribbled in this one to full-page sketches and drafts worked out at his composing table in the Maiernigg *Häuschen*? The latter possibility seems likely, given that our surviving notebook breaks off after only two additional pages: evidently Mahler was no longer interested in storing up first ideas, but had instead other tasks to accomplish. Moreover, the booklet already contains all the principal kernels for the symphony's first movement: introductory material, main theme, second idea,

---

[34] This short-score page for the first movement is reproduced in Reilly, "The Manuscripts," p. 81, illustration 6. The orchestral draft score is located in the Bruno Walter Collection, New York Public Library for the Performing Arts; photofacsimiles of several pages are included in Reilly "The Manuscripts," pp. 78, 81, and 83.

Gesangsatz, and a recapitulatory climax in the tonic. According to his own chronicle – and Mahler was generally accurate in recounting his works' genesis – three movements of the Seventh were composed in four weeks; this, too, suggests that he moved quickly from preliminaries to actual construction of the first movement.

The Seventh Symphony sketchbook embodies several characteristics of Mahler's compositional process that he had described to Bauer-Lechner (and occasionally to others) during the decade 1892–1901. His goal was the now much-touted concept of a "symphonic world," a coherent, organic musical whole without "patches and binding."[35] But as we have seen, such a world did not necessarily emerge in overtly coherent, systematic fashion; indeed, ideas seem to crop up in the notebook almost haphazardly. Once in 1893 Natalie had asked Mahler point blank how he went about composing. "God, how can one ask such a thing, Natalie!" was the exasperated reply, which continued thus:

> Do you know how to make a trumpet? You take a hole and wrap brass around it; that's about what happens in composing. No, seriously, how can it be described? It happens in a hundredfold different ways . . . Often I begin in the middle, often at the beginning, occasionally at the end, and the rest subsequently fits itself together here, there, and all around, until it rounds itself out into a whole and is finished.[36]

Such a process of groping for the right brass to wrap around a particular hole is at least as apparent from the notebook materials *not* culled for the Seventh as from those that were. In subsequent discussions with Bauer-Lechner, Mahler compared the process of composing to ordering the parts of a block puzzle, and to playing with bricks. When he had finally completed the draft of his Third Symphony, the ever-curious Natalie wanted to know how it had all come about; Mahler replied:

> I myself don't know; naturally the stones were at hand, but that suddenly a whole emerged from them must have occurred as with a block puzzle; for a long time one seeks in vain to discern its outline from the confusion of single cubes, until at one point, through the correct grouping of a couple of

[35] NBL2, pp. 35 and 198 (NBLE, pp. 40 and 178), summer 1895 and 12 October 1901.   [36] NBL2, p. 29 (NBLE, p. 33), July–August 1893.

principal stones, one fits with another, one gives way to another, and: the picture is there![37]

And at the time he was beginning work on his Fourth, Mahler told her that

> Composing is like playing with bricks, whereby a new building always arises from the same stones. The stones, however, have lain there ready and waiting from one's youth, the only time for collecting and storing them.[38]

The sketchbook gives us a partial glimpse of Mahler gathering blocks for a new work; determining their proper arrangement was the task he usually accomplished in preliminary drafts and short scores, written on full-size sheets in his composing hut. It is also noteworthy that, notwithstanding his notorious obsession over orchestration, we find virtually no indications of sonority in these early jottings. As he himself put it, "*what* one writes has always seemed to me more important than what it is scored *for*,"[39] and both surviving sketchbooks plus the various short-score drafts for his works confirm that such was indeed Mahler's order of priorities.

Several of the sketches for the Seventh we have examined – most notably the last three pages discussed above – reveal that, once underway, individual musical ideas could blossom quickly, in astonishingly complete form. As noted above, Mahler rarely sketches melodic material by itself; according to his Hamburg colleague, the composer Josef Bohuslav Foerster,

> Mahler assured me that almost never did a purely melodic line occur to him, but rather nearly always a theme, already embellished, developed, and in many ways linked to secondary thematic permutations. We took up the score [of "Todtenfeier"] again, and Mahler pointed out indisputable evidence for his words.[40]

Earlier in 1905, Mahler had delivered an impromptu discourse upon such organic interrelationships in his works, just after the second performances of his *Kindertotenlieder* cycle and the four individual Rückert songs;

---

[37] NBL2, p. 57 (NBLE, p. 60), 28 June 1896.
[38] NBL2, p. 138 (NBLE, p. 131), June–July 1899.
[39] GMB2, no. 198 (GMBE, no. 189), 4 December 1896.
[40] Josef Bohuslav Foerster, *Der Pilger: Erinnerungen eines Musikers*, trans. Pavel Eisner (Prague, 1955), p. 356.

present on that occasion was young Anton von Webern, who recorded the following remarks in his diary:

> The discussion turned to counterpoint . . . Mahler . . . admitted only Bach, Brahms, and Wagner as the greatest contrapuntalists . . . "Nature is for us the model in this realm. Just as in nature the entire universe has developed from the primeval cell, from plants, animals, and men beyond to God, the Supreme Being, so also in music should a larger structure develop from a single motive in which is contained the germ of everything that is yet to be."[41]

We have noted several instances of such organic development from small kernels in the Seventh Symphony notebook. Yet, as is typical of Mahler's surviving sketches, we find there scarcely a trace of the seemingly tortuous motivic working-out that so preoccupied Beethoven. Apparently Mahler's favored mode of writing was far more spontaneous; as he described his early sketches for the Andante of the Second Symphony to Natalie,

> the melody overflows in them [the sketches] in a full, broad current, rather in Schubertian manner: one thing plays forth from another, always expanding new branches about itself, with inexhaustible richness and variety, leading to a manifold intricacy . . .

> And only thus, in full strokes, can one properly create. It's nothing when somebody messes around with a poor little bit of a theme, which he varies and makes into a fugue, and must cultivate frugally for God knows how long, in order to get a whole movement out of it. I can't bear this economical system [*das Sparsystem*]; everything must be there in superabundance and flow incessantly if it's to amount to anything.[42]

---

[41] Cited in Hans Moldenhauer (with Rosaleen Moldenhauer), *Anton von Webern* (New York, 1979), p. 75. Two performances of the Mahler "Liederabend" with orchestra (29 January and 3 February, 1905) were sponsored by the Vereinigung schaffender Tonkünstler, the organization for contemporary music founded by Schoenberg and his circle, of which Mahler was honorary president (see also HLGF 2, pp. 572–76). Mahler's comments anticipate Schoenberg's now-popular notions of "developing variation" and "Grundgestalt."

[42] NBL2, p. 25 (NBLE, p. 29), July–August 1893. This would seem to contradict Bauer-Lechner's recollection from 29 June 1896 that "he filled up a bundle of sketch sheets and his pocket notebooks, as usual, with a hundred variants of a motive or a modulation, until he discovered just what he needed and how it had to fit into the overall context." Yet given Mahler's extreme reluctance to show

And so indeed the outer movements and scherzo of the Seventh must have flowed forth: the orchestral draft score of the first movement is inscribed at the end "Maiernigg 15. August 1905 / <u>Septima</u> finita,"[43] and that same day Mahler wrote his old friend Guido Adler: "Septima mea finita est. Credo hoc opus fauste natum et bene gestum . . ."[44] In the event, *hoc opus* would be judged his most problematic, even to the present day. That such a fascinating document of Mahler's creativity as this sketchbook should survive for the Seventh, of all things, seems a fittingly ironic trick of fate upon that master of musical irony whose half-humorous retort to those curious about his mode of creation was: "Blicke mir nicht in die Lieder!"

Footnote 42 (*cont.*)

 anyone his works-in-progress, it may be that Natalie actually saw very little of what those sketch sheets and notebooks contained. In any case, none of the materials surviving from her collection (which included sketches and drafts for *Das klagende Lied*, the Second and Third Symphonies, three *Wunderhorn* lieder, three Rückert lieder, and one of the *Kindertotenlieder*) provides evidence of such a laborious, repetitive process.

[43] Reproduced in Reilly, "The Manuscripts," p. 78, illustration 5.

[44] "My Seventh is finished. I believe this work auspiciously born and well produced . . ." Edward R. Reilly, *Gustav Mahler and Guido Adler: Records of a Friendship* (Cambridge, 1982), p. 103.

8 Prolonged counterpoint in Mahler

KOFI AGAWU

It's beyond words, the way I am constantly learning more and more from Bach (really sitting at his feet like a child): for my natural way of working is Bach-like.[1]

Thus Mahler described his mode of composing to Natalie Bauer-Lechner, his companion and confidante of the "*Wunderhorn* years," during the summer of 1901. But that summer was a time of stylistic change for the composer; this was the working holiday when he abandoned the *Wunderhorn* anthology for the poetry of Rückert, and began the *Kindertotenlieder* cycle, which opens with a memorable ritornello in two-voice counterpoint (for oboe and horn in the orchestral version). That passage is emblematic of a new linearity in Mahler, a contrapuntal orientation that left its most distinctive traces on his late works, *Das Lied von der Erde* and the Ninth Symphony. Yet already in the Fourth Symphony, completed in 1900, Mahler had manifest a more mature polyphonic technique than in earlier works, and the succeeding middle-period symphonies (the Fifth through the Seventh) are marked by an "unequivocally contrapuntal style," as Donald Mitchell puts it.[2] To posit the beginnings of Mahler's new contrapuntal manner in 1901 is, of course, only partially accurate. One need only recall the canonic third movement of the First Symphony (1888), for example, or the chorale style of the Eighth (1906) to cast in doubt any oversimplified bifurcation of Mahler's oeuvre into "linear manner" (post-1901) versus "vertical manner" (pre-1901). Nevertheless, it has been widely recognized that 1901 marks the onset of a more concentrated and overt contrapuntal tendency in Mahler, which is concurrent

---

[1] NBL2, p. 189 (NBLE, p. 170).   [2] MWY, p. 345; cf. also MSSLD, pp. 55 ff.

217

with the end of the *Wunderhorn* years and the continuation of his second maturity.[3]

In charting the stylistic course of a composer who worked with such heterogeneous musical materials as Mahler did, the usual approach is to make a list of "characteristics."[4] However useful that may be, it needs to be supplemented by stylistic conclusions based upon structural analysis: such is the approach adopted in this essay. My purpose is to study aspects of Mahler's harmony and voice leading through close examination of brief but representative excerpts, and thereby to identify common procedures in his music as well as their similarity or dissimilarity to eighteenth- and earlier nineteenth-century norms. The principal analytical focus will be upon "prolonged counterpoint" in two complex passages from "Der Abschied," the finale of *Das Lied von der Erde*.[5] Generally speaking, I adopt the methodological approach of Heinrich Schenker. It must be noted, however, that Mahler's music sometimes oversteps the boundaries of strict Schenkerian theory.[6] Thus, for example, in discussing what he terms

---

[3] A straightforward introduction to Mahler's style may be found in Guido Adler, *Gustav Mahler* (Vienna, 1916), trans. Edward R. Reilly in *Gustav Mahler and Guido Adler: Records of a Friendship* (Cambridge, 1982). The change in Mahler's style following 1901 has also been noted by Paul Bekker, *Gustav Mahlers Sinfonien* (Berlin, 1921, rpt. Tutzing, 1969), pp. 175–78. Synopses of many writers' stylistic observations are found in HLGF, especially in the appendices. Particularly vivid characterizations of Mahler's sounding surfaces may be found in TAME.

[4] Hans Redlich, for example, identifies "fingerprints of style" in his discussion of melody, harmony, and counterpoint in Mahler; see his *Bruckner and Mahler*, rev. edn., The Master Musicians Series (London, 1963), pp. 147–57.

[5] The term "prolonged counterpoint" is used by Felix Salzer in his *Structural Hearing: Tonal Coherence in Music*, new edn., 2 vols. (New York, 1962), vol. I, p. 191. My use of the term in this paper follows that of Salzer and Carl Schachter, and denotes "elaboration, development, manipulation, and transformation of [the] underlying principles [of 'strict' or 'elementary' counterpoint]" (see Salzer and Schachter, *Counterpoint in Composition* [New York, 1969, rpt. 1989], p. xix). Part 2 of their book is entirely devoted to techniques of prolonged counterpoint, and the concluding chapter demonstrates the application of these techniques to a wide range of compositions from ca. 1550 to ca. 1900; there are, however, no examples from the music of Mahler.

[6] Cf. also Allen Forte, "Middleground Motives in the Adagietto of Mahler's Fifth Symphony," *19th Century Music* 8 (1984), esp. 153–54.

"bridges" from strict counterpoint to free composition, Schenker cites passages of Brahms, Wagner, Bruckner, Wolf, and Richard Strauss, but not Mahler.[7] Schenker's approach to the analysis of chromatic music is, nevertheless, suggestive of how one might proceed, and I shall draw upon it here. While the modest scope of this essay does not permit a comprehensive account of Mahler's stylistic development, I hope that some of the strategies pursued here may contribute to such an account.

Diatonic foundations

Although one occasionally encounters a dense passage in Mahler in which tonal orientation is difficult to discern, his music is not only fundamentally diatonic but sometimes aggressively so. Certain of Mahler's precompositional models contribute to this: ländler, marches, minuets, waltzes, and horn calls, for example, are all traditionally diatonic at core. A more significant influence, however, must be the keen awareness of long-range dissonance and its resolution that Mahler developed during a lifetime of constant performance and study of earlier masters (Bach, Mozart, Beethoven, Berlioz, Schumann, and Wagner, among others), in whose works such a tonal dialectic plays a basic role. From this perspective, diatonicism is both a familiar natural background for a diverse variety of enriching procedures as well as a standard rhetorical option, to be exploited on the music's "surface" according to aesthetic need. The "enrichment" just mentioned is generally of two sorts: (1) the conjoining of competing diatonic systems either by linear succession or by superimposition; and (2) the "energizing" of diatonic scale steps through chromaticization.[8]

---

[7] Heinrich Schenker, *Counterpoint*, trans. John Rothgeb and Jürgen Thym, ed. John Rothgeb (New York, 1987), Pt. 6, "Bridges to Free Composition," vol. II, pp. 175–273.

[8] On the interaction between diatonic collections as a source of chromaticism, see William E. Benjamin, "Interlocking Diatonic Collections as a Source of Chromaticism in Late Nineteenth-Century Music," *In Theory Only* 1 (1976), 31–51. An adaptation of Benjamin's theory for the analysis of Mahler is Richard Kaplan, "The Interaction of Diatonic Collections in the Adagio of Mahler's Tenth Symphony," *In Theory Only* 6 (1981), 29–39. The transformation of scale steps is implicit in Schenkerian approaches; see, e.g., Matthew Brown, "The

A technical way of describing the diatonic foundations of Mahler's music, then, is to say that each movement is a large-scale "composing out" (*Auskomponierung*) of one of a small number of idiomatic diatonic progressions. Schenker lists these progressions at the beginning of *Free Composition*,[9] and some analysts of Mahler's music have identified instances of them. For a composer who spent a great deal of time in the theater, and whose language was strongly influenced by the additive musical processes especially characteristic of nineteenth-century Italian opera, the Schenkerian *Ursatz* is perhaps no more than a vision, a deep song or subliminal "first music" that guides tonal expression at different levels of structure. The frank theatricality apparent in some of Mahler's works is achieved in part through techniques of disjunction and discontinuity – procedures that, while not undermining the conceptual relevance of deep structures, may hinder the perceptual accessibility of such structures. This problem is not explicitly addressed in this paper, since all examples examined here are short extracts from longer works, which can easily be grasped, so to say, as "complete fragments." I raise the issue in passing only because any consideration of the larger contexts from which the present examples are drawn must ultimately contend with the recursive nature of deep structural functions.

Let us begin with a simple passage from one of Mahler's best-known works, the Fourth Symphony, in order to introduce a few elementary technical terms (see Ex. 8.1). This excerpt is a closed period in G; the tonic is thus prolonged, as Salzer puts it, by "motion through the framework of a single key-determining progression."[10] Three types of diminution may be identified. The first is arpeggiation, which is present at the outset in the melody notes d^2–( )–g^2–b^1. (Arpeggiations are part of Mahler's ordinary language throughout the Fourth Symphony, and occur with particular motivic significance in the finale, composed eight years before the remainder of the work.) The second type of diminution is the passing note, which

Diatonic and the Chromatic in Schenker's Theory of Harmonic Relations," *Journal of Music Theory* 30 (1986), 1–33. A valuable recent critique of trends in Mahler analysis is John Williamson, "Mahler, Hermeneutics and Analysis," *Music Analysis* 10 (1991), 357–73.

[9] Schenker, *Free Composition ("Der freie Satz")*, trans. and ed. Ernst Oster (New York, 1979). [10] Salzer, *Structural Hearing*, vol. I, p. 227.

Ex. 8.1   Fourth Symphony, 1st mvt., bars 4–7

occurs in both accented and unaccented forms (see c^2 and a^1 at bars $4/^4$ and $6/^1$ respectively).[11] Passing diminutions may also include chromatic notes: the $d\sharp^2$ at bar $5/^1$ is an accented chromatic passing note. The third diminution is the neighbor note: $f\sharp^2$ at $5/^3$ is an upper neighbor note (to the consonant e^2), and b^1 at $6/^4$ is a lower neighbor (to the passing seventh, c^2). The turn figures at $4/^3$ and $6/^3$ combine upper and lower neighbor-note motions into a double neighbor-note figure, the latter of which incorporates a chromatic passing tone, $c\sharp^2$.

The foregoing analysis of Ex. 8.1 as a closed harmonic progression, activated by familiar diminutions, clearly establishes the well-formed and indeed ordinary nature of Mahler's diatonic writing; a passage from a Haydn symphony could have been chosen to illustrate the same techniques of diminution. And the fact that, from the analytical perspective, Ex. 8.1 lacks both particularity and unique characteristics is in part a dimension of the Fourth Symphony's explicit neoclassicism. The analysis also implicitly reveals the potential for extensions, expansions, and interpolations within such simple diatonic structures. Indeed, were we to proceed further into the symphony, we would, for example, encounter many instances of the elongated appoggiatura in the slow movement. The appoggiatura, which is certainly among Mahler's principal means of achieving melodic intensity, often functions as an accented incomplete neighbor note. Even when rhetorically exaggerated, the appoggiatura retains its neighbor- (or passing-) note function. It is against this background of grammatical norms that Mahler's poetic flights are best appreciated.

---

[11] A superscript following a slash after a bar number identifies a specific beat within that bar; for example, $4/^2$ refers to the second beat of bar 4.

221

Ex. 8.2   Ninth Symphony, 1st mvt., bars 44–47

Cadential enrichment

A predisposition toward expressive variety is evident in Mahler's habits of punctuation – i.e., in his choice of cadence types to secure the closure of a given passage, movement, or work. While Mahler often writes fairly conventional cadences, like those associated with classical models in Ex. 8.1, he also punctuates less mechanically, deploying some of his more imaginative strokes at points of syntax that carry considerable traditional expectation.

A separate paper would be required to discuss Mahler's cadential practice in detail; the following is no more than a brief sketch of enrichment procedures found in a few of his cadences.[12] In addition to regular authentic cadences in which the dominant is prolonged by either a six-four chord or a neighboring augmented sixth,[13] Mahler often writes enriched authentic cadences such as the one shown in Ex. 8.2, from the first movement of the Ninth Symphony. Here the enrichment is of two sorts. The first is modal mixture: we enter the passage from the minor mode and quit it in the major. This local D minor to D major succession reflects the broader modal conflict that occupies the entire first movement of the

---

12   Valuable comments on cadential practice in the nineteenth century may be found in Robert Bailey, ed., *Wagner: Prelude and Transfiguration from "Tristan and Isolde"*, Norton Critical Scores (New York, 1985), pp. 118–25.

13   The six-four type is illustrated by Ex. 8.1; for a case of a neighboring augmented-sixth prolongation, see Mahler's Second Symphony, mvt. 2, bars 29–32.

Ex. 8.3   Ninth Symphony, 1st mvt., bars 53–54

Ninth.[14] The second procedure of enrichment is a modification of harmonic syntax. In place of the normal V^6_4–$^5_3$ progression, Mahler writes V^6_4–$^6_3$, denying the dominant chord its defining fifth (e), thus simultaneously weakening and enhancing the continuity of the cadence. Note, however, that the pitch e^2 occurs on the downbeat of the last quoted bar, where it functions as an appoggiatura to a melodically unrealized d^2, suggesting a 9–8 suspension. (Such lingering appoggiaturas are another issue that spans this entire movement.)

Example 8.3, also from the first movement of the Ninth, may be understood as a conflation of two cadence types – the authentic and the deceptive. The bass motion, A–D, collaborates with a melody descending from scale degree $\hat{5}$ to $\hat{1}$ to suggest an authentic cadence. The chord of resolution, however, is not D major but $B\flat^6$ major (with the bass note D functioning as the third of the $B\flat$ triad). Thus, despite the strong implications of the melodic line and bass progression, this is actually a V→VI or "deceptive" cadence. As a result, both of these standard cadence types take on added levels of meaning.[15]

One of the most memorable cadences in all of Mahler's music is that

---

14   The themes introduced in bars 7 and 27 embody the major and minor polarities respectively.

15   Mahler very likely became acquainted with "cadential conflation" in the music of Wagner, where full melodic cadential gestures are frequently undercut by deceptive harmonic resolutions in the orchestra; this is one of several techniques Wagner uses to prevent premature tonal closure prior to the arrival of a major structural articulation.

Ex. 8.4   Second Symphony, 1st mvt., bars 325–29

leading from the end of the development section into the recapitulation in the first movement ("Todtenfeier") of the Second Symphony. Example 8.4 summarizes the chordal content of these bars, showing an underlying V–i progression in C minor. But whereas the bass stabilizes and underwrites the intelligibility of the progression, the upper voices destabilize and challenge the sense of a generic $\hat{2}$–$\hat{1}$ melodic progression by piling on a series of added notes.[16] The third and fourth bars of the quoted passage contain all the notes of the C harmonic minor scale with only one "wrong" note: the passing eighth-note triplet f♯ in the fourth bar. After this striking vertical-ization of the C minor scale, it is entirely logical, and yet rhetorically sur-prising, that Mahler finishes on the "pure" and contextually definitive octave Cs.

The purity of resolution in Ex. 8.4 stands in contrast to the numerous cadences in which the concluding triad is incomplete, and the musical ear is left to fill in the rest of the chord.[17] In some cases, Mahler dispenses with the idea of a consonant close altogether, cadencing on a sonority that seems very much "on its way." Example 8.5, an excerpt from "Der Tamboursg'sell," is a case in point. Without the f♯s in the third and fifth bars, or the fs and d♭s in the fourth and sixth, this would have been a perfectly normal authentic

[16] By "generic $\hat{2}$-$\hat{1}$" progression I mean a generic top voice that would ordinarily involve those scale-degree functions. Mahler, however, sustains $\hat{5}$ in the top voice. For a highly detailed analysis of the entire "Todtenfeier" movement, see Stephen E. Hefling, "The Making of Mahler's 'Todtenfeier': A Documentary and Analytical Study," 3 vols. (Ph.D. diss., Yale University, 1985); concerning the rhetoric of this cadence, see his article "Mahler's 'Todtenfeier' and the Problem of Program Music," *19th Century Music* 12 (1988), esp. 32–34.

[17] E.g., the cadence in bars 419–23 in the third movement of the Ninth.

Ex. 8.5 "Der Tamboursg'sell," bars 133–38

cadence in C minor. Mahler both weakens and strengthens this normality, not by altering the elements of an authentic cadence but by adding to them, such that they remain embedded in a more complex pitch context.[18]

Chromatic enrichment: mixture

A familiar source of deep expressive effect and expanded tonal pro-cedures in Mahler is the interpenetration of major and minor modes, often simply termed mixture; among earlier composers, perhaps the most characteristic and memorable usages of the device are found in Schubert, for whose music Mahler felt particular affinity.[19] From his earliest songs

[18] The sonority in bars 136 and 138 (0157) is pitch-class set 4-16 (see Allen Forte, *The Structure of Atonal Music* [New Haven, 1973]). Both the presence of the defining fifth, C–g, and the semitonal approach to g from f♯ notwithstanding, the sonority sounds dissonant in context; it gains a measure of stability, however, by virtue of its position at the end of the four-bar phrase.

[19] Natalie Bauer-Lechner, "Mahleriana" (partially unpublished MS, Bibliothèque musicale Gustav Mahler, Paris), September 1901: "Beim Spazierengehen: 'Wenn ich als junger Bursch ein Schubert'sches Werk voll Entzücken spielte, war es meine größte Sehnsucht, daß ich selbst einmal, was mich erfüllte und bewegte, in solchem Inhalt, solchen Formen, ganz wie ich es wollte, ausdrücken könnte.'" ("While walking: 'As a youth, when I played through a work of Schubert and was thereby filled with enchantment, my greatest longing was that I myself might someday be able to express what filled and moved me exactly as I wished, in such content and such forms.'") Cf. also Herta Blaukopf, "The Young Mahler," p. 10 above. Of course mixture also occurs with varying frequency and expressive intensity in the works of many other nineteenth-century composers.

Ex. 8.6 "Rheinlegendchen," bars 1–10

Ex. 8.7 Seventh Symphony, 4th mvt., bars 8–11

Ex. 8.8 Sixth Symphony, 3rd mvt., bars 1–4

through his mature symphonies, Mahler, like Schubert, deployed mixture
with particular care – not merely as the simple juxtaposition of major and
minor over the same tonic, but as a more complex procedure whereby a
"secondary" harmonic field is activated.[20] Among Mahler's compositions
from 1901 and following years, the *Kindertotenlieder*, the first movements
of the Fifth, Sixth, Seventh, and Ninth Symphonies, and the opening movement of *Das Lied von der Erde* make particularly telling use of mixture.

In Exx. 8.6, 8.7, and 8.8, each of the three major-mode melodic fragments quoted embodies a musical narrative in which the minor mode is
encountered and dealt with as part of an ongoing discourse. In Ex. 8.6, the
lowered third scale degree ($c\natural^2$ in the seventh through ninth bars) functions
as an interpolation within a predominantly major-mode context. In Ex. 8.7,
$\flat\hat{3}$ arrives as part of an overall melodic ascent, $\hat{1}$–$\hat{2}$–$\sharp\hat{2}/\flat\hat{3}$ (= f^1–g^1–$a\flat^1$), thus
exploiting the enharmonic equivalence of $\flat3$ and $\sharp2$. The continuation of
this passage (not shown) treats further of this minor-mode interpolation

---

[20] For additional discussion of mixture, see Edward Aldwell and Carl Schachter,
    Harmony and Voice Leading (San Diego, 1989), pp. 355–66 and 503–09.

Ex. 8.9   Sixth Symphony, 1st mvt., bars 59–63

Ex. 8.10   *Das Lied von der Erde*, "Der Abschied," bars 413–16, from *Gustav Mahler: Sämtliche Werke, Kritische Gesamtausgabe*, Supplement Band II, edited by Stephen E. Hefling. © Copyright 1989 by Universal Edition A.G., Wien, All Rights Reserved. Used by permission of European American Music Distributors Corporation, sole US and Canadian agent for Universal Edition A.G., Wien

while leading the potent $\sharp\hat{2}$ on to its eventual destination, $\natural\hat{3}$. Example 8.8 also exploits the double meaning of $\flat\hat{3}$ and $\sharp\hat{2}$. Example 8.9, a famous passage of modal mixture from the first movement of the Sixth Symphony, contains four triads on A, two of them major (1 and 4), the other two minor (2 and 3). Such a distribution of major and minor colors hints at the sort of modal freedom characteristic of Mahler's late style.

A more intricate and fundamental instance of mixture occupies a closed four-bar passage from "Der Abschied" of *Das Lied* (Ex. 8.10),[21] in which the major and minor modes, while expressively poignant in their

---

[21] The excerpts from "Der Abschied" presented here and in Exx. 8.16 and 8.20 are taken from Mahler's own voice and piano version of *Das Lied von der Erde*, published as Supplement Band II in the *Kritische Gesamtausgabe*, ed. Stephen E. Hefling (Vienna, 1989). Bar numbers shown in these examples correspond to those found in the orchestral score of the work.

Ex. 8.11   "Rheinlegendchen," bars 17–32

fluctuation, are structurally interchangeable; they function not as two distinct keys, but as a larger referential construct on C that combines major and minor.[22] The succession of chords numbered 1–9 in Ex. 8.10 shifts modality as follows (m = minor, M = major):

1	2	3	4	5	6	7	8	9
m	M	m	M	M	m	M	M/m	m

Although the passage is framed by the minor and inflects its most striking gesture with $\flat\hat{3}$ – "*ein*-sam" – it is nevertheless exceptionally fluid in modal orientation.[23]

An excerpt from the *Wunderhorn* song "Rheinlegendchen" (summarized in Ex. 8.11) illustrates a secondary form of modal mixture, and also draws attention to the unifying function of repeated motives, which can compensate for relatively long spans between clear articulations of the prevailing tonal framework. The passage is tonally open, beginning in the tonic (A) and modulating to the dominant (E). This modulatory narrative proceeds in two four-bar phrases (bars 17–20 and 21–14), followed by an eight-bar unit (bars 25–32). The traditional minor-mode mediant (iii), reached at the end of the first four-bar phrase (bar 20), is replaced by its parallel

---

[22]   Robert Bailey has observed that by the time of Wagner's *Tristan*, the major and minor modes have become "equivalent and interchangeable" (*Wagner: Prelude and Transfiguration*, p. 116).

[23]   Salzer characterizes this passage as a "highly expressive use of mixture, both in melody and harmony" (*Structural Hearing*, vol. I, p. 181).

major (III♯) at the end of the second phrase (bar 24). This C♯ major triad then functions locally as V of f♯, the relative minor of A. But the relative minor is here only a possibility rather than an actuality, for Mahler once again opts for the parallel major instead (F♯, bar 25) . Thus, although mixture is operative through the implication that the relative minor is imminent, only the major form of the F♯ triad is actually sounded. Then, by way of a 10–5 linear intervallic pattern (bars 25–28), the music arrives at V/V in bar 28, which is in turn prolonged for four bars before cadencing in V.

Two additional enrichment processes may be observed in Ex. 8.11. The first concerns the descending tetrachord motive, a^1–g♯^{1}–f♯^{1}–e^1, which is heard in each phrase (in the longer third phrase comprising eight bars it begins upon A♯ and is considerably extended). This pattern provides motivic continuity spanning the slightly unusual harmonic progressions. Second is the "real" (as distinct from "tonal") transposition of bars 25–26 into 27–28, which yields the effect of an interpolation – a small, albeit open, harmonic world within the overall I–V progression. Such fragmentation, emphasized by the 10–5 pattern, gives considerable prominence to local events, which somewhat confound the listener's ability to perceive prolongations synoptically.[24]

Chromatic enrichment: interpolation

Interpolations such as that just examined proceed through closed or semi-closed harmonic progressions that seem rather like small worlds functioning somewhat autonomously within a larger harmonic succession. Structural coherence in passages containing interpolations often derives less from the linear semitonal relations of late chromatic music than from a new prominence of motive on different levels. The term "interpolation" allows us to acknowledge not only the many challenges to normative expression of tonicity (be it a single or a "double tonic") posed by a succession of small worlds, but also the structural significance of disjunctions and

---

[24] For a related discussion concerning Wagner's music, see Carolyn Abbate, "Wagner, 'On Modulation,' and *Tristan*," *Cambridge Opera Journal* 1 (1989), 33–58.

Ex. 8.12   Ninth Symphony, 3rd mvt., bars 109–32

discontinuities, as well as the integrative potential of motivic parallel-isms.[25]

Two passages from the Ninth Symphony will help focus our discussion of interpolation. The first (Ex. 8.12) comes from the famously contrapuntal Rondo-Burleske, a movement so saturated with what Salzer terms

[25] For a recent discussion of interpolations or "parenthetical episodes," see Matthew Brown, "Tonality and Form in Debussy's *Prélude à 'L'Après-midi d'un*

"independent voice leading" that it is a formidable challenge to discern the sort of hierarchically ordered linear organization operative in the previous examples examined here.[26] Our passage begins in F (bar 109), moves to C (bar 115), touches on F minor (bar 116), passes through C♯ minor (bar 120), hints at A major (bars 120–22), and finally returns to F (bar 131) – which, overall, suggests a monotonal structure. It would be difficult to argue, however, that the triad of F exhibits, to paraphrase Salzer, prolonged motion within the framework of a single key-determining progression,[27] for the overriding aural impression is of a consistent motivic process that throws into relief a series of apparently independent harmonic regions – in other words, Mahlerian interpolations.[28]

Consider the first three bars of Ex. 8.12: Two transpositionally equivalent and overlapping melodic motives follow one another: a^1–g^1–a^1–f^1 and f^1–$e\flat^1$–f^1–$d\flat^1$. Each is harmonized by three root-position triads, I–V–♭VI, the first in F and the second in D♭.[29] Outer-voice motion follows a 10–5 linear intervallic pattern (cf. bars 25–28 of "Rheinlegendchen," Ex. 8.11). The structural outline of the bass, F–D♭–A initiates an equal-interval cycle of major thirds, a characteristic segment of the whole-tone scale. Lacking potent and conventionally suggestive semitone relations and fifth spans,

faune'," *Music Theory Spectrum* 15 (1993), 127–143. On motivic parallelisms, see Charles Burkhart, "Schenker's 'Motivic Parallelisms'," *Journal of Music Theory* 22 (1978), 145–75. The ascendancy of motives as determinants of structure in later 19th-century music is discussed in Carl Dahlhaus, *Between Romanticism and Modernism: Four Studies in the Later Nineteenth Century*, trans. Mary Whittall (Berkeley, 1980), pp. 40–78.

[26] "Independent" voice leading is discussed by Salzer in *Structural Hearing*, vol. I, pp. 191–93.

[27] See Salzer, *Structural Hearing*, e.g., vol. I, chap. 2, and p. 227; see also n. 10 above.

[28] A comprehensive analysis of this movement may be found in Christopher Orlo Lewis, *Tonal Coherence in Mahler's Ninth Symphony*, Studies in Musicology, no. 79 (Ann Arbor, 1984), ch. 4.

[29] I–V–♭VI is the so-called "motto progression" of the Ninth Symphony, which is heard distinctly in three movements; the second (e.g., bars 261–64), third (bars 109–11, etc.) and finale (bars 3–4 and frequently thereafter). Further on this issue, see Lewis, *Tonal Coherence*, p. 50; Jack Diether, "The Expressive Content of Mahler's Ninth Symphony," *Chord and Discord* 2/10 (1963), 83–84; Deryck Cooke, "Mahler's Melodic Thinking," in his *Vindications: Essays in Romantic Music* (London, 1982), pp. 103–05; and Constantin Floros, *Gustav Mahler: The Symphonies*, trans. Vernon Wicker (Portland, Ore., 1993), pp. 281 and 284–85.

Ex. 8.13 Ninth Symphony, 4th mvt., bars 1–11

this type of partitioning effectively undermines the listener's feeling for an overarching hierarchy and instead focuses attention upon a chain-like, moment-by-moment additive process. On this reading, then, the succession of passages described above as "in D♭ major," "in C major," "in F minor," and so on, represents a larger-than-life interpolation between the framing articulations of F (bars 109 and 131) – not a composing-out of F major *Stufen* (structural scale degrees). This is not to imply a loss of tonal meaning; rather, such meaning is guaranteed by the motivic process even as the passage as a whole renounces traditional processes of *Auskomponierung*.

A second example of chromatic enrichment by interpolation is the opening period of the last movement of the Ninth (Ex. 8.13). While there is no doubt about the priority of D♭ (mostly major, inflected towards minor at the close of the excerpt), some moments in the period (see especially bars 8–9) seem beyond the boundaries of D♭ major, thus inviting interpretation

Ex. 8.14 Generating bar 3 of Ex. 8.13

1

I — V — vi – iii
10   5   10   5

2

I — V —♭VI iii

3

I — V$^{6-5}$♭VI iii$^{6-5}$

as interpolations. Scrutiny of the passage in light of the enrichment techniques discussed above reveals the unifying function of motives in a chromatic context built upon a diatonic linear foundation.

Let us proceed in the sequence of the excerpt. Bar 3 may be generated
from a simple 10–5 diatonic sequence (reminiscent of the Pachelbel
Canon) as shown in level 1 of Ex. 8.14. At level 2, vi is replaced by a borrowed
♭VI from the parallel minor. Level 3 introduces consonant suspensions
between adjacent chords, bringing us to the threshold of Mahler's actual
music. The next bar of the passage (bar 4, Ex. 8.13) remains within the
confines of a diatonic tonality, partly because of its cadential function,
which is embellished by means of the ubiquitous turn or double-neighbor
figure (first heard at 1/^{4} and now in the tenor at 4/^{2}) plus a decorated 4–3
suspension (bar 4/$^{3-4}$). Bar 5 includes an incomplete secondary dominant
in the approach to the subdominant (vii^{o6} of IV^6) and an elongated form of
the turn figure in the alto at bar 5/$^{3-4}$. In bar 6 three occurrences of the turn
figure (in the soprano, bass, and alto respectively) decorate its otherwise
straightforward VI–iii progression.

Bar 7 is an obvious variant of bar 3, and may accordingly be generated
after the model of Ex. 8.14, as shown in Ex. 8.15. A 10–5 diatonic sequence

Ex. 8.15   Generating bar 7 of Ex. 8.13

(level 1) is enriched by transferring the original melody of bar 3 into an inner voice plus adding a countermelody above it (level 2), and then mixing the mode (level 3). The fifth sonority at level 3 completes an overlapping I–V⁷–♭VI progression in B♭♭, or ♭VI (the progression is also notated enharmonically, in A, for clarity). Thus (as in "Rheinlegendchen") bars 7/¹ to 8/¹ are held together by a "real" (as distinct from a "tonal") transposition; this is obvious from the bass pattern d♭–A♭–B♭♭, A–E–F, and F–c–(d♭). The last is incomplete: the arrival on d♭ is postponed for two bars, presumably to avoid a premature return to the tonic. (The fragment from the Rondo-Burleske quoted in Ex. 8.12 shows the origin of this bass pattern.) Bar 8, in addition to participating in the sequence, functions as a variant of bar 4, substituting a plagal cadence for the earlier authentic one, but retaining the same motivic gesture. It also shares with bar 6 a threefold occurrence of the turn figure (bass, tenor, and alto respectively). Bar 9 expands upon what Riemann terms the pre-dominant sonority: in place of the typical progression from IV⁶ to a (German) augmented sixth and then to V, Mahler reverses the positions of the first two sonorities, adds dissonance to the IV⁶ (g♮), and respells the augmented sixth (not B♭♭, but A). The essential progression remains that from an augmented sixth chord to a dominant, but it now includes an interpolation in the second half of bar 9. Finally, bars 10–11 provide closure for the period through an authentic cadence, and by reiterating the motivic gesture previously heard in bars 4 and 8.

The integrative role of motivic material in this passage is a more complex manifestation of the process encountered in the "Rhein-legendchen" excerpt discussed above (Ex. 8.11); here again, motives lend coherence to a context of extended tonality. Bars 3–4 expose the referential motive, to which bars 5–6 offer a counterstatement embodying a nearly identical rhythmic pattern. Then bars 7–8 recompose bars 3–4, to be followed in bars 9–10 by another variant of the melodic contour from bars 3–4. Note that within this process of developing variation, the melody in bar 9 reproduces exactly the pitch content of bar 2, thus hinting at another motivic relation. Just as bars $2/^4$–$4/^4$ contain a hidden canon (between soprano and tenor voices) that serves to smooth over the apparent disjunction in tonal orientation between bars 2 and 3, so the repetition of melodic span from bar 9 in the following bar cements the relationship between these apparently tonally disjunct bars (9 and 10). Motive and harmony are related; harmonic "purple patches" (to use Tovey's redoubtable term) sound like interpolations which the motivic process stencils over.

Prolonged counterpoint

Hitherto we have analyzed small fragments of Mahler's music to show the function of diminutions at relatively local structural levels. The next set of examples includes analyses of two slightly more extended passages. Both are from the "Der Abschied" of *Das Lied*, and both magnificently demonstrate not only the integrity of line in Mahler, but also the role of prolonged counterpoint as a basic form-building device.[30]

The first passage, bars 172–99 of "Der Abschied" (Ex. 8.16) is an instance of a full Mahlerian period – that is, a coherent melodic-harmonic-

---

[30] For convenience, the following analyses are based upon Mahler's own voice and piano version of *Das Lied von der Erde* (KG, Supplement Band II). Bar numbers shown here, as well as the singer's text, correspond to the orchestral score of the work.

Ex. 8.16 *Das Lied von der Erde*, "Der Abschied," bars 172–200, from *Gustav Mahler: Sämtliche Werke, Kritische Gesamtausgabe*, Supplement Band II, edited by Stephen E. Hefling. © Copyright 1989 by Universal Edition A.G., Wien, All Rights Reserved. Used by permission of European American Music Distributors Corporation, sole US and Canadian agent for Universal Edition A.G., Wien

rhythmic unit founded upon a single tonality (B♭). The excerpt is preceded by a pentatonically based passage outlining the mediant of B♭ (bars 166–71), but the pentatonic elements are quickly absorbed into the prevailing diatonic/chromatic complex of the period under consideration here.[31] One reason that this twenty-eight-bar passage has clear periodicity is that it provides the basis for three subsequent modified strophic variations, beginning in bars 199, 229, and 245. Later, in the second half of "Der Abschied," the passage will return in yet another variant, transposed up a step from B♭ major to C major (bars 460–508).[32]

The first issue to consider is the claim advanced above that the passage is monotonically organized in B♭. (Ex. 8.17 displays a voice-leading graph of the entire period.) It begins and ends on a B♭ major chord (bars 172 and 199 respectively), with recurrences of B♭ in bars 178 (major) and 191 (minor); furthermore, each of these chords is spaced with scale degree $\hat{3}$ or $\hat{♭3}$ in the top voice. These articulations of B♭ effect a periodic return to centrality, not so much through the dynamism of a sharply polarized V–I progression, but rather through a circular surrounding of B♭ – "solar" rather than "polar" tonicization.[33] This distinction does not, however, imply that dominant chords are insignificant in the passage; on the contrary, local dominants precede each B♭ chord, producing a clear sense of cadence. Nor are these dominants equivalent in function: the dominant seventh of bars 188–89 is structurally more important than the others, owing both to its occurrence near the end of the passage (as the period is being rounded off) and to its role in clarifying the rather complex linear structure of the preceding bars, as we shall see. The overall tonal profile of the passage, then, stems from the

---

[31] A discussion of pentatonicism in *Das Lied* as well as a detailed analysis of "Der Abschied" will be found in J. Randall Wheaton, "The Diatonic Potential of Strange Sets: Theoretical Tenets and Structural Meaning in Gustav Mahler's *Der Abschied*" (Ph.D. diss., Yale University, 1988).

[32] For a detailed study of the form of "Der Abschied," see MSSLD, pp. 339–432. See also the diagram "Overall Structure of 'Der Abschied,'" based on a formal analysis by Robert Bailey, in Stephen E. Hefling, "*Das Lied von der Erde*: Mahler's Symphony for Voices and Orchestra – or Piano," *Journal of Musicology* 10 (1992), 329.

[33] The distinction between "solar" and "polar" arrangements of keys stems from eighteenth-century theory and is briefly discussed by Leonard G. Ratner in *Classic Music: Expression, Form and Style* (New York, 1980), pp. 48–51.

Ex. 8.17   "Der Abschied," analysis of bars 172–99

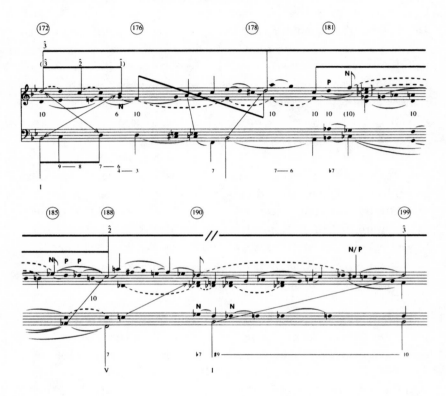

tension between a shadowy, polarized I–V–I progression and the periodic assertion of I throughout the passage.

Of course the periodic return of a given chord, even if preceded by its dominant, is not by itself a sufficient condition to establish tonic centrality. It would need to be shown that the music between any two occurrences of the B♭ chord is hierarchically subsumed by that chord, and thereby represents a composing-out of B♭ *Stufen*. The ensuing detailed consideration of Ex. 8.17 will shed light on this processes of *Auskomponierung*. We will proceed through the sequence of the passage in five overlapping segments: bars 172–76; 176–78; 178–81; 181–88; and 188–99.

Ex. 8.18   Generating bars 172–76 of Ex. 8.16

The principal event in the first segment (bars 172–76) is a 10–6 voice
exchange between treble and bass, which prolongs B♭ major. Ex. 8.18 suggests a hypothetical origin of the passage in three stages: first, the 10–8–6
voice exchange as it occurs in eighteenth-century music ($\hat{3}$–$\hat{2}$–$\hat{1}$ in the treble
directly counterpointed by its retrograde, $\hat{1}$–$\hat{2}$–$\hat{3}$, in the bass); second, an
embellishment of the same voice exchange through 9–8 and 7–6 suspen-
sions (this stage is also common in eighteenth-century repertoire); and
third, a twist: the addition of a 4–3 appoggiatura within the texture of the
final sixth chord (not impossible, although less likely, in eighteenth-
century music).

The first-inversion tonic chord in bar 176, which concludes the first
segment and initiates the second, progresses through its dominant to a
root-position tonic in bar 178. The melodic motion of these bars is an
ascending middleground unfolding of a sixth, f^1–d^2, culminating in a
double neighbor-note (or "turn") embellishment at the goal of ascent, d^2
($\hat{3}$) in bar 178. The corresponding bass includes a suspended pair of chromatic passing notes (e/c♯), which briefly displace treble from bass (the diagonal lines in the graph indicate the underlying structural simultaneity).

Ex. 8.19   "Der Abschied," bars 178–88, voice leading

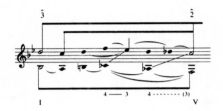

The third segment, bars 178–81/^{1}, is a prolongation of the tonic through its first-inversion dominant, which seems to effect a lower-neighbor gesture in both bass and treble. Two Mahlerian fingerprints enliven this familiar eighteenth-century progression. The first is an "added" overlapping polyphonic voice (bars 179–80) that creates a 7–6 suspension (a^2–g^2), recalling the suspensions in bars 173–74. The origin of this upper voice is an implied b♭^{1} (octave doubling of the root) in bar 178; now projected above the primary tone (d^2, $\hat{3}$), this strand of the texture would presumably initiate a stepwise descent (to f^2) in the next segment. The second fingerprint is the substitution of B♮ for B♭ in the bass of bar 181/^{2} in conjunction with the chromatic passing tone a♭ in the tenor range: the resulting (incomplete) diminished seventh chord strongly implies motion to ii (C minor), wherewith the turn-embellished d^2 of the upper voice would pass up to e♭^{2}. This, then, would suggest that an upper-voice middleground descent from $\hat{3}$ to $\hat{2}$ has taken place, and that $\hat{2}$ is now prolonged (and covered) by the local ascent c^2–d^2–(e♭^{2}) of bars 181–82, as summarized in Ex. 8.19.

But in segment four (bars 181–88) matters become complicated. In place of the expected ii, Mahler substitutes a "deceptive" resolution: ♭II (C♭ major). The f^2 appoggiatura in the upper voice of bar 182 must resolve (4–3), particularly since e♭^{1} is already sounding below it; but as is often the case in his later works, Mahler allows for assumed resolution through register transfer (which might also be thought of as "absorption into the voice-leading texture"). For the moment, it must be assumed that c^2 ($\hat{2}$ in B♭) has temporarily descended to c♭^{2}, as shown in Ex. 8.17; whether it will ultimately function as a passing note (to b♭^{1}) or as a lower neighbor (to c^2) is clarified only a good bit later in the music.

Meanwhile, the melody dips down to g♭^{1}, and ascends rather listlessly through chromatic passing notes. The underlying harmony shifts some-what unexpectedly to G^7 in bar 185 – V/ii in B♭ – which defines the upper-voice b♮^{1} (enharmonically, c♭^{2}) as the third of the chord, and thereby also the leading tone (or lower neighbor) to c^2. The ensuing leap to e♭^{2} is a common-place anticipation of the next expected sonority – C minor – that typically precipitates a downbeat 2–1 appoggiatura (d^2–c^2 in this case); in addition, e♭^{2} may also be heard as a lingering suspension from the three previous bars of C♭ harmony, the long-range resolution of the f^2 introduced back in bar 182. The pitch d^2 arrives in bar 186, but once again there is a deceptive har-monic resolution, to A♭ (♭VI/ii in B♭); the appoggiatura in the upper voice passes only gradually toward resolution via d♭^{2}, and when the c^2 finally arrives in bar 188, it has solid harmonic support: V^7 of B♭.

Thus, in the fifth and final segment, bars 188–99, the principal har-monic motion is a V^7–I progression with, once again, displacements between treble and bass articulation. The composing out of this progres-sion admits of two different explanations. In the first, upper voice $\hat{2}$ in bar 188 moves to ♭$\hat{3}$ in bar 190; it is then prolonged through bar 199, whereupon it is transformed into ♮$\hat{3}$. On this reading, the essential progression from dominant to tonic is complete between bars 188–91, and the remainder is a prolongation – via mixture – of the tonic. A second (and to me preferable) explanation regards the d♭^{2}/c♯^{2} as an extraordinarily long accented passing note between c^2 in bar 188 and d^2 in bar 199. In this view, the arrival on a tonic pedal in bar 190 represents a partial harmonic resolution (note the inner-voice activity throughout the ensuing bars), but not a linear-melodic resolution. That is why Ex. 8.17 shows a diagonal line linking the bass B♭ in bar 190 to the treble d^2 in bar 197.

From the broadest perspective, this period may be interpreted as a classic Schenkerian interruption structure:

$$\hat{3}\text{–}\hat{2} \; // \qquad \hat{3} \ldots \qquad (\hat{2}\text{–}\hat{1}?)$$
$$\text{I–V} \; // \qquad \text{I} \qquad (\text{V–I})$$

Yet the displaced points of resolution – whether of suspensions, neighbor notes, passing notes, or familiar dominant-tonic progressions – plus the implication of modal mixture are tonal procedures lending a strong sense of fluid mobility and unpredictable dynamism to the passage. The broad span is traversed via circuitous paths.

Ex. 8.20 *Das Lied von der Erde*, "Der Abschied," bars 81–97, from *Gustav Mahler: Sämtliche Werke, Kritische Gesamtausgabe*, Supplement Band II, edited by Stephen E. Hefling. © Copyright 1989 by Universal Edition A.G., Wien, All Rights Reserved. Used by permission of European American Music Distributors Corporation, sole US and Canadian agent for Universal Edition A.G., Wien

The second extensive excerpt to be considered here, bars 81–97 of "Der Abschied" (Ex. 8.20), is more "harmonic" than the previous one; it projects a large-scale ii–V–I/i progression in C. This eighteenth-century model with its succession of descending fifths in the bass provides a strong background against which we can hear Mahler's varied yet firmly rooted foreground (see the graph in Ex. 8.21). As before, we will proceed in the sequence of the passage.

Prolongation of ii (bars 81–83). Mahler's foreground in these bars may

Ex. 8.21   "Der Abschied," analysis of bars 81–97

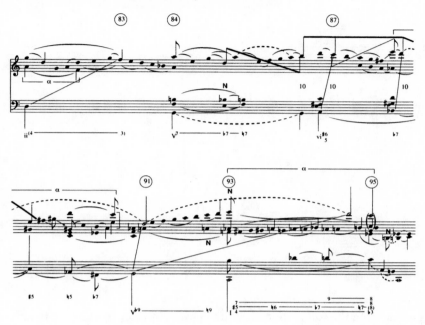

be generated in four stages, as shown in Ex. 8.22.[34] Level 1 contains a regular upper neighbor-note configuration. This is truncated at level 2 to yield an accented upper neighbor, or 4–3 appoggiatura.[35] Level 3 retains the appoggiatura while incorporating a descending passing motion in the middle voice to fill in the interval between notes lying a fifth and third above the bass (a^1–f^1). (The descending third is one of the most prominent motives of "Der Abschied," and three notable instances of it are marked "α" in Ex. 8.21.) Level 4 extends the auxiliary note g^2 so that its point of resolution

---

[34]   In the orchestral score the bass D/d is a quarter note for cellos and contrabasses (pizzicato) in bar 81, and it clearly functions as structural bass throughout bars 81–83; this is less apparent in the piano score, where Mahler represents the structural bass only as a grace note.

[35]   In the foreground of the Mahler passage, this g^2 is a suspension by register transfer from the preceding sonority; such a "neighbor" could also be an accented passing note.

243

Ex. 8.22 Generating bars 82–3 of Ex. 8.20

occurs after the completion of the inner-voice motion; from here it is but a small step to Mahler's foreground as analyzed in Ex. 8.21. The ii chord, then, is prolonged partly by a 4–3 suspension and partly by stepwise, inner-voice motion within the chord itself.

Prolongation of V (bars 84–92). Two occurrences of the dominant chord (in bars 84–86 and 91–92) provide the framework for this prolongation. Although the two dominants do not have the same articulative and structural weight – the latter is more important than the earlier one – they are inextricably linked. In bar 91, the abandoned but still operative dominant is regained, and the expectation of tonic resolution is intensified. It is in this sense that we may speak of a dominant prolongation across the span of bars 84 to 92.

The principal agent of prolongation is the familiar linear intervallic pattern, 10–10–10, which we encountered in the previous passage. Here, however, two of the sonorities framed by outer-voice tenths differ in chord quality from the traditional 10–10 pattern: the first (bar 86) is supported by the dominant seventh, the second (bar 87) is a half-diminished triad in first inversion, and the third seems at least initially like an augmented-sixth embellishment of the preceding 'deceptive' resolution ($V–vi^{\sharp 6}_{5}$). The upper voice in bars 86–89 thus composes out the interval $b^2–d^3$ (a component of the dominant). Since the stepwise outer-voice motion ensures a coherent contrapuntal progression, Mahler is able to enrich this traditional linear-intervallic pattern through a variety of striking local harmonies.

A less prominent although still significant prolongational device is neighbor-note motion, heard in the treble and inner voices in bars 84–86 (prolonging the initial dominant) and, more significantly, as the bass approaches V in bars 90–91: here two chromatic neighbor notes, an upper (A♭) and a lower (F♯), provide a prospective prolongation of the dominant.

One memorable detail in this prolongation of V is the persistence of pitch class A♭ (or G♯) from bar 88 through bar 94. When first heard in bar 88, it functions as the augmented sixth (or seventh?) of the chord on B♭. In bar 89 it becomes the fifth of the augmented triad on C, yet serves another function, as follows: Although the augmented triad in bar 89 may seem to provide a preliminary, incomplete resolution to the tonic, it functions more obviously as an extension of the vi chord ("deceptive" prolongation of V) in bar 87. This is owing to the prominent linear tritone unfolding, $d^3–g\sharp^2$, in the upper voice, which pulls toward resolution in A minor. Partial resolution occurs in 90/4 (the verticality $a^1–c^3$), but by then, as noted above, the bass is homing in on G through neighbor-note motion. In bar 91, A♭ is back as a ninth above the dominant bass, and sets up a strong expectation of resolution through semitone descent. The culmination of this linear prolongation occurs in bars 93–95, where the long-awaited resolution to the tonic occurs. Even as the bass arrives on C (bar 93), A♭ persists as part of the suspended dominant ninth; the pitch eventually ascends chromatically to b♮^{1} in bar 94, which remains temporarily unresolved in bar 95, blurring a potentially trite V–I cadence in C minor.

Prolongation of I/i (bars 93–97). The last five bars of this excerpt are taken up by resolution to, and prolongation of, the tonic chord. At first it seems the resolution will be to the major (the pitch e♮^{3} in bar 93, although functioning as an appoggiatura to the ensuing d^3, reinforces the major-mode orientation of the passage thus far). But significant minor mixture is audible (chiefly in ♭$\hat{6}$, the persistent A♭ discussed above), and when closure is finally complete, it is explicitly minor in coloration (bars 95–98). We have already noted several ways in which major-minor juxtaposition and combination are significant in Mahler. Here mixture gives expressive profile to the culminating tonic of an expanded ii–V–I/i cadential progression, and facilitates the transition from a C-centered passage to an F-centered one (beginning in bar 98). More significantly, however, "Der Abschied" as a musico-poetic whole is a large-scale progression of mode from C minor to C major, whereby the major arrives with finality in the transfiguring coda ("Die liebe Erde . . ."). The minor-mode cadence in bars 93–98, prepared by implication of the major, is a poetic indication that the moment of transcendence is not yet.

Conclusion

I began this essay by positing that the foundations of Mahler's music are essentially diatonic, based on the composing-out of structural diatonic progressions. I then described and analyzed techniques such as mixture and interpolation by which Mahler's music enriches traditional diatonic progressions. Finally, I analyzed two complex passages from "Der Abschied" of *Das Lied von der Erde*, demonstrating that they are essentially well formed by traditional contrapuntal standards, and at the same time drawing attention to numerous, occasionally urgent ways in which voice leading enriches traditional paradigms.

Mahler's claim that "my natural way of working is Bach-like," quoted at the head of this essay, assumes expanded significance in light of the foregoing discussion. At one level, Mahler's Bach is the Bach of the Passions and cantatas, the Bach who perhaps inspired the alternating recitative and aria-like sections in "Der Abschied," as Mitchell has argued.[36] But the Bach referred to in this essay is the Bach of diminutions and of carefully controlled counterpoint. This aspect of Mahler's compositional practice, then, shows a direct and self-conscious link with the past. Bach is not filtered through a series of nineteenth-century understandings; he is appropriated whole by Mahler.

At the same time, the rhetoric of romantic and post-Wagnerian music is fully in evidence throughout the passages analyzed here, especially those from *Das Lied*. Super-charged chromaticism, climactic moments embod-

---

[36] MSSLD, pp. 356–57, 363, et passim.

ying "discharges of ecstasy" (Mitchell),[37] long, unyielding appoggiaturas, and vocal gestures associated with the theater: these are expansions upon the trim eighteenth-century syntactical procedures. The result of this confluence of influences is a "contaminated" ground, an original syncretism.

One task for subsequent analysts is to return this understanding of harmony and voice-leading to Mahler's peculiar sounding surfaces, to seek a more accurate representation of his style based on this contrapuntal logic. Several recent writings on Mahler have already indicated the fruitfulness of such an approach.[38] Largely unexplored, however, is the possibility of "timbral syntax" – i.e., the extent to which Mahler's opulent sound coloring may be cogently interrelated with his fundamental harmonic-contrapuntal syntax. Such a study would probably reveal important facets of Mahler's particular appropriation of consonance–dissonance relations; it might also provide us with a more secure means for characterizing his musical textures, which continue to hold a strong fascination for us.

[37] MSSLD, p. 344

[38] Among them are Peter Bergquist, "The First Movement of Mahler's Tenth Symphony: An Analysis and Examination of the Sketches," *Music Forum* 5 (1980), 235–94; Carolyn Baxendale, "The Finale of Mahler's Fifth Symphony: Long Range Musical Thought," *Journal of the Royal Musical Association* 112 (1987), 257–79; Richard A. Kaplan, "Interpreting Surface Harmonic Connections in the Adagio of Mahler's Tenth Symphony," *In Theory Only* 4 (1978), 32–44; Forte, "Middleground Motives," 153–63; Stephen E. Hefling, "The Composition of Mahler's 'Ich bin der Welt abhanden Gekommen,'" in *Gustav Mahler*, ed. Hermann Danuser, Wege der Forschung, vol. 653 (Darmstadt, 1992), pp. 96–158; John Williamson, "The Structural Premises of Mahler's Introductions: Prolegomena to an Analysis of the First Movement of the Seventh Symphony," *Music Analysis* 5 (1986), 29–57; John Williamson, "Mahler and Episodic Structure: The First Movement of the Seventh Symphony," in *The Seventh Symphony of Gustav Mahler: A Symposium*, ed. James L. Zychowicz (Madison, Wis., 1990), pp. 27–46; and Williamson, "Mahler, Hermeneutics and Analysis," pp. 357–73.

9 Dissonance treatment and middleground prolongations in Mahler's later music

JOHN WILLIAMSON

The starting point for this essay was not directly connected with Mahler. In an article on Chopin, Eugene Narmour notes that "in addition to the usual structural dissonances found in the style of this period, certain melodic patterns in [Chopin's] music generate a rather large pool of dissonant sonorities that actually come to function structurally, though not necessarily transformationally, on some level."[1] By uncovering situations in which melody and harmony are incongruent, Narmour seeks to reverse the usual Schenkerian assumption that melody emerges from voice-leading; rather, melody becomes a method of structuring harmony (a principle demonstrated by some intermittently convincing analysis), and also of structuring harmonic dissonance. Dissonances that others have taken to be expressive decorations of underlying structural consonances turn into structural entities in the course of Narmour's argument. For the student of Mahler, such an approach raises the possibility of reviewing the nature of what is prolonged, and of what prolongs – categories which are far from being open and shut. Analysts are still uncertain about models for prolongations at middleground and background structural levels in Mahler (let alone models for transformation in any rigorous sense). There is, however, a degree of consensus concerning Mahler's specific foreground contrapuntal-harmonic techniques, many of which were identified before analysts turned to Schenkerian methods in the effort to extend their insight beyond style characteristics as viewed in the narrow context of Mahler's contempo-

---

[1] Eugene Narmour, "Melodic Structuring of Harmonic Dissonance: A Method for Analysing Chopin's Contribution to the Development of Harmony," in *Chopin Studies*, ed. Jim Samson (Cambridge, 1988), pp. 77–78.

raries. But it is far from clear how such techniques coexist with Schenkerian orthodoxy (both as analytical model and as arbiter of canonical repertory). To be sure, the straightforward application of Schenker to Mahler's music is by no means proven universally valid; it may be that what deviates from the Schenkerian paradigm in Mahler actually constitutes a Mahlerian norm, resulting in special forms of dissonant prolongations and incomplete structures at the middleground (and, more tentatively, background) level. Recent research on such issues as tonal models dependant on dissonant prolongations, directional tonality, "alternatives to monotonality," and incomplete forms of the Schenkerian *Ursatz* open up distinct possibilities for analysts of Mahler.[2] But an equally urgent task is to examine his specific forms of foreground dissonance treatment from the perspective of their possible extension into the middleground. In short, it remains to be established whether the expressive features of Mahler's foreground yield models for prolongation.

The antithesis between expressive decoration and structural prolongation that looms so large in Narmour's essay raises fundamental questions of methodology. Alternatives to analysis (as traditionally understood) are now more than ever being invoked as means of uncovering the underlying concerns of Mahler's music. Writers such as Carolyn Abbate and Anthony Newcomb have demonstrated that models of critical musicology, some of which bear strong links to rhetorical and semiotic approaches (although not always explicitly acknowledged), may play a role in discussing Mahler.[3] This is not simply a matter of making Mahler's music "speak," as Adorno and Floros in their different ways have attempted to do.[4] Rather, it is

---

[2] See, e.g., Robert P. Morgan, "Dissonant Prolongations: Theoretical and Compositional Precedents," *Journal of Music Theory* 20 (1976), 49–91; Harald Krebs, "Alternatives to Monotonality in Early Nineteenth-Century Music," *Journal of Music Theory* 25 (1981), 1–16; and Charles Burkhart, "Departures from the Norm in Two Songs from Schumann's *Liederkreis*," in *Schenker Studies*, ed. Hedi Siegel (Cambridge, 1990), pp. 146–64.

[3] Anthony Newcomb, "Narrative Archetypes and Mahler's Ninth Symphony," in *Music and Text: Critical Inquiries*, ed. Steven Paul Scher (Cambridge, 1992), pp. 118–36; Carolyn Abbate, *Unsung Voices: Opera and Musical Narrative in the Nineteenth Century* (Princeton, 1991).

[4] Constantin Floros, *Gustav Mahler*, 3 vols. (Wiesbaden, 1977–85); TAM and TAME.

thinking of music in the mode of narrative, as opposed to evaluating what such a narrative might mean; narrative and plot are now issues of a critical musicology that has to a degree been formed on grounds that analysis had thought its own. The present essay will first consider some models of prolongation in Mahler's symphonies after 1900 (with particular stress upon the Fifth, Sixth, and Seventh) before concluding with brief consideration of the role that narrative and rhetoric might have in Mahler studies, focusing especially upon two ideas presented by Kofi Agawu: that a tension exists in Mahler between public and personal voices, and that symbols may evolve from signs.[5]

Much Mahler analysis explores matters of motivic variation (including Adorno's rather distinct notion of "variant"), counterpoint, and heterophony. Although variation is a subject that can hardly be avoided (whether at foreground or middleground levels), Mahler's treatment of counterpoint presents the analyst with many of the composer's most distinctive types of prolongation. Discussion of counterpoint, however, requires that a number of important distinctions be made. Although the fugues in the finale of the Fifth Symphony or the first movement of the Eighth have their traditional aspects, it would be misleading to claim that Mahler's handling of counterpoint is orthodox as regards the tensions in part writing, or the rhythmic and melodic balance of lines. Problems emerge that Mahlerians have perhaps not formulated well. It is not quite sufficient to catalogue the peculiarities of Mahler's harmonic language in isolation, as is vaguely apparent in an article to which all Mahlerians return (more in frustration, perhaps, than in certainty of enlightenment): Hans Tischler's essay on "Mahler's Impact on the Crisis of Tonality," which, although published in 1951, actually summarizes portions of his dissertation completed in 1937.[6] Although Tischler does present a valuable index of Mahler's harmonic praxis, he also slips into his harmonic taxonomy the notion of dramatic key symbolism. This stands in Tischler's essay as a (perhaps) inevitably hermeneutic attempt to offer a structural basis within

---

[5] V. Kofi Agawu, *Playing with Signs: A Semiotic Interpretation of Classic Music* (Princeton, 1991), p. 136.

[6] Hans Tischler, "Mahler's Impact on the Crisis of Tonality," *The Music Review* 12 (1951), 113–21 (see also Tischler, "Die Harmonik in den Werken Gustav Mahlers," diss., University of Vienna, 1937).

Ex. 9.1   Fifth Symphony, 1st mvt., bars 165–67

which harmonic phenomena might operate in Mahler's music. But the problem has been stated rather differently, from a more technical standpoint, by a non-Mahlerian in a review of Peter Bergquist's essay on the opening movement of the Tenth – a standpoint reflecting the manner in which, until the 1980s, Mahler analysis tended to formulate hermeneutic concepts in order to explain formal as well as technical aspects of the symphonies. Noting Bergquist's definition of Mahler's late style as "harmony overgrown with counterpoint," William Drabkin in effect issued a call for an "examination of just how Mahler makes his 'ivy' cling to the harmonic wall he has built."[7] This seems a fair demand, even if the specific areas Drabkin turns to – voice exchange, neighbor-note harmonies, and mixture of major and minor modes – are in one form or another already widely noted by anyone with an interest in Mahler. But quite apart from its fairness, Drabkin's challenge reminds us that hermeneutics will not solve all problems of symphonic cohesion.

Discussion of specific harmonic and contrapuntal phenomena in Mahler from the Fourth Symphony onwards should acknowledge a general underlying factor of his writing: parallel and similar motion are frequently associated with dissonance treatment, often apparently in opposition to the venerable contrapuntal ideal of contrary motion. In a relatively simple extract from the first movement of the Fifth Symphony (Ex. 9.1), neighbor notes and passing notes (including chromatic ones) combine with particularly striking effect in the third bar, where the move to f^2 / c^2 in the upper

---

[7]   William Drabkin, review of *The Music Forum* 5 (1980), in *Music Analysis* 1 (1982), 207.

Ex. 9.2   Sixth Symphony, 4th mvt., bar 386 ("Schoenberg's chord")

parts (violins and trumpet) takes place in parallel fourths. Both neighbor notes (e♮² and b♮¹) clash with their resolutions in middle parts. And contrary to earlier ideals of contrapuntal motion, the two melodic lines are rhythmically identical; they reach the caesura at the end of the phrase simultaneously. (Yet as though aware of this, Mahler animates the dominant seventh in the third bar with syncopations in the trombone parts.) So widespread are such melodic combinations in the foreground of Mahler's music that they frequently serve to generate irregular dissonances and dissonant complexes. Unconventional progressions are at least as likely to arise from the combination of polyphonic writing with neighbor-note substitution as from the "invention" of higher dissonances. Schoenberg drew attention to the chord in the finale of the Sixth Symphony shown in Ex. 9.2; what particularly interested him was not whether it could be related to a root, but that it should be "judged according to [its] origin," which he believed to be melodic.[8] But he might equally well have declared it polyphonic: the point cannot be carried by considering the chord in isolation. The unconventional in later Mahler is regularly a function of voice-leading context.

Discussion of Mahler's voice leading must from the outset acknowledge the fundamental diatonicism of his style. It goes without saying that he knew how to handle the full gamut of nineteenth-century chromaticism (including diminished and half-diminished sevenths, Neapolitan and augmented sixths, the augmented triad, etc.). What distinguishes him from many contemporaries is not the relative incidence of such resources but the frequent simplicity of his bass movement, especially (but not exclusively) in his early works.[9] A composer who deals in tonic pedals and tonic–domi-

---

[8] Arnold Schoenberg, *Theory of Harmony*, trans. Roy E. Carter (London, 1978), p. 330.   [9] Cf. also TAM, pp. 41 and 152–53 (TAME, pp. 27 and 115).

Ex. 9.3   Sixth Symphony, 4th mvt., bars 518–19

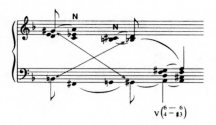

$$V\left(\begin{smallmatrix}6 & - & 6\\ 4 & - & \sharp3\end{smallmatrix}\right)$$

nant alternations and drones will inevitably tend to treat chromaticism initially as a surface phenomenon. It is no accident that Mahler often favored the flattened supertonic as a melodic event (combining it particularly with dominant harmony), rather than the full Neapolitan sixth chord. On such simple foundations rests Mahler's fondness for neighbor-note effects; where others might favor the structural neighbor note with consonant support, he prefers to bring out the full piquancy of the chromatic neighbor note within its diatonic surroundings – whereby it seems more like an irritant than an integrated event. His frequent cadential use of the dominant minor thirteenth reduced to its most basic form, an augmented triad, really does not need to be explained away by the mechanics of third-construction; it is a simple instance of neighbor-note substitution.

Not so simple, but founded on similar premises, is the approach to cadence at the recapitulation in the finale of the Sixth Symphony (bars 518–20; see Ex. 9.3). The background of this progression ("background" more in Hans Keller's sense than Schenker's) is a typical neighbor-note cadential preparation. The neighboring chord, which would typically be a six-three in such a context, often with the sixth augmented, is prolonged by a voice exchange (no less typical), and also by further neighbor notes. When the dominant bass arrives for the cadential progression, a vestige of the neighbor chord (g♯) still overlaps with the six-four, resolving to a only as the fourth falls to the leading note. The sixth (f) above the bass never resolves to the fifth; the result is that an augmented triad constitutes the dominant in the perfect cadence. Thus Mahler modifies a familiar progression by obscuring its details through unresolved neighbor tones; the brutality of the scoring at this point combines with the riot of incidental notes to

253

Ex. 9.4   Sixth Symphony, 4th mvt., bars 521–30

produce a particularly opaque effect that is intensified by the arrival of the bass on D_1 in bar 520. But D is not allowed to remain as tonic; instead the German sixth of C is superimposed upon the D pedal, as though it merely represented the dominant of the dominant (Ex. 9.4). C supplants D minor as tonic, and Mahler proceeds directly from D to C in the bass, telescoping the progression V/V–V–I by omitting its middle term. Mahler here writes a progression of adjacent roots which he might have rationalized, had he thought it necessary, by invoking Sechter's notion of a theoretical inter-mediate root related to the others by fifth and fourth.

Tischler has stressed the significance of Mahler's avoiding the "usual classical cadences."[10] This is an exaggeration, of course; it would be better to say that Mahler conceals the normal cadence forms through elision and suspended neighbor notes, the two techniques illustrated side by side in Exx. 9.3 and 9.4. Tischler suggests that instead of writing V–I, Mahler would prefer V–IV–I or II–I. These forms certainly exist, but the $\hat{2}$–$\hat{1}$ step in the bass is often likely to be harmonized in such a way as to suggest V/V–I rather than II–I, thus highlighting the elision of the dominant while still alluding to its function. The form V–IV–I in the middle-period instrumental sym-phonies is often in reality V–IV$_5^6$–I. The significance of IV$_5^6$ is exemplified in the very important cadence of bars 519–23 in the first movement of the Seventh Symphony.[11] In preparing this striking plagal cadence, Mahler first emphasizes V$_4^6$ by recalling the characteristic rhythm of the movement's slow introduction (bars 512 ff). The $_4^6$ does not lead to a $_3^5$ but, after a few

---

10   Tischler, "Mahler's Impact on the Crisis of Tonality," p. 113.
11   Mahler's early pocket-notebook sketch of this passage will be found on p. 208 above.

Ex. 9.5   Sixth Symphony, 4th mvt., bars 126–29

bars, settles on IV$^6_5$ for a buildup of cadential tension that is released onto the tonic. This example is particularly noteworthy, partly because it is typical of Mahler's practice, partly because the traditional dominant is replaced, but mostly because it has great importance in the overall structure of the movement; the subdominant is accorded greater weight in terms of orchestration, duration, and elaboration than any dominant resource in the immediate vicinity.

All three instrumental symphonies of 1901–06 provide instances of the often radical manner in which Mahler had begun to treat voice leading. (Interestingly, these are found with particular regularity in the outer movements, which presented the greatest difficulties to orchestrate, including the two-movement Part I of the Fifth). Alongside local harmonic and contrapuntal events that feature standard chromatic chords, altered scale degrees and neighbor-note effects, we encounter absence of the leading note in certain contexts, parallel triads with altered notes, and advanced treatment of pedal notes. Example 9.5 comprises the prolongation of a Neapolitan sixth in the finale of the Sixth Symphony: the noteworthy feature of this passage is that once again the highlighted passing harmony is an augmented triad, producing the angular line f–g♯–b♭ in an inner part. This idiom may be a Mahlerian fingerprint, but whether it should be characterized simply as a harmonic phenomenon is debatable.

That question is sharpened a few bars later when Mahler's irregular voice leading becomes so acerbic that even he felt compelled to insist in a footnote, "Das Es der 1. Posaune ist richtig [the E♭ in the first trombone is correct]" (Ex. 9.6). The upper voice, purely as a melodic event, would be unexceptionable in A minor; but it is harmonized with parallel triads – both descending (in the trumpets) and ascending (trombones). Such

Ex. 9.6 Sixth Symphony, 4th mvt., bar 131

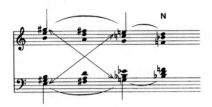

parallelism is not uncommon in Mahler, but it is seldom conventional, or precisely parallel. Pages of the Seventh Symphony's opening movement feature part-writing analogous to that found on the lower staff of Ex. 9.6, but the unchanging parallel motion of the upper staff is less common. Fundamentally, the progression prolongs the dominant of A minor, first through a 10–8–6 voice exchange, then via consonant support of the neighbor note d^2 by a B♭ triad. In the course of the voice exchange, however, the leading note (g♯) is flattened to g♮ in the bass; thereby the mixture of mode that characterizes the symphony's familiar motto theme is extended into a prolongational model by means of the voice exchange (and its intervening harmony). As the exchange is completed, Mahler harmonizes the g♮ with an e♭^{1} in the trombone chords, directly against the e♮^{2} of the woodwind's decorated melodic line – hence the footnote for the average orchestral player (and the perhaps-below-average conductor). Yet why did he want e♭, since the e♮ would have fit just as well? In any case, e♭ or e, the progression flashes past amid such a kaleidoscope of orchestral color that the average listener probably takes little notice of the deliberate clash. Did Mahler want to relate the e♭ to the B♭ triad in order to disguise the otherwise clear dominant status of the prolongation? Such ambiguities are common in his last works. That they arise here from two streams of triads is particularly interesting in view of Debussy's practice during the same period. But whereas Debussy's chord streams encourage talk of both organum and impressionism, Mahler's reasons for such procedures seem less clear.

The outer movements of the Seventh Symphony contain the most striking examples of triads in parallel or near-parallel motion, which may perhaps arise from a "thickening" of melodic lines into chordal streams; the only principle (if it can be termed such) that seems to govern his practice is the extent to which neighbor-note substitution occurs from passage to passage. On the whole we may say that the parallel $^6_3$s of the predominantly diatonic finale (e.g. bars 296–98) stand closer to orthodoxy than the chromatically inflected triadic streams of the first movement (e.g. bars 242–44), though even in the finale the diatonic g♯² of the woodwind chord stream clashes with a g♮¹ in horns and strings at bar 297; different voice-leading laws operate within different coloristic strata. But even to refer to "triadic streams" perhaps misses a vital point, since Mahler's nervously brittle orchestration seems to discourage such impressionistic terms; rather, Mahler projects his closely grouped triads at his audience with a vehemence quite alien to most orchestration of the period.

There has been no consistent attempt to categorize the chordal streams found in Mahler's middle-period instrumental symphonies. The most striking description of them depends in part on a concept of harmony that has until recently been somewhat marginal to writings on harmony and voice leading in the English-speaking world. The passage that Ernst Kurth chose to illustrate Mahler's practice comes from the first movement of the Sixth; of bars 209–14 (see Ex. 9.7), Kurth wrote:

> Here two chord progressions are simply placed against each other like two counterpointed lines; only these seem expanded from lines of notes to lines of sounds. The energy of their movement extends over the individual chords with all their clashing atonal effects. – So too neighboring harmonies often grow from neighboring notes, free flowing harmonies from passing notes, even whole chords of anticipation (which press into other chords not yet quitted) from notes of anticipation.
>
> It is one of the principal characteristics of developments around 1900 that the unit of sound swells up beyond the individual note to the whole chord.[12]

Kurth wanted to see the explanation for the accurately observed phenomenon in his concept of harmony as a product of energy; melodic energy means proliferation of voices, and involves not merely notes but chords. In the passage cited, Kurth conceded certain "impressionistic" charms [*Klangreize*] but stressed a potential harshness that looked back toward

---

[12] Ernst Kurth, *Romantische Harmonik und ihre Krise in Wagners "Tristan,"* 3rd edn. (Berlin, 1923), pp. 368–69.

Ex. 9.7   Sixth Symphony, 4th mvt., bars 209–14

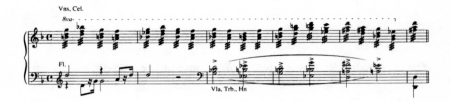

"the pre-classical polyphonic linear principle." Without such appeals to earlier periods for justification, it is difficult to find any rationale for the passage in anything other than Mahler's unique praxis. The dissonances all depend on some element of substitution or alteration, whether they arise from Mahler's ubiquitous fluctuation of mode, his no less characteristic $\hat{5}$–$\flat\hat{6}$ melodic gesture (expressed both linearly and as a simultaneity), or his elliptical cadences. One line ends with the Phrygian second descending to a local tonic (D) while the lower line clashes against it with the normal second scale degree resolving conventionally to the local tonic in the familiar horn-fifth idiom (Ex. 9.7).

Kurth spoke of atonality in relation to the clashes of this example. The currently more disreputable slogan, polytonality, emerges tentatively in Tischler. Mahler, he maintained, "never employed polytonality," although "many passages produce a similar impression."[13] That is rather loosely said; it might have been better to point out that in Mahler's last period many passages *appear* to be on the verge of bitonality, although the visual impression often disappears in performance owing to the enharmonic properties of the notes Mahler has chosen (as, for example, in the wonderful overlap of D minor and B flat minor at bar 211 of the Ninth's opening movement, which tantalizes the eye and, at least to the end of bar 212, the ear as well). A line that stands out bitonally from its surroundings can often be explained away by the usual forms of Mahlerian dissonance treatment when its "bitonal" characteristics are enharmonically reinterpreted. If polytonality must be adduced, it should be understood as a potential polytonality that often resides in details which decorate more conventional progressions. In

[13]   Tischler, "Mahler's Impact on the Crisis of Tonality," p. 115.

Ex. 9.8 Sixth Symphony, 2nd mvt., bars 533–39

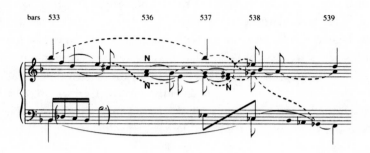

Ex. 9.8, an analytical graph of a D minor passage in the second movement of the Fifth (bars 533–9), the combination of d^2 and d♭ in bar 533 may be explained by Mahler's fondness for ambiguity of mode, or the d♭ may be looked upon as an anticipation of the ensuing neighbor-note complex involving c♯². Both provide means of prolonging the B♭ in the bass within the sphere of D minor, and the neighbor-note reading in particular shows how Mahler may create the fleeting illusion of tonal ambiguity in numerous places. The peak of tension in this spot is a German sixth (bar 538) that could resolve within E♭. But the resolution twists into D minor, which has been the other potential tonality in the section. The overall impression of this passage is of a suspension of movement within otherwise conventional harmonic progressions. B♭ achieves a degree of substance through the illusory prolongation involving D♭ (which recalls an important motive from earlier in the movement) and through the suggestion of E♭ in bar 537; yet B♭ is firmly flanked by D. This whole section, from the end of the celebrated D major chorale to the beginning of the shadowy A minor coda, derives its tension from $\hat{5}$–♭$\hat{6}$ motion in D minor, and it constitutes a summation of precisely the neighbor-note tension that first appeared in the funeral march which opens the whole work (first movement, bars 1–20). Mahler's ability to build whole sections of a movement around such tensions is even more apparent in the Scherzo of the Seventh, his most extended essay in fantastical counterpoint and orchestration, which begins with the same $\hat{5}$–♭$\hat{6}$ scale degrees in D minor.

Although Schoenberg writes of frequent "fluctuating and suspended tonality" in Mahler, his first symphonies of the twentieth century tended to confine such ambiguity to relatively restricted areas involving the initial establishment of or departure from a key; in this context, Tischler points to "cadence-less modulation" in which a "sudden shift is chromatically camouflaged," and he illustrates it with an example from the slow movement of the Sixth (bars 169–73).[14] The passage begins in B, then moves to Eb. The means of modulation, however, is simply the enharmonic equation of B major (with an added minor seventh) and the German sixth of Eb. There is little that is surprising in this. Wolf or Strauss might very well have resolved the augmented sixth chord to a cadence involving $^6_4$ and $^5_3$ in Eb rather than simply moving, as Mahler does, to a root-position Eb major triad; his stylistic fingerprint in this case probably amounts to little more than a procedure that would hardly surprise us in Schubert. The lack of a cadence is obvious, but the chromatic camouflage is no more than a familiar progression decorated, as usual, with some contrapuntal detail. This brings us back with a vengeance to Drabkin's criticism of Bergquist. The next few examples, therefore, have been selected as instances of how Mahler uses his specific harmonic-contrapuntal techniques on a larger scale to control structural pivots.

In the finale of the Sixth, the interplay between the keys of A minor and C minor is of crucial significance. The principal tonal center of the movement is of course A, but at several points Mahler attempts to disguise this by stressing C. One such occasion is the beginning of the Allegro moderato, launched in C minor, which key has been prepared at great length during the chorale section of the slow introduction (including a particularly weighty perfect cadence in bars 94–96). The first stages of the Allegro (bars 98–113) present several motives that will be prominent in the sonata-form exposition about to ensue. These motives initially combine to confirm C minor all the more emphatically; the graph of Ex. 9.9 commences with this carefully defined C. The first prolongation of real interest is a descent in the bass from Ab to E♮ (bars 104–07): the trumpet part descends parallel to this, first in tenths, then more daringly in elevenths (a change in interval succession effected by the falling semitone b^1–bb^1). As a result, E in the bass coincides with ab^1 (first horn) in the parallel line.

---

[14] Schoenberg, *Theory of Harmony*, p. 383; Tischler, "Mahler's Impact on the Crisis of Tonality," p. 117.

Ex. 9.9 Sixth Symphony, 4th mvt., bars 104–14

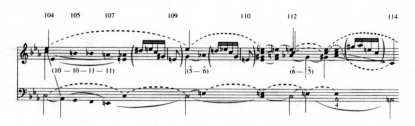

Interpreted with respect to the e♭¹ that persists throughout the passage, the resulting linear motion is the familiar augmented triad with a neighboring note (E–A♭–C plus E♭), which in the foreground of bars 108–09 is enharmonically reinterpreted by the oboes as a possible dominant of A minor. Typically, however, Mahler is in no hurry to complete the shift to A minor, but instead alternates harbingers of A with the still far-from-super-seded C. The e♭² is motivically retained in the topmost part while the bass line alternates C and E♮; the oboes' figure in bars 109–10 is characteristically bounded by e♭ and e♮ in different octaves, retaining in a new shape the modal uncertainty of the symphony's motto, which has recently recurred in bars 96–97 of the finale. And this ambiguity is further intensified by the role of the g♯/a♭: in bars 110–11, the g♯¹ oscillates semitonally with a♮¹, effecting the traditional leading-note resolution of A minor. But in 112–13 g♯/a♭¹ alter-nates with g♮¹, producing the ♭6̂–5̂ gesture that Mahler, in common with numerous other nineteenth-century composers, invokes almost as a basic affect. The prolongation of C thus overlaps with a prolongation of the dom-inant of A, yielding an area of ambiguity centered upon the augmented triad, which provides the framework for proliferating surface detail such as the trumpet and oboe motives of the passage.

This leads back to consideration of the chord Schoenberg character-ized as "only superficially annexed to the old system" (Ex. 9.2), by which he means the traditional method of explaining harmonic phenomena on the basis of roots and third-construction.[15] The chord is more easily explained in context by reference to a chromatic transition that began in A major

[15] See n. 8 above.

Ex. 9.10   Sixth Symphony, 4th mvt., bars 381–95

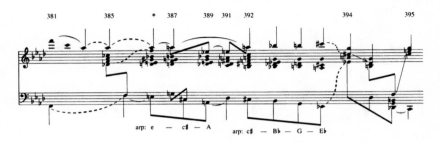

(bar 364), moved through F♯ major and minor (bar 372), and from there to F minor. Schoenberg's chord (marked "*" in Ex. 9.10) occurs in the context of F minor, which is of fleeting significance, both locally and in the movement at large. Here it is the starting-point for another gradual chromatic transition analogous to that in the slow introduction at bar 39; both employ a variety of chromatic resources in a tonally unclear context before escaping into C minor through augmented sixths.[16] In the later passage, the background progression is derived from seventh chords plus neighbor notes that regularly sound with the chord on which they depend, producing ninths or even wider dissonances. That is the most obvious explanation for Schoenberg's chord (bar 386), inasmuch as only b♭^{1} and f^2 of the upper staff are foreign, enharmonically or otherwise, to the seventh chord on E below. From the bass motion f–e that precedes the chord, it would be legitimate to regard the arpeggiated motion of the lowest part (which is filled in by semiquavers in the basses) as a prolongation of an A major dominant seventh, which moves to a seventh on D that, in this context, functions as V/V in C; the next bass arpeggiation (bars 392–93) again prolongs an augmented sixth, with step-wise chromatic motion above. A plausible background progression for the passage as a whole is the relatively straightforward combination of seventh chords and inessential notes shown in Ex. 9.11. Here again, chromatic neighbors prolong already dissonant chords. Through the layout of his various seventh chords and

---

[16]   For a brief comparison of the two chromatic transitions, see John Williamson, "Mahler, Hermeneutics, and Analysis," *Music Analysis* 10 (1991), 368–70.

Ex. 9.11 Sixth Symphony, 4th mvt., bars 389–95

their neighbor notes, Mahler contrives to give the semblance of tonal ambiguity, which rightly excited Schoenberg, even if it can ultimately be rationalized within a traditional framework. Yet such rationalization fails to convey the sheer brutality of this section, which fulfills some of Kurth's criteria by expanding the dissonant note into the dissonant sound-complex while all too clearly throwing over any suggestion of impression-istic "charm."

Each of these harmonic-contrapuntal transitions depends for its effect on traditional economy of voice leading. The contrapuntal lines by which Mahler engenders a high level of chromatic dissonance follow the law of shortest movement, disturbed by occasional leaps of thirds and (to a lesser extent) fourths in the bass. The next example, however – from the coda to the finale to the Seventh – relies on the use of the pedal, and ranks among the most striking instances of control and dissolution of tension in Mahler's music. It is also the only extended chromatic section in a pre-dominantly diatonic movement. An extended rondo, the finale of the Seventh is correspondingly more discursive than the sonata-form move-ments from which the majority of the examples discussed above have been taken. The section in question (Ex. 9.12) is developmental and precedes the final statements of the movement's "C" and "A" themes (at bars 517 and 539 respectively). Since these elements are quite conventionally diatonic (a parody minuet and a rather pompous march, both in the major), the pre-ceding development serves to create an area of tension that Mahler high-lights by quoting the main theme from the extremely complex first movement. The pedal notes controlling this section succeed each other

Ex. 9.12 Seventh Symphony, 5th mvt., bars 446–518

through descending chromatic motion. The A (bars 455 ff.) suggests untonicized D major, against which the dissonances that result from overlapping imitations are diatonic, until the intrusion of the minor third (bar 457), a resource by now familiar. The ensuing G♯ (bars 462 ff.), which supports C♯ minor, is the basis for a more complex section that reintroduces the first movement's main theme. Here the dissonance treatment is more extensive, involving the familiar motion between $\hat{5}$ and ♭$\hat{6}$ and climaxing with the most formidable dissonance thus far in the movement, as the bass shifts to G♮ (bar 475). This in turn is topped in C minor by another case of almost-parallel motion analogous to the movement of tenths and elevenths in the Sixth Symphony's finale, and hinging on the same type of chromatic displacement – here f♯–f. The climax chords are again rich in semitonal dissonance, which then evaporates in a B major section that seems to be pure comic opera. The "Turkish" music of this passage is a typical change of scene in a movement that, since Adorno, has frequently been described as tableau and explained in metaphors of the dramatic stage.[17] The continuing bass descent next leads to B♭ (bar 492), of mixed mode; but thanks to the motion $\hat{5}$–♭$\hat{6}$, first a g♭, then a complete B major triad is imposed on the pedal F, causing the contrary motion of the outer parts to accelerate toward the first root position triad for some time, which is the cue for a climax in D flat major that combines material from the outer movements (bars 506 ff.). This then dissolves into C for the final appearance of the minuet theme, but still over a pedal, once again dominant. Many of the same sonorities dependent on neighboring and passing notes reappear in this context, but the pedals are used to control a wavelike pattern of tensions (to employ a Kurthian metaphor) that threatens repeatedly to topple into the same kind of harmonic frenzy noted above in the finale of the Sixth. The strong divergent thrust of the outer parts, which ultimately come to span six octaves at the turn to D♭, is the chief means of control, and exemplifies the traditional solidity of contrapuntal construction that, at a fairly deep level, underlies many of Mahler's more radical surface procedures. Thus, a strong tension between structural levels manifests itself in Mahler's later music. The localized parallel motion is often braced by a deeper underlying contrary motion.

Kurth's image of the dissonant note that expands into the dissonant chord or chord stream is a suggestive one, which has its parallel within a Schenker-based viewpoint. The foreground incidents that generate tension – the neighbor note, modal ambiguity, and (to a lesser extent) the voice exchange – underlie and model transitions that more properly belong to the middleground, and usually result in elliptical voice-leading,

---

[17] TAME, p. 137 (TAM, p. 180); Bernd Sponheuer, *Logik des Zerfalls: Untersuchungen zum Finalproblem in den Symphonien Gustav Mahlers* (Tutzing, 1978), pp. 397–401.

Ex. 9.13   *Das Lied von der Erde*, "Von der Jugend," bars 70–86

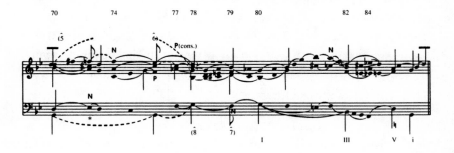

complex dissonances, and a curious ability to keep two (or more) tonal possibilities in an uncertain equilibrium. Generally the latter are related by third and fourth, although the last example discussed illustrates the possibilities for semitonal relationships in the roles of C, D♭, and B. A final example, taken from *Das Lied von der Erde*, suggests how Mahler's processes gradually come to accommodate a musical vocabulary that has expanded to appropriate elements of modality and pentatonicism. That *Das Lied von der Erde* as a whole depends on a pentatonic complex in which major (C) and relative minor (A) are held in a state of equilibrium is not a particularly contentious statement. In its way, this kind of structure is as historically interesting as the more chromatic processes seen in the middle-period works (it forms, for example, the basis for several works and movements by Mahler's contemporary, Hans Pfitzner).[18] What operates over the span of the whole work can also be seen at middleground level. In the third movement, "Von der Jugend," an oscillation between G minor and B♭ major (bars 70–86) reflects the general structural tension of the work, but also decorates it with some of Mahler's habitual dissonance treatment (Ex. 9.13). Thus the foreground oscillation in an inner voice, $\hat{5}$–♭$\hat{6}$ (e.g., cellos, bar 70), is quite orthodoxly expanded in an upper part into a model for a prolongation (bars 70–78). But the seventh scale degree is used in both flattened and leading-note forms to generate melodic tension (e.g., f♯^{2} in bar 70), harmonic complexity (at "*" in Ex. 9.13), and a neighbor-note relationship ($\hat{8}$–$\hat{7}$) that governs the motion between G minor and B♭ major.

---

[18]   John Williamson, *The Music of Hans Pfitzner* (Oxford, 1992), pp. 73–5.

Although f$\sharp^2$ is initially favored in the melodic line of bar 70, it is f$\natural$ ($\hat{5}$ of B$\flat$) that comes to predominate, leading to the curious cadence of bars 85–86, in which the dominant of G minor contains the flattened seventh rather than the leading note. This cadence form is rather rare in Mahler; while it may result from the collision of his music's normal vocabulary with a specific feature of pentatonic complexes, it is nevertheless entirely consistent with the manner in which foreground motives generate middleground processes.

The examples considered in this essay present aspects of Mahler's style that, while commonly acknowledged in his melodic and motivic writing, also generate structures of more than foreground application. It is not my contention, however, that they extend much farther than the rich and densely organized middleground of Mahler's symphonies, since few structural backgrounds modifying the traditional Schenkerian paradigms have been presented in the analytical literature, other than Robert Bailey's "double tonic complex" – a notion invoked primarily to account for Mahler's practice of sometimes ending in a key other than that in which he started. This, it must be said, is a matter that affects whole works rather than individual movements (apart from one or two striking exceptions such as the last movement of the First Symphony and the first movement of the Third). There is thus plenty of room for argument about the precise relevance to the symphonic movement of attempts to replace the traditional polarity of tonic and dominant with double-tonic relationships involving keys a third apart (which attempts are perhaps best represented by Christopher Lewis's analysis of the Ninth Symphony).[19] But when recent efforts to view Mahler's music as narrative are set alongside the findings of music analysis, it emerges that simply to proceed from local dissonance treatments to prolongational models related to them, and then on to a Schenkerian background, may not be entirely adequate as a technical account of Mahler's practice. Anthony Newcomb's recent essay on the Ninth Symphony suggests the possibility of viewing areas of melodic, rhythmic, and tonal instability as aspects of a conceptual paradigm derived from the theory of narrative. The result is to set areas organized at length

---

[19] Christopher Orlo Lewis, *Tonal Coherence in Mahler's Ninth Symphony*, Studies in Musicology, No. 79 (Ann Arbor, 1984).

around traditional harmonic relationships in a "plot archetype" that also finds room for the areas in which neighbor-note and modal tensions seem to predominate. In its alternation of stable and unstable, the first movement of the Ninth is structured as a series of crises, confrontations, and collapses (a choice of words that deliberately echoes Adorno).[20]

Newcomb's approach finds a new context for material that, in the Schenkerian view, served to prolong. The antithesis between the structural and the expressive is reinterpreted as a process in which both serve to advance a quest modelled upon the notion of the *Bildungsroman*.[21] But so specific a conceptual paradigm is hardly necessary if the factor of tone is taken into account, and in particular the differentiations of tone involved in what Carolyn Abbate refers to as the "narrating voice." The type of procedure that she describes in "Todtenfeier," – the juxtaposition of "two unrelated musics" analogous to the role of operatic song and narrative within larger surroundings – might equally well describe the first movement of the Ninth, although in that case the song seems to be the context for the unstable areas (a reversal which constitutes an interesting gloss on her critical and analytical assumptions).[22] In such a picture of musical continuity, the distinction between an underlying model for diatonic prolongation and fore- and middleground models that may involve departures from the norm of nineteenth-century common tonal practice may itself reflect a procedural norm for Mahler's music. What Abbate offers is a specifically narrative mode within music (manifesting itself through narrative moments rather than over the complete span of a piece) that shares with the rather different approach of Newcomb a tendency to reject older hermeneutic models (music as autobiography, "one-for-one mapping of plot events") in favor of processes defined as "oscillations" and "disjunctions" (although these do rely in a generalized way upon specific literary models).[23]

The distinction between moments when a song-like tone stands out from its background does not necessarily depend, therefore, upon a distinction such as Kofi Agawu makes:

---

[20] Newcomb, "Narrative Archetypes," pp. 119–22.   [21] Ibid., p. 120.

[22] Abbate, *Unsung Voices*, pp. 148–55.

[23] Newcomb, "Narrative Archetypes," p. 120; Abbate, *Unsung Voices*, pp. 141–48.

The paradox of Mahler is another case in point. His unabashedly public angle plays on the listener's familiarity with various topics including marches, ländler, bugle-calls, chorales, and so on; yet that same compositional voice contrasts with, or sometimes merges into, an extremely personal and – some might claim – autobiographical one.[24]

But in Mahler all these manifestations of the public voice possess the potential of a music within inverted commas, and thus (to speak in as yet tentative metaphors) may be taken as a form of intrusive narrative; yet together they make up a highly distinctive personal voice. Mahler's public voice itself seems to imply a highly personal context for the conjunction of numerous generic references. All forms of antithesis in discussing Mahler's music – stable against unstable, narrative intrusions against a larger and less closely defined background, public against personal – overlook *inter alia* the extent to which certain models for prolongation are common to both elements in the antithesis.

To achieve a more comprehensive picture of cohesion in Mahler's music, it is not sufficient either to rely upon images of organic continuity in which dissonant elements are viewed as prolongational, or to posit models of narrative that stress antithetical voices of one kind or another. A more illuminating idea in Agawu's semiotics is the notion of "transformation of sign into symbol."[25] In this context, Mahler's elaboration of surface dissonances into underlying models for middleground cohesion generates a tension between their role as functional signs within the syntagmatic aspect of his music and their symbolic value as agents of disjunction and disruption. The major–minor signals, which are common to all Mahler's style periods, symbolize an extroverted tension that is allowed to proliferate within the structure until structure itself fractures into antitheses of narrating voices. In this context Drabkin's question of how Mahler achieves his specific techniques of prolongation becomes also a demand for a clarification of Mahler's tone, and for demonstration of how functional signs become referential through historical association. The use of neighbornote formations that counter the norms of musical process achieves its status in Mahler through disruption of functional signs, thus establishing a potential for referentiality. Modal ambiguity, which already carries a refer-

[24] Agawu *Playing with Signs*, p. 136.   [25] Ibid., p. 137.

ential charge from earlier composers, becomes a means of organizing areas of tonal and harmonic transition. The possibility of studying Mahler in semiotic terms lies in the tension between the topics of ostensible discourse (the material of Agawu's public voice) and the underlying cracks in the texture of the discourse. Within this field of tension, the question of expression and structure assumes guises that defy conventional musicological boundaries between history, genre, criticism, and analysis.

10 "... his fractures are the script of truth." – Adorno's Mahler

PETER FRANKLIN

In considering the more problematic features [Hintergründen] of the Mahler renaissance, one must not overlook Theodor W. Adorno's Mahler book, which appeared in 1960. Its effect on the world of the cultivated, on many musicologists, many composers, has been immense. The Mahler-image of many avant-garde composers was decisively shaped by him (mention need only be made of Dieter Schnebel, Peter Ruzicka, Helmut Lachenmann, György Ligeti).

. . .

There is no question but that Adorno sharpened our understanding of many technical compositional features of Mahlerian music, such as major–minor alternation, the elaboration of variants, and his montage technique. It was nevertheless of considerable consequence for Mahler reception in the past twenty-five years that Adorno completely ignored Mahler's authentic programs and, with them, the composer's own worldview.[1]

I quote here from a 1986 paper on the history of Mahler reception in which Constantin Floros unwittingly encouraged the discomfort with Adorno that has long been evident among English-speaking musicologists, especially in Anglo-American Mahler studies. Adorno was then and is now difficult to deal with; if German scholars found him problematic and were beginning to consign him to history, might he not justifiably be avoided altogether by the rest of us? Had many non-German-speaking Mahler scholars really read and fully absorbed *Mahler: Eine musikalische*

---

[1] Constantin Floros, "Zur Wirkungsgeschichte Gustav Mahlers," in Paul Op de Coul, ed., *Fragment or Completion? Proceedings of the Mahler X Symposium Utrecht 1986* (The Hague, 1991), p. 188. The translation is my own.

Physiognomik when Floros gave his 1986 paper in Utrecht? Five years had still to pass before Edmund Jephcott's English translation would appear in 1992.[2] The first sign of a sea-change in mainstream Mahler scholarship was in Donald Mitchell's *Gustav Mahler: Songs and Symphonies of Life and Death* (London, 1985), where lengthy quotations from Adorno's account of *Das Lied von der Erde* appear in endnotes. These were introduced with evident admiration suggestive of an almost epiphanic discovery.[3] Here were the seeds of a productive response to Adorno's reading of Mahler. Ten years on, however, one wonders if Anglo-American Mahler scholarship is not still trying to maneuver around Adorno, rather in the way that musicology in general has maneuvered around the implications of feminism, if we are to believe Susan McClary. In her view, the discipline has attempted to "pass directly from pre- to post-feminism without ever having to change – or even examine – its ways."[4] McClary's remarks about Adorno in her introduction to *Feminine Endings* will serve as a convenient springboard to my exploration of what might occupy us between the pre- and post-Adorno phases of Mahler interpretation:

> Writing between the world wars, from the historical vantage point of the horrific collapse of German high culture, Adorno dismisses with contempt those who would regard this music [of the German canon] as a set of icons and insists upon treating it as a medium within which the bourgeois contradictions between individual free will and social pressure to conform were played out in increasingly pessimistic ways. The illusion of total order and control cherished by traditional musicologists is shrugged away by his readings, which focus unremittingly on human dilemmas rather than on transcendent truth.[5]

---

[2] Theodor W. Adorno, *Mahler: Eine musikalische Physiognomik* (Frankfurt am Main, 1960 [2nd edn. 1963]) [hereafter cited as TAM]. The complete text also appears in Theodor W. Adorno, *Gesammelte Schriften*, vol. XIII: *Die musikalische Monographien*, ed. Gretel Adorno and Rolf Tiedemann (Frankfurt am Main, 1971), pp. 149–319. It has been translated into English by Edmund Jephcott as *Mahler: A Musical Physiognomy* (Chicago, 1992) [hereafter cited as TAME]. Parenthesized page citations in my text refer to the English translation.

[3] MSSLD, p. 125 and passim (e.g., pp. 451–2, nn. 20 and 21, and p. 466, n. 70).

[4] Susan McClary, *Feminine Endings: Music, Gender and Sexuality* (Minneapolis, 1991), p. 5.   [5] Ibid., p. 28.

This points to "problematic features" of Adorno lying beyond the fact that he is a difficult, theoretical Marxist-Hegelian who wrote in such a way as to repel trivializing consumption of what he had to say. More specific concerns addressed by his critics include (1) that his aesthetic views were dominated by a preoccupation with high culture in a specific historical context, and (2) that his critical perceptions were shaped to the point of deformity (as some have suggested[6]) by his response to German fascism in the 1920s and 30s. Is anxiety about his "effect" also, as McClary implies, related to the suspicion that he presents some kind of threat to the discipline of musicology as traditionally constituted? It would probably be fair to say that such a threat has been perceived most directly in his work on individual composers, particularly in his tendency to write in a seemingly accusatory, negatively critical manner. Concrete negation has never been an easy pill for musicians to swallow. As ardent a musical negator as Arnold Schoenberg seems never to have understood even remotely that Adorno was on his side in *Philosophy of New Music*.[7]

Adorno *is* difficult to read, as Max Paddison has explained in his recent, impressively thorough introduction to Adorno's musical aesthetics, a volume that usefully complements the growing body of Adorno's writings translated into English.[8] Adorno's dialectical method relied on what he called a "constellation" technique, where ideas and images spiral around their subject matter, creating almost three-dimensional intellectual structures that are best grasped as totalities. Readers impatient for signposts and clearly stated goals may understandably find his writing cryptic and even hermetic in its density, rather like the fragmentary marks on the edges of a time-brittled, eighteenth-century lady's fan. If only it could be opened it might reveal a complete painted landscape. Any attempt to elucidate Adorno must steer a judicious course between destructive reduction and over-zealous theoretical explication. While I shall have things to say about the complete range of his writing on Mahler, the 1960 book (*A Musical Physiognomy*) will inevitably be my main focus. Unlike Adorno's better-known musical monograph on Wagner, or the *Philosophy of New Music*, the

---

[6] See Terry Eagleton, *The Ideology of the Aesthetic* (London, 1990), pp. 358–59.
[7] See H. H. Stuckenschmidt, *Arnold Schoenberg: His Life, World and Work* (London, 1977), pp. 495 and 508.
[8] Max Paddison, *Adorno's Aesthetics of Music* (Cambridge, 1993).

Mahler volume is in a sense less directly occupied with illustrating and analyzing the phenomenon of modern cultural decline than with elucidating the work of a composer Adorno seems to recognize as having been engaged in an enterprise almost parallel to his own. Mahler was less amenable to consistent theoretical critique and contextualization than perhaps any other composer whom Adorno confronted. In commenting on the "hint of cunning triumph" that he detected in the composer's death mask in 1960,[9] Adorno might almost have been provoked by the realization that there was always some feature of Mahler which resisted even his own formidable critical method. Mahler seemed always to have got there first, and to have achieved the unachievable in a manner that both surprised and fascinated Adorno. Frequently lyrical and ultimately celebratory as it may be, his picture of Mahler is no less marked by theoretical and interpretative complexity than is any of his other works on music, literature, or aesthetics. For this reason it is best to begin with a specific instance of his approach, whose ramifications may then be traced in the constellation of ideas of which it is a part.

I

An important hint missed by readers of the English translation of *Mahler: A Musical Physiognomy* is the dedication, in a facsimile of Adorno's handwriting, that appears at the start of the German text. On an otherwise blank page we find:

Plate 10.1   Adorno, dedication of *Mahler: Eine musikalische Physiognomik* to his wife (reproduced by permission of the Theodor W. Adorno Archiv, Frankfurt am Main)

It is a simple matter to add the omitted words – "dich lieb ich immer, immerdar!" ("I love you always and forever!") – since the quotation is the final vocal phrase of Mahler's song "Liebst du um Schönheit." In this dedication to his own wife, Gretel, Adorno appropriates the song that Mahler had given as a private gift to *his* wife, Alma, in 1902. Apart from indicating that this book might have had a rather particular personal significance for Adorno, the musical quotation with its suppressed text is in fact the emblematic equivalent of what Adorno will often call an "individual element" when discussing a musical work. It is in perfect accord with one of the preoccupations of his aesthetic theory that this element should subsequently be revealed to be a significant component in his larger picture of Mahler's music. Early in his final chapter ("The Long Gaze") Adorno alludes specifically to the same concluding phrase of "Liebst du um Schönheit" to illustrate the pre-history of what he feels to be the peculiar expressive quality of Mahler's late music. Relatively traditional tonal formulae, he suggests, are forced to acquire expressive significance, expressive meaning that goes so far beyond their conventional implications as to convey "extreme states of the soul" (p. 145). The closing phrase of the Rückert setting is seen by Adorno as an early, isolated example of such expressive saturation, which he accounts for as follows (pp. 146–47):

> In the song "Liebst du um Schönheit"... the singing voice closes on an A, the submediant, forming a discord with the tonic triad, as if the feeling found no outlet but suffocated in its excess. What is expressed is so overwhelming as to render the phenomenon, the language of music itself, indifferent. It does not finish its utterance; expression becomes a sobbing.

There is much to be said about this observation, which clearly does not seek to imply that Mahler had somehow failed to express in music what Rückert's words suggest. The shadow of such an interpretation might nevertheless contribute to the suspicion that Adorno's treatment of

Footnote to page 274
9 In the closing section of the "Epilegomena" to the 1960 Vienna Memorial Address; see Adorno, *Quasi una Fantasia: Essays on Modern Music*, trans. Rodney Livingstone (London, 1992), pp. 109–10; see also n. 25 below.

Mahler is marked by underlying negativity. It is a suspicion that will be harbored by those who have read, perhaps, of his undoubtedly negative assessments of the finale of the Seventh Symphony and much of the Eighth (to which I will return below). In this instance he is in fact celebrating a passage in which relatively conventional music becomes mimetically expressive in such a way that it rejects conventional nineteenth-century means of musical extension and closure, and prefigures the expressionism of Schoenberg and Berg. But there is more to it: the expressive burden, Adorno proposes, is "so overwhelming as to render the phenomenon, the language of music itself, indifferent." What he means is perhaps that the music, the "phenomenon" of the song, as an example of a historical genre (the German lied) with precedents and norms that are sufficiently accommodated for it to be recognizable as such, does not itself stop at this point. Rather than ending on what would have been a tonic six-four chord of C major with an added submediant in the voice part, four bars of postlude freeze and formalize the yearning "espressivo" in chromatic figuration and suspensions that sink to final resolution on a conventional tonic chord. It is, however, music from which the expressive subject is literally absent, lost in an inexpressible fullness of emotion on that unresolved A.

Taking as his starting point an intra-musical event analytically described, Adorno characteristically reviews that event in a context of interpretation which goes beyond, but does not traduce, the analytical observation. Here the interpretation could be said to draw upon experience of how one might expect the song to be performed, how the singer and the pianist might enact their momentary dissociation. This kind of interpretation relies considerably upon what Adorno would call the "historical" nature of the musical material and its cultural meaning. But further still: the moment could be taken as an example of how in Mahler the cultural (the historical or determined) aspect of the music as genre, as form, is in tension with the expressive impulse of an implied "subject" within it. (We need not necessarily think of that subject as the historical Mahler or Rückert.) This is not, Adorno would argue, a programmatic interpretation of the conclusion of "Liebst du um Schönheit." Adorno (ostensibly like Mahler himself after 1900) was no friend of program music or the New German school that practiced it. Instead, he believed himself to be reading from, rather than "into," the music he discussed.[10] The content of music he sought to decipher in words was fundamentally musical in nature, given that musical material for Adorno was, as I have indicated, always historical, always to some extent received rather than spontaneously generated, always more than mere configurations of notes unaffected by accretions of cultural meaning.

I will return to the matter of how and why Adorno has been questioned and criticized within Mahler studies. For the moment it will be helpful to remain with this image of a music that is somehow divided against itself and to see how it defines Adorno's reading of other, larger-scale aspects of Mahler's symphonic style, the "primary experience" of which he describes as one that is "inimical to art, needs art in order to manifest itself, and indeed must heighten art from its own inner necessity" (p. 6). Once again we are confronted by a complex construction of both positive and negative implications. The notion that there is in Mahler something "inimical to art" inevitably resonates with what Adorno alludes to in the first sentence of his opening chapter as "the judgment on Gustav Mahler passed not only by the Hitler regime but by the history of music in the fifty years since the composer's death" (p. 3). Certainly many people in that centenary year of 1960 still regarded Mahler's symphonies as inimical to good musical taste, as little more than cautionary examples of ends outstripping means in a period of late romantic hyperbole. But what Adorno means by "inimical to art" is aimed specifically at traditional bourgeois art, with all its unexamined ideological baggage.

One item of that baggage was the notion that large-scale musical works, particularly non-operatic ones, were born of genial inspiration, and that their content inevitably unfolded some kind of "dramatic" progression toward triumphant resolution and affirmation. Audiences had come to expect music to realize the romantic dream of its own transcendent

---

[10] Adorno's term for the kind of analysis he practised was "immanent" (*immanente Kritik*). The peculiar problems of the notion of immanence, with its mystical and theological implications, require careful theoretical consideration, however. Wherever possible, I have avoided using Frankfurt-school jargon words, albeit in the knowledge that clarification can entail oversimplification. For a brief, perhaps cautionary, example of an attempt to explain "immanent analysis," see Paddison *Adorno's Aesthetics*, p. 60.

implications and resonantly to enact transcendence in such a way as to drench the social experience of the symphony concert with the organ-and-choir aura of sacred ritual – to realize the nineteenth-century vision of arrival in Heaven as part coronation, part festival mass. Mahler's own vision was defined by such expectations (recall his excited description of the Third Symphony's first movement – "angels – bells – transcendental" – in a letter to Fritz Löhr.)[11] But so too, as Adorno might have put it, was Mahler's vision tormented by them.

When he describes the straightforward satisfaction of such expectations as "affirmative," Adorno means that their positive implications are social and cultural as much as they are subjective – that they affirm the status quo and thus earn their reward as consumable commodities. Mahler, on the other hand, takes these expectations of his art so seriously, Adorno implies, that his relentless quest after some sort of grounded certainty runs up against the spectre of its own willfulness, its potential untruth. The result is a music that quite literally questions its own artfulness and thus progressively, modernistically presages its emancipation from myth and ideology. Once again the idea is clarified in the context of a specific example: the First Symphony. Here in the eruptive, rupturing climaxes of the first movement, written at the very outset of Mahler's career as a symphonist, Adorno finds a noisy anticipation of the localized tension between expressive Subject and musical Phenomenon that characterizes the end of "Liebst du um Schönheit." These are the extraordinary moments that Adorno describes as achieving "breakthrough" (*Durchbruch*). He is specific about the relevant instance in this movement: Six bars before fig. 26 the introduction's distant fanfares erupt "quite out of scale with the orchestra's previous sound or even the preceding crescendo" (pp. 4–5). Here and elsewhere, when Adorno writes of musical events that he himself has clearly felt and experienced deeply, his repertoire of images broadens, opening shafts into his own childhood memories through the layers of cultural mediation that have covered their first immediacy. He speaks of the music expanding "with a physical jolt," the rupture (*Riß*) intervening as if from outside the music:

> For a few moments the symphony imagines that something has become
> reality that for a lifetime the gaze from the earth has fearfully yearned for in

[11] GMB2, no. 146 (GMBE, no. 137), 29 August 1895.

278

the sky. With it Mahler's music has kept faith; the transformation of that experience is its history. If all music, with its first note, promises that which is different, the rending of the veil, his symphonies attempt to withhold it no longer, to place it literally before our eyes ... So an adolescent woken at five in the morning by the perception of a sound that descends overpoweringly upon him may never cease to await the return of what was heard for a second between sleeping and waking. Its physical presence makes metaphysical thought appear as pale and feeble as an aesthetic that asks whether, in a formal sense, the moment of rupture has been successfully achieved or merely intended – a moment that rebels against the illusion of the successful work.[12]

It is nevertheless clear that this question will not go away, either for Mahler or for Adorno. The implication is that the tension between the moment of expressive truth in "Liebst du um Schönheit" and the given need for formal closure that defines its character as art, as song, has here been heightened to breaking-point. The music seems determined to "overreach itself" (p. 6), to break through to some utopian state, beyond the music itself, that is sufficiently unlike mere "music" as to make any subsequent formal recapitulation impossible. Symmetrical closure would signify a self-defeating reversion to the invocation-to-breakthrough, which the actual breakthrough should have made redundant. Suggesting that Mahler's symphonies are therefore inevitably "rooted in what music seeks to transcend" (p. 6), Adorno immediately and not surprisingly alludes to the Scherzo of the Second Symphony and its perpetual motion – an unbroken music whose most extreme form must logically be defined by "aimlessly circling, irresistible movements" (p. 6). Although he fails to elaborate on the fact, all that we know about that Scherzo and Mahler's own figurative "programs" for it supports Adorno's implied reading of it as a musical illustration of failed transcendence.[13] The trio's "breakthrough," symbolized by the unheeded visionary sermon of St. Anthony, fails effectively to dispel the formally returning Scherzo material, which thus takes on the character of an anti-music, repressively circling in a kind of "empty activity devoid of autonomy" that Adorno interprets in Mahler as an image of the

---

12 TAME, p. 5 (TAM, pp. 11–12).
13 See NBL2, p. 40 (NBLE, pp. 43–44 and 232), GMB2, no. 167 (GMBE, no. 158), and AMML4, pp. 213–14.

Hegelian *Weltlauf*: "the perverse 'course of the world' . . . which confronts consciousness in advance as something 'hostile and empty'" (p. 6).

It is movements like this that make others, such as the finales of the First and Second Symphonies, and later those of the Seventh and Eighth, so problematic, so much in need of a specific effort of interpretation if they are to be saved from the accusation of empty capitulation to the demands of triumphalism. When Adorno notoriously declares "Mahler was a poor yea-sayer" (p. 137), he means it partly in the congratulatory sense that Mahler was by nature no tub-thumping dealer in empty-headed affirmation. That is why Adorno sought out complicating dialectical contradictions in Mahler's grand and triumphant finales, why he admired the finale of the ultimately self-negating Sixth Symphony above all others, and why, by implication, he might have welcomed the return to the opening music of nature in the finale of the First Symphony.[14] The reasons are significant, and worth reconstructing.

Lovers of that symphony stand to be particularly hurt by his characterization of its opening string pedal (Adorno's model for the adolescent sound-hallucination described earlier):

> Reaching to the highest A of the violins, it is an unpleasant whistling sound like that emitted by old-fashioned steam engines. A thin curtain, threadbare but densely woven, it hangs from the sky like a pale gray cloud layer, similarly painful to sensitive eyes. (p. 4)

As is typical of Adorno's method, only later in the first chapter is his response to that opening pedal clarified, during a wider interpretation of Mahler's "sounds of nature." As always, his implied argument is a fascinating one that raises doubts and questions while simultaneously bringing one back to the music with renewed attention. Is he stretching the point to accommodate a tendentious extension of his critique of bourgeois enlightenment, we wonder, or is he simply right? Or both?

His reconsideration of the "tormenting pedal point" (p. 15) comes in

---

14 His actual reading of the affirmative conclusion of the First Symphony appears to have been predictably negative. In TAME, p. 52, we find the following: "In the Finale of the First Symphony laceration is intensified beyond all mediating measure into a totality of despair, behind which, to be sure, the nonchalant triumphal close pales to an affair of mere management."

the course of examining what the direction *Wie ein Naturlaut* actually meant for Mahler. The concept of Nature, according to Adorno and Horkheimer's *Dialectic of Enlightenment* (1944), is entirely an ideological category within bourgeois thought: a false image of the way the world is, rendered timeless and ahistorical in order to disarm the Otherness that it fixed and controlled. "What men want to learn from nature is how to use it in order wholly to dominate it and other men."[15] Later sections of *Dialectic of Enlightenment* offer as a significant example the instrumental masculine view of woman as a conceptual embodiment of (dominated) "nature":

> Woman as an alleged natural being is a product of history, which denaturizes her. But the desperate will to destroy everything that embodies the allurement of nature, the attraction of the physical, biological, national, and social underdog shows that Christianity has miscarried.[16]

Nature is being invoked in an explicitly "dialectical" way here, encompassing two opposed concepts, each of which relies in some sense upon the other. Nature implies that which is other than history, culture, technological progress, yet its ideological function in bourgeois society reveals its character to be precisely dependent upon those things. Mahler's "sounds of nature," suggests Adorno, are no less dialectical in character because they are defined by the language of cultivated, artistic music to which they are deliberately contrasted, and which in fact they negate (p. 15). This they do by insisting on awkward registers, on crudely "elemental" figures in which Mahler's symphonic writing "seeks to catch the disordered voices of living things" (p. 14). Here Adorno's underlying philosophical and political preoccupations facilitate what is arguably a remarkable insight into the implications of Mahler's once-notorious proclivity for "banal" musical material and effects, and of the strange, anti-universalist accent of his musical language that Adorno likens to speaking music in Austrian, or in the manner of a Bohemian Jew.[17] If the good bourgeois German symphony were defined by its rationalized order and the sanitized relationship between its tasteful material and structural norms, then Mahler's symphonies were conspicuous for their fractured "brokenness," for their refusal

---

[15] Theodor Adorno and Max Horkheimer, *Dialectic of Englightenment*, trans. John Cumming (London, 1979), p. 4.   [16] Ibid., p. 111.

[17] See Adorno, *Quasi una Fantasia*, p. 82, and TAME, pp. 23 and 149.

to domesticate or prettify the natural sounds, the childlike melodies, the musical waifs and strays they find a home for. Here, suggests Adorno, the musical and the social are as one. As rationalized bourgeois society sought to control and repress its own residue of alienated individual elements, those that "didn't fit," so Mahler's music, by its very difference, gives the lie to the kind of music, the kind of symphony that would do the same in terms of its hierarchical prohibition of the popular, the coarse, the vulgar. In his symphonies, suggests Adorno, the nineteenth-century triumph of rationalization, as catalogued and defined by Max Weber, is mockingly accused by its own liberated, unruly residue: by what has escaped and at the same time been marginalized by the rationalization process (p. 17).

He does not follow this line of thought through to a complete critical reading of the finale of the First Symphony, but it might consistently have focused upon the return of the "sounds of nature" and their structural, motivic relationship with the triumphal march that closes the work. Already implied is the question whether its triumph is not actually of a negating, anti-affirmative kind: an affirmation, rather, of energetic forces that threaten the whole world of "artistic" illusion and taste that had, in a sense, given birth to them. (This is precisely how Adorno will interpret passages in the first and third movements of the Third Symphony [pp. 36–37 and 77–80].) The rift between Subject and Phenomenon, between expression and form, models the alienation of the individual in modern society, and even threateningly suggests an alternative. Decipher this music, Adorno seems to encourage, and you may discover that its ostensible faults and shortcomings are in fact what redeems it from mythology and false consciousness. Its "fractures," as he puts it later, "are the script of truth" (p. 166).

II

The threat posed by Adorno to conventional musicology, as well as to certain articles of faith implicit in celebratory Anglo-American Mahler scholarship since 1960, can be directly equated with Adorno's interpretation of the threat often posed by Mahler to the aesthetic norms of his culture. That threat manifests itself in Adorno as an implicit challenge to those who support less disturbing, more straightforwardly affirmative or spiritually transcendent readings of Mahler's music. It is a challenge, on one hand, that insists upon precision of response to the historical musical "text," and, on the other, questions the assumptions underlying alternative readings. Some might argue that Adorno's own interpretations go beyond what music, Mahler's or anyone else's, could demonstrably be construed to signify or express. That might, however, be no more than a straw grasped from the wreckage of a less teleological, less dialectical kind of idealism than Adorno's, the character of which is clarified in his interpretation of Mahler as a culminating or terminal representative of "serious" music in the Great Tradition. Beyond Mahler, the whole project of twentieth-century avant-garde modernism threatens to shrink into a practically enacted, theoretical footnote to that same tradition. (Paddison notes and explores how Adorno's Mahler interpretation was potentially at odds with aspects of his earlier writing on New Music.[18])

The claim that Adorno's readings are somehow "ideologically" slanted or biased is one that can readily rebound upon the accuser. Even as indispensable and learned a Mahler scholar as Constantin Floros, whose 1986 symposium paper led us into this essay, is unconvincing when he becomes more explicit about what he means by accusing Adorno of ignoring Mahler's own worldview and "authentic programs." Floros is disinclined to accept Adorno's subtly nuanced reading of the Fourth Symphony as significantly knowing in its childlike manner ("The bells in the first measure ... really are fool's bells, which, without saying it, say: none of what you now hear is true" [p. 56]); he therefore confidently asserts, "In reality [*in Wirklichkeit*] the Fourth Symphony is a meditation on life after death ... [Mahler] believed firmly in transcendence and the transcendent mission of music."[19] – Perhaps; but is there not something too final about that "in Wirklichkeit"? Is not part of the reality of that symphony and its conclusion that it defines itself against the finales of the Second and Third Symphonies, that its significance lies in its difference? Life after death and transcendent missions themselves sound hollow and tendentious beside Adorno's arguably much more Mahlerian, more music-specific response:

---

[18] Paddison *Adorno's Aesthetics*, ch. 7 ("The Disintegration of Musical Material"), e.g. pp. 263–64 and 269–70 ff.

[19] Floros "Zur Wirkungsgeschichte Mahlers," p. 189.

The G Major episode . . . following the exposition of the first movement of
Mahler's Fourth Symphony, a blissful passage, lies before the listener like a
village before which he is seized by the feeling that this might be what he
seeks. (p. 44)

Its image-world is that of childhood. The means are reduced, without heavy
brass; horns and trumpets are more modest in number. No father-figures are
admitted to its precincts. The sound avoids all monumentality . . . (p. 53)

Mahler's theology, again like Kafka's, is gnostic, his fairy-tale symphony as
sad as the late works. If it dies away with the words of promise "that all shall
awake to joy," no one knows whether it does not fall asleep forever. The
phantasmagoria of the transcendent landscape is at once posited by it and
negated. Joy remains unattainable, and no transcendence is left but that of
yearning. (p. 57)

Dissatisfaction with Adorno's negative response to the Eighth
Symphony, on the other hand, is imperiled at once by the ambivalence with
which that work has consistently been received by Mahler scholars. Others
have found it worrying and anomalous. Henry-Louis de La Grange is
consequently forced to demolish Adorno's estimation of Mahler's
"mißglücktes Hauptwerk" ("abortive magnum opus") with a large cannon
aimed widely at the entire body of what he calls "the 'intellectual' wing
among the Mahlerians . . . conditioned as even they are by the traditional
idea of Mahler as an introspective composer whose preferred mood is one
of suffering and intimations of death."[20] We know what he means, but the
implication that the only alternative to Adorno's reading of the Eighth is an
anti-intellectual, unquestioning submission to its affirmation seems precisely to underline Adorno's worries. Here is de La Grange's peroration:

Let us give ourselves up to the physical joy produced by the torrents of
sound of the Veni Creator and the final Hymnus. Let us accept without

---

[20] Henry-Louis de La Grange, "The Eighth: Exception or Crowning Achievement?"
in Eveline Nikkels and Robert Becqué, eds., A "Mass" for the Masses: Proceedings
of the Mahler VIII Symposium Amsterdam 1988 (Rijswijk, 1992), pp. 131–32
(quote from p. 132). His phrase "mißglücktes Hauptwerk" refers to a sentence
early in Adorno's section on the Eighth: "Das Hauptwerk ist die mißglückte,
objektiv unmögliche Wiederbelebung des kultischen" (TAM, p.182; Gesammelte
Schriften, vol. XIII, p. 283), which Jephcott translates "The magnum opus is the
aborted, objectively impossible resuscitation of the cultic" (TAME, p. 138).

question the contrapuntal intricacy of the double fugue, whose simultaneous lines and antiphonal refinements fill our ears with ten times, a hundred times more notes than our minds can take in.[21]

Adorno is fully prepared to explain why he is *dis*inclined to give himself up to such things:

> What Durkheim imputed to religions at about the time the solemn festival performances from *Parsifal* to the Eighth Symphony were coming into being, that they were self-representations of the collective spirit, applies exactly to at least the ritual art-works of late capitalism. Their Holy of Holies is empty . . . Like no other composer of his time, Mahler was sensitive to collective shocks. The temptation that arose from this, to glorify the collective that he felt sounding through him as an absolute, was almost overwhelming. That he did not resist is his offense . . . If on this one occasion one were to speak of Mahler in the language of psychology, the Eighth, like the Finale of the Seventh, was an identification with the attacker [*Angreifer*]. It takes refuge in the power and glory of what it dreads; its official posture is fear deformed as affirmation. (pp. 138–39)

The appeal of Adorno's approach to the Eighth, perhaps also to the Finale of the Seventh, will be to those whose response to Mahler is both emotional and intellectual, to those who might abandon themselves to it and then worry – to the kind of composer (I am tempted to suggest) who might complete such a symphony and then go on to write *Das Lied von der Erde*.

Summaries of Adorno's account of the Eighth can easily miss the evidence of tension in it, of a critic struggling against his own experience of having been "swept away." His description of Webern's clearly magnificent performance is moving for its briefly confessional tone ("the dignity of the magnum opus in some places breaches its concept and thereby realizes it: perhaps this can only be measured by someone who still has the 'Accende' in Anton von Webern's Vienna performance in his ears" [p. 140]). A little later he notes: "When in the *Faust* music the boys' choir sings 'Jauchzet laut, es ist gelungen,' a shiver passes for a second through the listener as if success were really achieved" (p. 141). One is forcefully reminded here of comments Mahler wrote to Bruno Walter in 1909 about his seeming to hear "answers" to his questions while conducting, and about the "burning denunciation of

---

[21]   de La Grange, "The Eighth," p. 142.

the Creator" voiced in some of his own works – the focusing of a vital, visionary energy that nevertheless dissipated as soon as the music ended.[22] Might we not, in this respect, regard Adorno as one of the most authentically Mahlerian of all Mahler's critics? His ambivalence and worry about the experience of affirmative music derive from a cultural position and intellectual personality arguably so close to Mahler's own as to render his interpretations an almost documentary historical significance.

The assumption must be that a composer as dialectical as Mahler deserves an equally dialectical response. It is interesting that in the same Eighth Symphony symposium in which de La Grange made his enthusiastic plea against Adorno and on behalf of that work, two other participants engaged more productively with Adorno's reading of it. Mathias Hansen edged cautiously around Adorno's verdict, historicizing and contextualizing it both in Adorno's Schoenberg-dominated perspective on the problems of New Music after the Second World War and in his attempt to forge a consistent developmental interpretation of New Music's progressive character. However, Hansen's subsequent cultural-historical inquiry into comparable manifestations of affirmation around the time of the Eighth Symphony led him, via Hofmannsthal's "conservative revolution," to a consideration of the politics of anti-modernist manifestations of *Geist* that were rooted in the Austrian Catholic Baroque and strongly affiliated to Goethe; ultimately, his findings seem to gloss Adorno's interpretation of the Eighth in a judiciously sympathetic manner.[23] An alternative approach was provided by Alexander von Bohrmann, who made the provocative proposal that the contradictory dialectical element which Adorno missed in the Eighth was in reality already a property of the Second Part of Goethe's *Faust*. Interpreting the "Veni Creator" text (not least in Mahler's setting) as an expression of pre-dogmatic piety, Bohrmann dwelt on the implications of its linkage with the specific section of *Faust* that experimentally deconstructs the autonomous subject. A poststructuralist reading, he suggested, might even counter Adorno's skepticism about the Eighth by uncovering a critique of metaphysics embedded within it.[24]

[22] GMB2, nos. 404 and 429 (GMBE, nos. 382 and 407).

[23] Mathias Hansen, "Mahlers Achte im Spannungsfeld von Geschichte und Tradition," in *A "Mass" for the Masses* (see n. 20 above), pp. 78–87.

[24] Alexander von Bohrmann, "Metaphysik der Unmöglichkeit? Zum Text von

III

Hansen's and Bohrmann's responses to Adorno are indicative of what might prove to be Adorno's most fitting legacy: a critical scholarship that takes the implications of its interpretative strategies as seriously as he did, while exploring both the evidence for and the alternatives to his sometimes over-dogmatic assertions. These can certainly tire even the most tolerant of readers. When Adorno is out of sympathy with what he is writing about, his approach can be crushing in its relentless self-assurance. This is notoriously the case in his dealings with forms of mass culture, but one equally wishes that Richard Strauss, or Sibelius, even Stravinsky, might be permitted some contradictory advocacy as he consigns them to the scrap-heap of history. That he could and did change his mind over details, however, is demonstrated in the course of his long-developing response to Mahler.

Inevitably it is Adorno's late, centenary-year writings on Mahler which dominate what we know of that response. They included, along with the *Musikalische Physiognomik*, three extended radio programs (introducing the Ninth, Fourth, and Sixth Symphonies respectively), an essay entitled "Mahler's Topicality [*Aktualität*] (On His Hundredth Birthday)," and the important "Memorial Address" delivered in Vienna, with its subsequent "Epilegomena."[25] Three later pieces include a rebuttal of Hans Mayer's view that Mahler was insensitive to the literary qualities

Mahlers VIII. Symphonie," in A *"Mass" for the Masses* (see n. 20 above), pp. 92–99. By limiting my consideration of constructive engagement with Adorno's reading of Mahler to this particular symposium, I do not mean to overlook valuable responses to Adorno in the work of other German-speaking scholars. Particular mention should be made of the important study of Mahler by Hans Heinrich Eggebrecht, *Die Musik Gustav Mahlers* (Munich, 1982; new edn., 1986).

25 The three radio-program scripts appear in *Gesammelte Schriften*, vol. XVIII, as "Aus dem Ersten Mahler-Vortrag" (the first part of this had in fact been identical with the "Gedenkrede"), "Zweiter Mahler-Vortrag," and "Dritter Mahler-Vortrag," pp. 584–622. "Mahlers Aktualität (seinem hundertsten Geburtstag)" also appears in *Gesammelte Schriften*, vol. XVIII, pp. 241–43. The "Wiener Gedenkrede" and its "Epilegomena" (1961) were incorporated into *Quasi una Fantasia* (*Gesammelte Schriften*, vol. XVI, pp. 323–50); in the English trans. (n. 9 above), pp. 81–110, they appear as "Centenary Address, Vienna 1960" and "Afterthoughts."

and integrity of his poetic texts, and a 1969 piece on the Tenth Symphony.[26] What should not be overlooked, however, is that Adorno had published two rather significant pro-Mahler essays three decades earlier: the first, called "Mahler Today," in 1930 in the Universal Edition magazine *Anbruch*; the second, "Notes on Mahler" ("Marginalien zu Mahler") in 1936, in the journal *23*.[27] In both, his later assessment is clearly present in outline. "Mahler Today" is particularly interesting, however, for its relatively positive reading of the Eighth Symphony as a consistent example of the anti-bourgeois element in Mahler, which Adorno was eager to equate with that of the more obviously progressive Schoenberg. Rather than as a cathedral built erroneously out of "disqualified" materials, the Eighth is here interpreted as a "revolutionary camp" in which the architectural quibbles of self-appointed "building police" were entirely irrelevant:

> Mahler's ecclesia militans is a salvation army, better than the real one; not petit-bourgeois temperate, not retrospectively converted, but determined to call the oppressed to the true battle [*richtigen Kampf*].[28]

The date of that first Mahler essay, in which Adorno seems to equate the Eighth's "collective" voice with that of the unruly revolutionary rabble in the first movement of the Third Symphony,[29] has obvious significance. Given the circles he moved in, he would have been familiar with all the arguments both for and against Mahler in the 1920s, and also with their increasing political resonance. Adorno brought to the hearing of Mahler as educated an ear as did the composer's detractors, but he would inevitably have recoiled from their often xenophobic and anti-semitic intentions, and would have weighed ever more carefully his own powerful, and no doubt contradictory, experiences of the music in light of both the tortuous support Schoenberg accorded Mahler's music and the passionate attach-

---

26   "Zu einem Streitgespräch über Mahler" (1968), and "Fragment als Graphic: Zur Neuausgabe von Mahlers Zehnte Symphonie" (1969), *Gesammelte Schriften*, vol. XVIII, pp. 244–50 and 251–53. One additional late essay, "Zu einer imaginären Auswahl von Liedern Gustav Mahlers" (1964), was included in the volume *Impromptus* (*Gesammelte Schriften*, vol. XVII, pp. 189–97).

27   "Mahler Heute" (1930), and "Marginalien zu Mahler" (1936), *Gesammelte Schriften*, vol. XVIII, pp. 226–34 and 235–40.

28   Adorno, "Mahler Heute," p. 229.   29   See TAME, pp. 36–37 and 77–80.

ment his own teacher, Alban Berg, felt for it.[30] Adorno's relative silence prior to 1960 on the subject of Mahler may simply have been a function of the composer's having departed from the scene too early to have been at the cutting edge of contemporary music in Adorno's own harshly contemporary world. Only gradually, perhaps, had Mahler's much-vaunted status as a precursor of modernism been submerged by the discovered "actuality" which came to pervade Adorno's published work on Mahler. His later intensive reexamination of Mahler's output took place at a time when score-reading and the concert experience could be supplemented by long-playing records. By 1960 he had refined and extended his earlier response to Mahler in light of his hitherto uncompromising equation of compositional authenticity with the most advanced techniques.

Adorno's philosophical standpoint vis à vis the circumstances of production in late capitalist mass culture had demanded an unshaking commitment to alienated opposition, to the point of hermetic resistance to consumable comprehensibility. (This was an aspect of his musical philosophy that influenced Thomas Mann in his discussions with Adorno during the gestation of *Dr. Faustus*.[31]) Mahler, Adorno knew, was not "original" in either materials or technique. Adorno also notes in his "Memorial Address" of 1960 (formulated after *Eine musikalische Physiognomik*, and regarded by him as a kind of synopsis of the book) that Mahler emphatically did not, like Hofmannsthal's fictional Lord Chandos in 1902, choose the proto-modernist path of expressive renunciation:

---

[30] Schoenberg's views on Mahler were formally expressed in his short "Gustav Mahler: In Memoriam," published in the Mahler-commemorative edition of *Der Merker* in March 1912, and also in the extended Prague lecture of the same year, first published in translation in Dika Newlin's original edition of *Style and Idea* (New York, 1950; see Leonard Stein, ed., *Style and Idea: Selected Writings of Arnold Schoenberg* [London, 1975], pp. 447–72). Berg's passion for Mahler is affirmed not least by Adorno himself, in *Alban Berg: Der Meister des kleinsten Übergangs* (1968), where he records that at Webern's performance of Mahler's Eighth Symphony, he and Berg were almost thrown out for their "rowdiness": "Berg was so carried away with enthusiasm for the music and its interpretation that he began to talk loudly about both, as if the performance were for us alone" (see Adorno, *Alban Berg: Master of the Smallest Link*, trans. Juliane Brand and Christopher Hailey [Cambridge, 1991], p. 10).

[31] See, e.g., Thomas Mann, *The Genesis of a Novel*, trans. Richard and Clara Winston (London, 1961), pp. 121–26.

although Mahler came from the margins of society and never disowned the experience derived from his background, he is not far removed from Hofmannsthal's high-born Lord Chandos who finds the words crumbling in his mouth because they no longer say what they ought. But unlike Chandos, Mahler did not conclude that the only solution was to fall silent.[32]

Instead, Adorno suggests, Mahler embarked upon what ought to have been an impossible enterprise. Reendowing regressive tonal formulae with the power to express what they had never, or no longer, intended, he turns them into "explosive expressions of the pain felt by the individual subject imprisoned in an alienated society." They became, for Adorno, "cryptograms of modernism, guardians of the absolute dissonance which after him became the very language of music":

> Unstylized outbreaks of horror, such as the one in the first trio of the Funeral March in the Fifth Symphony, in which the inhuman voice of command seems to cut across the screams of the victims, were no longer really compatible with the language of tonality, least of all within the compass of the march. The scandal is that he achieved it nevertheless and succeeded in expressing the truly unprecedented with a traditional vocabulary.[33]

The frisson of shock behind that sense of what was "scandalous" in Mahler consistently animates the 1960 book. Although its eight chapters begin with the First Symphony and end, memorably, with *Das Lied von der Erde* and the Ninth, their sequence is only secondarily conditioned by chronology. Adorno's main concern is to reconstruct Mahler's musical "physiognomy," as he saw it, in painstaking theoretical stages. The chapter titles deliberately avoid highlighting conventional musical categories until the latter half of the book (specifically in chapters 5 and 6: "Variant – Form," and "Dimensions of Technique"). At first, after the opening "Curtain and Fanfare" chapter, Adorno addresses the issue of Mahler's "tone": on occasion childish, mimetically mannered, a little foreign, popular, even downright plebeian. Exploring the way in which that tone is quite literally heightened by "tonal" means (the chapter-title "Ton" could be translated simply as "Sound," but is clearly intended to have the same figurative

---

[32] *Quasi una Fantasia* (n. 9 above), p. 85.   [33] Ibid., pp. 85–86.

implications that the word has in English), Adorno examines Mahler's
alternation of major and minor modes. His suggestion is that Mahler capi-
talizes on and focuses their traditional symbolic association: expressive
particularity and Otherness (minor) is opposed to symbolic generality
(major). In this he already anticipates the theme of his third chapter,
"Characters," in which he elaborates upon the insight that the events and
processes of conventional form acquire specific, "characteristic" qualities
and meaning in Mahler, not least those of "breakthrough," "suspension,"
"fulfillment," and "collapse." Adorno inevitably adds to these the more
specific and detailed characters, or "topoi," that Mahler remobilizes from
romantic literature and opera, and from the imagery of *Des Knaben
Wunderhorn.* These, Adorno suggests, Mahler employs autonomously –
meaning that they are removed from their domesticated role in Bieder-
meier painting or sentimental literature and permitted to muster the unre-
stricted energies of the banal, even of outright kitsch, that potentially
threaten not just the taste but also the very structure of Mahler's symphonic
"novels" (the literary comparison is explored in Adorno's fifth chapter).
Form itself, potentially refigured as a character in its own right, is no longer
a dominant, meaning-bestowing "given," but becomes a goal, a quest after
some initially inconceivable, perhaps utopian balance between details and
whole.

If Adorno regarded the Finale of the Sixth Symphony as the central
focus of Mahler's oeuvre in this respect (a movement whose literally self-
destructive form he describes as its primary inspiration, one rich in what
he calls fields of disintegration[34]), his remarkable final chapter, "The Long
Gaze," is devoted to Mahler's last completed works. These are interpreted
as exemplary exercises in the scandalous, triumphant impossibility that
had defined his entire creative project, as Adorno saw it. In them, the childhood memory of utopia is retained in the knowledge that it is not only lost,
but that happiness itself can perhaps only ever be recognized as lost happiness. Making frequent comparative references to Proust, Adorno finds in
late Mahler an incomparable mixture of innocence and experience. The

---

[34] The term "Auflösungsfelder" is introduced in TAME, chap. 3, p. 45, initially with
reference to the Ninth Symphony; it returns in Adorno's extended discussion of
the Sixth's Finale on p. 99.

simple tonal formulae of old are uttered once more, but as familiar phrases "lit up" by experience (p. 147):

> someone who says something familiar, but behind which his whole life stands, says something more and other than what he says. Music becomes a blotting paper, an everyday thing that becomes saturated with significance ...

Much of the last chapter is devoted to *Das Lied von der Erde*. Its exoticism is examined as a possible cover for Mahler's confrontation of his own Jewishness. The tone, the "aroma" of his style now defines an artistic arena in which psychology and philosophy seem to converse: "by the euphemism of foreignness the outsider seeks to appease the shadow of terror. That, and not merely the expression of a sick man's premonition of individual death, endows the last works with their documentary seriousness" (p. 150). Their scrupulous avoidance of any easy indulgence in "hope" is precisely what is hopeful in them. If the message of the Ninth Symphony is that the individual "has power over no content but his own, however fragmented,"[35] that individual also hears and reflects upon the very marches whose purpose is to drag him away. Discerning a striking, quasi-political message in the Ninth Symphony's fractured subjectivity, Adorno observes that at the end of Mahler's life, his concept of freedom was once again embodied in the image of the trampled, the defeated. Characteristically offering an ostensibly negative assessment as his highest accolade, Adorno alludes briefly to "Der Tamboursg'sell": "Bereft of promises, his symphonies are ballads of the defeated..." (p. 167).

IV

That, for Adorno, was the ever more contemporaneous truth traced in the fractured script of Mahler's music – a music over which (as he finally reminds us) the night would soon fall, a music which recognizes the darkness in all its negativity while remaining true to its memory of the light. We might find that reading tendentious, too conveniently tailored to his own pessimistic world view. It is nevertheless here that the productive challenge

---

[35] TAME, p. 166 (TAM, p. 216). I have amended Jephcott's faulty translation ("this individual is capable of no content ...") of "dies Individuum keines Inhalt mächtig ist ..."

of his critical writing lies. While it might be difficult to agree whole-heartedly with Constantin Floros's point about Adorno's ignorance of Mahler's own worldview, Mathias Hansen and Alexander von Bohrmann, as we have seen, provide useful examples of how constructive dispute with him might be informed by contextual, analytical, perhaps even documentary scholarship. The cost might be that the mythical, heroic Mahler of the first biographies, even the celebrated and venerated object of later scholarship, will become humanized and historicized. Questions remain to be asked about aspects of Adorno's political worldview; they must also be asked about Mahler's. How do we interpret his relationship to cultural power? Extended and reassessed knowledge of Mahler the conductor, of Mahler the man, might constructively inform revised approaches to his works, be they provoked or inspired by Adorno.

To be troubled by his interpretations is to become aware of just how much there is still to be said about Mahler, and indeed, about his current reception. Would Adorno's *Physiognomik* have been the same in 1990 as it was in 1960? If his approach does still harbor a threat, then it is perhaps less to those who would reclaim the Fourth Symphony or *Das Lied von der Erde* as offering spiritual consolation and intimations of "life after death" than to those who would ignore such matters altogether and recolonize Mahler's works as the decontextualized subjects of "objective" analysis, with all its hidden agendas and inherited desire to separate pure musical sheep from heteronomous goats. We need not endorse Adorno's observation, made in his section on the Eighth Symphony, that "sheep and goats should not be separated even by one on the side of the goats" (p. 140). It is nevertheless hard to read him closely or for long on Mahler without gaining sympathetic comprehension of statements such as the following (from the Memorial Address); Susan McClary's otherwise perhaps overgeneralized account of Adorno's project is vindicated by them:

> If one wanted to turn him simply into another great composer, to reestablish the undoubted sublimity of his work simply by asserting it, that would be to accept the standard of the juste milieu and cheat him of what he truly deserves ... His musical language ... challenges that accepted idea of music as a pure, unmediated art – a view held on to all the more tenaciously as human relations themselves become ever more elaborately mediated, the more thoroughly administered the world becomes.

. . .

Mahler's music is critical, is a critique of aesthetic illusion, a critique even of the culture in which it functions and whose already used-up elements it accommodates.[36]

Perhaps what Adorno feared has already happened; if so, his greatest threat is to the Adagietto-Mahler of the compact-disc compilations. Restore that movement to the complete Fifth Symphony, thoroughly understood; restore that work to Mahler's complete oeuvre, and we stand once again to be neither charmed nor simply uplifted by him, but questioned, challenged, attacked. In 1936 Adorno had observed: "Those who hate Mahler have understood correctly that the Sixth's falling hammer is heading for them."[37] The supreme conundrum of his Mahler book lies in its implicit suggestion that the most intense and seriously concentrated kind of listening, the kind that he advocated throughout his career as the proper mode of attention to "great" music, will in Mahler's case be rewarded by the disturbing, perhaps liberating deconstruction of some of its guiding historical assumptions. Adorno himself was not fully immune to that threat; in its way it provoked the peculiarly fruitful truthfulness of his reading of Mahler.

[36] From *Quasi una Fantasia, Gesammelte Schriften*, vol. XVI, pp. 325 and 329, my own translation. Cf. *Quasi una Fantasia*, trans. Livingstone, pp. 83 and 88: although the latter generally reads well, Livingstone's translation can wander far and wide around Adorno's text. On p. 83 he not only reorganizes Adorno's paragraphing (occasionally helpful, given his tendency to write in unbroken paragraphs of some pages in length) but also inexplicably omits an entire paragraph of the German text (*Gesammelte Schriften*, vol. XVI, pp. 324–25, from "Aber etwas vom Zwielicht jener letzten Scherzos . . ." to ". . . verdrängt Mahler").

[37] "Marginalien zu Mahler" (see n. 27 above), p. 237.

Index

Printed in the United States
148982LV00005B/8/A

9 780521 033176